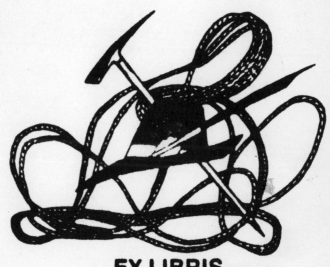

EX LIBRIS
Dana Q. Coffield

ALONE TO EVEREST

Earl Denman

EARL DENMAN

ALONE
TO
EVEREST

COWARD-McCANN, Inc.
NEW YORK

Library of Congress Catalog Card
Number 54-11487

Manufactured in the United States of America

To Mary

And so my mind like sullen clay awaits
The Maker's hand, the touch of which creates
A drinking gourd, a flowered vase, an urn,
From the dull earth to which my thoughts return.

E. L. D.

Contents

7

ILLUSTRATIONS

List of Maps

Introduction

THE TITLE of this book requires a few words of explanation. I have called it *Alone to Everest* because the underlying idea was my own, and I set out without a companion. By giving it this title I do not wish to imply that I was really alone throughout. Far from it. There were men who joined in wholeheartedly with me, and others who were indispensable behind the scenes. In truth I do not know how to pay sufficient tribute to folk of the calibre of Kabanza, Chief Tomasi Sebukweto, Robeni, Ndabateze, Tenzing, Ang Dowa and others without whose assistance I could have accomplished little or nothing. In particular, my undying thanks go out to Kabanza, Tenzing and Ang Dowa, who are the real heroes of my story. And, in speaking of this book, I am indebted to those who have helped with suggestions, words of encouragement, and with the labours of typing and preparation.

It should be explained that the original manuscript was written while the British expedition of 1953 was on its way to Everest. The success of this expedition made it necessary to revise the concluding pages. In these I may seem to write from the bitterness of defeat; but I am not bitter. There has been time in which to reflect, and in that time I have been again to the hills and forests. If there is an underlying sadness to my story, it is because sadness has prevailed to the end.

I have told of my Congo and Uganda ventures as an unseparated preliminary to my Everest story because the entire undertaking was one. To have told of the one without the other would have given a wrong impression of the whole. I would most certainly never have gone to Everest without success on all eight of the Virunga mountains.

I have introduced no false embellishments to my story. It would have been useful to claim that I saw gorillas, instead of only hearing them on the Virunga mountains. But alas, I did not see them.

My spelling of Tibetan place-names is of course uncertain, and my knowledge of that country's fauna is very limited. In other respects, it should be remembered that I was travelling extremely simply, and with the barest of essentials for survival. I did not have in mind the writing of a book as a certain follow-up to my two mountain ventures. I kept a diary, but even with this I had to contrive by writing in an exceedingly small hand, thus economising in bulk and weight. I did not possess a single scientific instrument for measuring either heights, distances or angles. I was, in fact, so utterly poor that I could not afford a watch for myself! Tenzing had one, but I did not. In the Congo and Uganda there was not one of us who had any direct means of telling the time. These are the ways of the needy.

My camera was a cheap second-hand one, with punctured bellows. Add to this my own inexperience, and I was lucky to get away with any photographs at all. On Everest, my photography was further handicapped by the poor quality gloves which I wore, and ultimately I was forced to put my camera away, as something quite impossible to deal with under the circumstances. Nevertheless, most of the photographs which appear in the book are my own. The others—showing Vishoke and Mikeno—were kindly lent me by the Institut des Parcs Nationaux du Congo Belge, to whom goes my grateful thanks.

There was a time when I was terribly ashamed of my poverty, and never admitted it to anyone. It depresses me to tell it now, but I am no longer ashamed to do so. The interest of story, I think, is enhanced because of it.

It may be wondered, what adventures actually took place? The answer depends largely upon what is meant by "adventure." If the word conveys events of excitement and stirring interest, then there was adventure aplenty. If by implication it means serious misfortune, injury or death, then there was none. There was a certain amount of lawbreaking, but what of it? We are all lawbreakers in some way or another, or if we are not, then we would like to be.

It may be asked why men climb mountains. I cannot speak for others, but my own answer becomes clear as my story develops. It will serve also, I am sure, for those who were with me, though they were men who could not easily express the reasons for their actions. The general truth, perhaps, is that all who climb mountains feel compelled to do so. Apart from this, there can be only a few personal reasons which vary with the individual.

It is only right, in view of the fact that this story is mainly about myself and the simple men who were with me, that there should be no Introduction by an " outsider," however eminent he might be. That is why I have myself given these few extra details.

An exception has been made by the inclusion of the original field notes on gorillas by Mr. C. J. P. Ionides, Senior Game Ranger, Tanganyika Territory. Mr. Ionides is one of the very few naturalists with field experience of the mountain gorilla, which he gained while collecting a specimen for the Coryndon Museum, Nairobi, during September 1946. A special words of thanks is due to him for these notes.

Finally, I am most grateful to the one who made possible my second, but altogether ill-fated, attempt to reach Everest, and also to the manufacturers who were willing to place their products at my disposal. My lasting regret is that I could do nothing to justify the confidence these people had placed in me. Althongh I have not dealt at any length with this second attempt, it was of tremendous importance to me—more than any reader will ever know—and to those who helped, I would like to end with a word of apology.

EARL L. DENMAN

I. *Background*

IN THIS age of self-inquiry, and of inquiry into the lives of others, it is common to look for motives. In my own case it is perhaps true that childhood glimpses of the Canadian Rockies formed a lasting impression —a first link in a chain of events leading from one mountain range to another. I like to think it was so, for Canada was my birthplace, and though I had no option but to leave it at an early age, I still retain a nostalgia which distance and time cannot remove, no matter how much allegiance is owed to another country.

It is impossible for me to look with the same nostalgia towards England, for I was never really happy there. How could I have been? As a family we had only left Canada in the forlorn hope of gaining relief for a completely paralysed father, and in England our savings were whittled away to nothing, so that we lost altogether our previous carefree prosperity. Also, the narrowness of the British mentality and way of life at that time depressed me. Perhaps, as a result of my early days in Canada, I felt cramped in England.

Of my father I only recall a dark, broad-shouldered man, for he remained bed-ridden throughout the whole of seven painful years: painful for himself and for my mother, who nursed him, and painful for the children—all boys—who could not escape the harsh, grinding responsibilities and sacrifices which each had to bear at a time when schooling and games should have been their only concerns.

Standing out clearly, like a snow-capped mountain summit framed by dark storm-clouds, is the memory of my mother's valiant struggle and her determination never to forsake her children or to relinquish the pride which she had inherited from good British stock. She became worn down in the end, but not before her victory had been won, for she had by then set her sons firmly on the highroad of life, through school and to work.

Although I did not see her during the last years of her life, I remember as
yesterday her hair, which had changed from the deepest black to grey,
and then to snowy white, but which in her last days gained a glorious
golden sheen. Life had withheld much from her, but in the end it set this
crown of gold on her head, as though in recognition of her selflessness.

Against this background I grew up with an ambition and determination
without which I would have been a good deal happier. I thought a lot
and developed the far-away look of a dreamer, for it was always the distant
heights which fascinated me and drew me to them in spirit. I was not
sure what could be accomplished by means of tenacity and little else, but
the target was set high and each rebuff only saw me all the more determined
to see at least one major dream through to its fulfilment.

Livingstone, Speke, Burton—these were my heroes, and though settled
in England I already belonged at heart to Africa. Indeed my whole world
was Africa, but it was not the true Africa. In it there were only wide
savannahs and deserts, wild life, forests, lakes and rivers, and of course
mountains. There was no place in this Africa of mine for large cities, and
though I had heard of Johannesburg I half believed the story that lions still
roamed its streets. Or, at any rate, I would not admit into my dreamland
a Johannesburg made up of mine dumps and sky scrapers, milk bars and
American cars.

What intrigued me most about Africa was the Belgian Congo, and
Ruwenzori, which sounded all the more fascinating and familiar as " The
Mountains of the Moon." Snow at the equator! It was a rich thought,
and not a dream. I would get there some day. I would. I did.

The story of my impecunious youth is of no concern to others, and to
myself the memory of it is best forgotten. Only the briefest of facts, which
have in some way a bearing upon my story of Everest, need be told.

At one stage, having served a five-year apprenticeship as an electrical
engineer, and then having branched out as an assistant mains engineer, the
time came for me to broaden my horizon. And so, each Friday, the
Electrical Times would be scanned, with an eye always for a suitable post in
Africa. There was no more than a slender chance of this, but eventually
the time came when I was to pack my bags and head for the Anglo-
Egyptian Sudan. This was far from the ideal, but at least it was Africa.
I had dreamt of mountains, but had to be content with a barren desert.
Instead of bracing snow-laden winds I had to endure the oppressive, sand-
bearing *haboob*. In the Sudan, I seemed farther away than ever from the

real magnet which had attracted me to Africa, and I resigned myself un-
willingly to the stifling heat and the monotony, and whiled away my spare
time by becoming the owner of a *jemel beta el khalla* ("camel of the desert"
—as opposed to a town-bred camel), whom I called Cuthbert, and who
provided me with many adventures.

Two years had to elapse before my first leave became due, and then
five full months had to be taken outside the Sudan but I could not go
overseas because of the war. Without hesitation, I decided on the Belgian
Congo, though means of transport beyond the southern borders of the Sudan
were few and far between, and I was warned of serious consequences if
I should overstay my leave. One of my objectives was, of course, the
Ruwenzori massif, and a secondary desire was to reach Lake Kivu, the
last of the large Central African lakes to be discovered by the white races.

A nine-days' voyage by Nile steamer took me to Juba, after which
I travelled by whatever means were available, usually contriving to gain
a place, though not always a seat, on lorries going to and from the gold
mines of the Congo. Most of the lorries carried dry fish for Africans
employed on the mines, so that travel was never free from the strong smell
of salted fish.

The lack of transport of my own made travelling very difficult, and the
chance to do any actual climbing seemed to recede as I approached the
mountains. In fact I skirted the long Ruwenzori range first to the west
and then to the east, without ever seeing beyond the foothills. The snow
peaks, wreathed in cloud and mist, were never visible. I had all but given
up hope, and had left the Congo for Uganda, when an unexpected chance
turned up, and by means of a series of journeys in fish lorries driven by
Indians, I returned to the Congo where, at the foot of the snow-capped
Mountains of the Moon, I found an enterprising Belgian in the early stages
of building a hotel. The mountains at this point rise abruptly from the
plains with no true foothills as on the eastern, or Uganda, side.

The Anglo-American explorer, H. M. Stanley, was the first to record
these mountains, which lie between Lake Edward and Lake George to the
south, and Lake Albert to the north. As far back as the time of Ptolemy,
they were known as The Mountains of the Moon, though it is open to
question whether these mountains, or the Virunga volcanoes, are the ones
which suggested this name to the Arabic imagination. Stanley called them
Ruwenzori—Mountains of Rain. The valleys are very deeply cut, especially
on the Congo side, and small lakes are numerous. The vegetation is

stimulated to fantastic growth by a combination of equatorial heat and a rainfall that is exceptional even for a mountain area. The Duke of Abruzzi, in 1906, was the first to scale the main peaks, the highest of which he named " Margherita " after the Queen of Italy. No gorillas live on Ruwenzori, in spite of the stories of some writers. Their nearest habitat is the forest to the west of Lake Edward.

There was neither time nor equipment to enable me to do anything spectacular in the way of real climbing on Ruwenzori, but two results of my short stay on the mountain range were to have an important and far-reaching effect upon my future mountaineering activities, and indeed upon my whole life. Firstly, it was here that I proved the feasibility of going with none but simple Africans, in perfect harmony, thus setting a mode of procedure that was to hold good on all future occasions. We travelled lightly and therefore quickly and cheaply.

Secondly, it was while in camp on Ruwenzori, just below the snow line, that I first came to think about Everest. I was sitting alone, gazing far to the south, when my thoughts strayed to the Virunga or Mufumbiro mountains which lie in that direction, and some of which I had glimpsed while in the neighbourhood of Lake Kivu before my climb on Ruwenzori.

They are eight in number, and the idea suddenly came to me that I would like to be the first to climb all eight of them. Transport would be a problem, but companionship would not. I would go with none but the black men who lived in the vicinity. The idea grew into something vital and worth while. It would give me a purpose for going to the mountains, a purpose for which I had been searching within myself. It would give me a chance to know some African people intimately and the wild beasts which live side by side with them. It would give me, also, a chance to get to grips with myself and the problems with which I battled. There was already something about the Virunga mountains which excited my imagination. Ruwenzori had done so, and now it was the turn of the Virungas. My mind was made up. There was no one to dissuade me.

Then, without any apparent effort of thought, the original conception broadened into a tremendous ambition—that of going alone to Everest. If I were successful on the eight Virunga mountains—but only if entirely successful—I would go to Everest in the same simple way.

II. Descriptive—of the Virunga Mountains and Gorillas

T HE ALBERTINE RIFT, which forms part of the great Central African rift system, contains the lakes Albert, Edward, Kivu and Tanganyika. To these may be added Lake George, though this, connected by the Kazinga Channel to Lake Edward, is considered by some to be in a subsidiary rift. The area is drained by the Nile and Congo rivers and their tributaries. Forming a watershed between the two principal rivers is the chain of Virunga or Mufumbiro mountains which lie to the north of Lake Kivu, dividing it and Lake Tanganyika from the Nile Basin. These volcanic cones have been built up along an east to west cross-fracture of the main Western Rift.

The major peaks are eight in number, and may be considered in three distinct sectors. (See pp. 45 and 83.) Nyiragongo and Nyamlagira lie to the west of the Goma to Rutshuru road, in what is known as the Nyamlagira sector of the Albert National Park; Mikeno, Vishoke and Karisimbi are triangularly disposed in a remoter part of the Park on the opposite side of the same road; the remaining three—Muhavura, Mgahinga, Sabinio —are situated in that order from east to west and form part of the boundary between Ruanda and the Western Province of Uganda Protectorate.

Various methods of spelling have been adopted for the mountains collectively and for most of the individual peaks. These have arisen, no doubt, because of the difficulty of distinguishing names as they are pronounced by Africans who have no knowledge of writing or of any language other than their own. For instance, the group is known as the Bufumbiro in Uganda, whereas Virunga, or Birunga, is the name most widely used in the Congo. This is a term in the Wanyaruanda language commonly applied to volcanic cones. Mufumbiro, or Mfumbiro, is another local name and means

19

" place where there is fire "—an apt description, as names given by indigenous Africans so often are. Another interpretation is " Cooking Pots," another vivid name.

For my own use I have tried to keep to the simplest and most phonetic spelling, and the only real difficulty in pronunciation is with Mikeno, which never differs in spelling but is invariably mispronounced " Mikeeno," whereas it is " Mi-kay-no " to all Africans of the vicinity. Vishoke is sometimes spelt Visoke (and even Bishoke and Bissokeh), but local Africans pronounce the *h*, and tend to put stress on the second syllable.

Mikeno (14,130–14,556 ft.) is by far the most difficult of the group as a mountaineering proposition, and it is quite certainly the least climbed of all Africa's high mountains, including Mount Kenya. Karisimbi, " the white shell," is the highest, and Vishoke the most remote of the eight volcanoes. The height of the former is variously estimated at between 14,780 ft. and 15,020 ft., while the latter ranges between 12,144–12,370 ft. The divergence in each case arises from a multiplicity of causes, including lack of a visible summit as well as the common errors, human and mechanical, connected with surveying.

Nyiragongo (11,385 ft.) is a composite volcano, still active, with one large and two subsidiary cones. The other live volcano, Nyamlagira (10,046 ft.), is the least impressive of them all, being wide at its base and having no steep gradients. Sabinio, on the other hand, is a fine mountain in every respect, and is second in age to Mikeno, whose name means " the barren." Both volcanoes have lost their craters, but Sabinio does not show the effects of erosion so markedly as Mikeno, the summit of which is truly barren. The height of Sabinio is estimated to be somewhere between 11,970 ft. and 12,150 ft.

Muhavura, with an altitude of about 13,550 ft., is the highest of the three mountains bordering on Uganda. It most closely meets the popular conception of a large volcano complete with a crater summit, and it dominates one of the most delightful parts of Africa—a lake region which for sheer rugged beauty is unexcelled anywhere in the world. A densely forested saddle joins Muhavura to Mgahinga, which rises to nearly 11,400 ft.

The eight volcanoes provide a barrier some 45 miles in extent from east to west. On the opposite side of Lake Victoria, which lies in the centre of the great Rift Valley, they have their counterparts in a similar volcanic region that is dominated by Kilimanjaro, which is the highest, and Mount Kenya, which is the oldest, of the system as a whole.

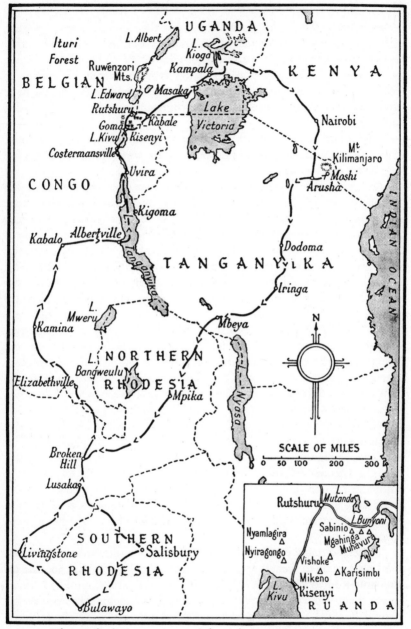

The Author's journey to and from the Virunga Mountains

These were the mountains which at that time occupied my thoughts, although I knew less about them than has been told here, and could gather little reliable information. I had caught glimpses of all but Vishoke while on my visit to Lake Kivu. Mikeno I knew very little about, but enough to hold it in respect as a difficult climb under any conditions. Could it be climbed by a lone white man unaccompanied except by unskilled natives?

Then there was a great deal of doubt as to the true nature of Sabinio. One writer claimed it was difficult, but another wrote quite casually about it. What was the real truth?

As a very first move it was necessary to gain permission to enter the Mikeno sector of the Albert National Park, in which Mikeno, Vishoke and Karisimbi are situated. This area is a " strict nature reserve " in which permission to reside is limited to a few indigenous Africans and entry is forbidden to all but an occasional scientific party. The object of this strictness is to retain all types of fauna and flora in their natural state as far as possible, and for this purpose it was at first thought necessary to prevent even the traditional firing of cultivable grass and bushland by local natives.

At Rumangabo, according to my information, there was a Conservateur, or warden, from whom permission could be gained on the spot for the ascents of Nyirangongo and Nyamlagira, but he had no authority to grant entry into the Mikeno sector. For this it was necessary to write to the controlling body in Belgium. Even if permission were given, which was most unlikely in view of my lack of scientific standing, would it be possible to recruit guides and porters and move from one sector to another without any transport of my own? Would any international complications debar me from reaching the three mountains which form part of the boundary between Uganda and the Belgian Congo? Then there was the matter of financing an expedition, no matter how modestly. My bank balance stood at £650. Was this sufficient for the undertaking, with Everest to follow if all went well? Would language difficulties bar the way to success?

These and many other problems confronted me, but to be quite frank, I did not face up to them squarely. The truth was, I think, I did not dare to. Probably if I had allowed myself to dwell on every stumbling-block, every single thing that could possibly go wrong, I would have become so depressed I should never have made a start at all. So, wittingly or not, I stopped to think neither about method nor madness, nor the possibility or otherwise of the whole undertaking. I just went piecemeal from one idea to another, and from one act to another, never grappling with too many problems at once.

Mine was a hard way to learn because it was a lonely one. But always at the back of my mind was the fear that I should be talked out of it if I told my plans to anyone else. There are always so many people ready to offer discouragement, and so few to see that failure, though painful, is better than frustrated longing.

My methods, I know, were in nearly all respects crude, but I saw no strangeness in them because they came naturally to me. During my early days on mountains the opportunity of climbing with more experienced men never came my way, and so I made my own trips with none but native Africans as guides and porters, and these I came to look upon also as friends and companions. Because I was unable at first to provide myself with clinkered boots, I dispensed with footwear altogether and climbed barefoot. Eventually I became so accustomed and hardened to walking and climbing in this simple manner that I found an added joy in it, and before long I could proceed happily beyond the snow line on any African mountain and over practically all kinds of ground without harm. To travel light became so much of a habit with me that any really non-essential article of equipment I looked upon as an encumbrance.

Money, on the other hand, was never an encumbrance—the trouble was there was never enough of it: but, looking back on my mountaineering ventures, it is easy to see that they would have lacked much of their excitement if they had been backed by greater financial resources. Thus, I think, the loser gains.

Disregarding my future security I had left the Sudan to participate, rather unspectacularly, in the war. I do not like war, because I am not the warrior type. Nor do I bow easily to discipline. The petty restrictions of Service life irked me, and the final months of hostilities found me man-œuvring for permission to climb the eight Virunga mountains, all of which I wanted to tackle from Belgian territory if possible.

A letter was sent in the first instance to Colonel R. Hoier, who was Conservateur des Parcs at the time and stationed at Rumangabo. In his reply, the Colonel provided me with the address of the Institut des Parcs Nationaux in Brussels and gave useful information about the mountains. He gave it as his opinion that the best season for climbing was the period July–August, when the weather could be expected to be good but the visibility poor. The months of December, January and February were also stated to be favourable, with the rider that " one is never sure, and usually there will be rain at every new moon and full moon."

The reply to my letter to the President of the Institut des Parcs Nationaux shows the very considerate attitude adopted by the Belgian authorities; as well as the complexities of the task confronting me.

The letter reads:

MONSIEUR,

During the last meeting, the Direction Committee of our Institut examined your request and decided, notwithstanding the strict character of our rules, to give it a partially favourable answer.

The volcanoes Nyiragongo and Nyamuragira can be reached through the General Tourist Organisation of the National Albert Park.

The climbing of the volcanoes Muhavura, Gahinga, and Sabinio, all three situated in a sector from which we systematically keep visitors away, we recommend you to begin from the north slopes of these volcanoes, which are in British territory where nothing forbids your presence.

Finally, for the group Mikeno, Karisimbi, Vishoke, we decided to take in your favour a measure of exception as far as the first two are concerned.

You are authorised, in consequence, to occupy the Kabara cabin of our Institut, situated in the Mikeno–Karisimbi sector. Starting from this place you will be able to climb the Mikeno, then with the possibility to also occupy the Lukumi cabin, start afterwards the climb of Karisimbi.

Before starting these various climbs, we would be grateful to you if you would contact the Conservateur of the National Park in residence at Rumangabo. A tax of 500 frs. will be asked for the double climb of the Mikeno-Karisimbi. The usual charge, on the other hand, will be required for the Nyamuragira and Nyiragongo.

In addition, we would like to remind you of the general dispositions in force, in those parts from which it is prohibited specially, not only to kill, wound or even disturb the wild animals, but also to disturb the natural resources of any kind, by harvesting or taking samples of original materials either vegetable or mineral, or by excavating works etc.

Assuring you, Monsieur, of our distinguished consideration,

LE PRESIDENT

This was only a beginning, but a very encouraging one. It will be noticed that permission to climb Vishoke was withheld, but this did not concern me greatly at the time.

Immediately I received this letter, I wrote to the Conservateur to tell him of my impending visit. I already held Col. Hoier in high esteem, so that it was disquieting to learn that he was about to retire. He wrote, in his quaint English: " As I am probably going home to Belgium in May, I shall not be here when you come, but my successor, the Commandant van Cools, shall be glad to help you with the trip in the Park. You do pass in the park places where the gorillas quite often are seen; all the same it is really a luck to get on them. Hope you will get it."

I hoped so too, for apart from the primary object of climbing, there was a strong desire to encounter the mountain gorillas in their natural habitat.

It is estimated that between 500 and 600 [1] of these animals live in the vicinity of Mikeno and Karisimbi, though it is quite impossible to determine their number with anything approaching true accuracy. The first specimen, or type specimen as it is called, was obtained from the Karisimbi region by Oscar Beringe during a hunting trip undertaken while on leave from Tanganyika, where he was engaged on railway construction work. His discovery was made about the year 1902 or 1903, so that the mountain gorilla did not become known until fully 50 years after the West African type form had been secured by the famous French explorer Paul B. du Chaillu. In honour of its discoverer, the Central African subspecies was named *Gorilla gorilla Beringei*, though many writers have caused confusion by giving Beringe's name as Beringer, and consequently turning the scientific name into *Beringeri* instead of *Beringei*. (The name *Gorilla gorilla gorilla* distinguishes the lowland forest species inhabiting West Africa.) The mountain species is the larger of the two, but its arms are said to be shorter. There are differences in skull proportions, and in particular, the palate of the mountain gorilla is longer. Also its pelage is thicker and longer.

[1] Col. Hoier's figures.

In adult males, the lower part of the back is banded with grey, while the lower extremities of body and head are greyish brown. Very old animals have a grey or silver patch on the loins. The body is large and thickset, almost square. The arms are very long, the legs short, weak and noticeably bowed. The enormous hands are beautifully made. The feet are broad and have big toes that are like thumbs. The face, chest, palms of the hands and soles of the feet are hairless. The " white " of the eye is black, and the iris bright reddish brown. Males attain considerably greater dimensions than females, and the latter lack the silver appearance on the back.

" They are very noisy animals," writes Mr. Ionides. " Not only do they break off large branches while feeding, but they make several sounds of their own. There is a vocal sound which seems to be conversation. There is a sharp barking roar of alarm, shriller in the case of females and deeper and of greater volume when made by the males. A curious sound rather like that of two empty bottles being struck together is made by the cupped hands striking the cheeks. There is also the well-known drumming made by striking the cupped hands against the chest.

" Like most primates, these apes are very alert and will at once make off on getting the scent or sight of a human. However, if the male fears danger to his family, he may demonstrate against an intruder, or even charge if seriously worried or alarmed on rare occasions, though I do not think that gorillas are normally savage animals, and I consider that such demonstrations and charges are purely defensive.

" Gorillas are easy to spoor from their habit of tearing up the vegetation while feeding. I think they are entirely herbivorous, and do not eat any animal food, as baboons (*Papio* sp.) do upon occasions. Their food on Mount Sabinio, at least during the month of September 1946, seemed to consist mainly of young bamboo shoots, a species of ground fungus, a species of red berry from a tree and wild celery. Gorillas are strictly diurnal and sleep at night. For this purpose beds are made of grass. The big male of a troop, probably owing to his great weight, makes his bed on the ground. The females and young bend down bamboos and then put grass on them, thus making a sort of spring mattress. The beds are very much fouled beyond where the animals sleep. At dawn they start feeding in the more open forest lower down and continue eating during the day, going higher up into the dense bamboo as the sun gets up. In the evening they descend to the lower, and rather more open parts, though all the forest is very thick. The big male usually feeds a little apart from his family."

There are two isolated gorilla habitats in the Belgian Congo, one bounded roughly by the extinct volcanoes Mikeno, Karisimbi, Vishoke and Sabinio, and the other to the west of Lake Edward and Lake Kivu. A third habitat lies outside the Congo in the Kayonza forest of Kigezi District, Uganda Protectorate. Gorillas of the Lake Edward region live at a comparatively low altitude: only one has been recorded as shot at slightly over 2,000 ft. They are inclined to resemble more closely the West African species, at least in bodily proportions, and the scientific subspecies name given to them is *Gorilla gorilla rex pygmaeorum*. On the other hand, the gorillas of Kayonza have not been separated from *G.g.beringei*.

T. A. Barnes and the American naturalist, Carl Akeley, gained a name for themselves through their exploits in shooting and capturing specimens of the mountain gorilla, but since the formation of a strict nature reserve mainly for protection of these animals, they have remained more or less unmolested. In the Lake Edward habitat, the capture of gorillas was allowed under permit until it was realised that it was impossible to capture the young of the species without killing the adults. Between February 1, 1948, and March 31, 1949, twelve captures were made under the supervision of a Game Officer, but for these twelve captures, another twelve deaths resulted, and it was decided that no more captures should be made. So, for a number of years, the Governor-General has issued no more permits, and shooting has only taken place in legitimate cases of self-defence.

There have been occasional reports of gorillas attacking human beings, and there is one authentic case on record of an old male, driven out of a troop, attacking natives and causing panic in the Goma district of the Belgian Congo early in 1948. Unprovoked attacks of this nature are rare, however, and most of the fantastic stories about these primates can be altogether discounted. In any case, I intended to keep to my promise, made by letter to the Institut in Brussels, not to take any firearms into this wild life sanctuary. My practice has been to go unarmed on all occasions, and I have by now encountered at very close range practically every kind of wild animal in Africa without coming to any harm.

III. *Eight Peaks and Many Problems*

A PART FROM obtaining permission to climb, there was nothing that could be done before demobilisation, though I contrived during a short period of leave to make a haphazardly prepared expedition to the Chimanimani mountains in the Melsetter district of Southern Rhodesia. These delightful mountains, bordering on the Manica e Sofala region of Moçambique, were fairly remote at the time, and it was not until December 1949 that the area was set aside as a National Park with the object of making it accessible to visitors. Again my only companions were natives, and our only shelter from the rain and cold was a rock cavern ideally situated between the two main peaks. This thoroughly satisfying little venture would not have been possible without the kindliness and hospitality of Mr. Gideon Martin, a direct descendant of the Little Trek leader and a man who was completely under the spell of Chimanimani, which he looked upon as his own. An Afrikaner, freedom-loving and reserved, he would never have given me access to Chimanimani if he had not become assured of the sincerity of my feeling for these and other mountains.

Shortly after this brief interlude, the war dragged to an end. For me it meant freedom to go where I pleased within the limits of my passport, but at first I found it difficult to shake off the lackadaisical habits which service life instils. Food, clothing and lodging, which had been provided for so long, were now once again to be my direct concern. All travel arrangements, which had been attended to by R.T.O.s in war time, became my own responsibility again. In the first few days of civilian life, one has to regain one's forgotten self-reliance.

Starting out from Bulawayo on Saturday, April 3, 1946, I met with my first difficulty at the Northern Rhodesia border. It was said at the time that unbelievable restrictions were brought to bear on British subjects wishing to pass from the one Rhodesian territory to the other, and so it proved, with the result that I was turned back for some trifling irregularity.

Gloomy days followed, and an official letter which ended " and so I can only advise the abandonment of your projected trip to the Belgian Congo " did nothing to console me. But the gloom did not last, for after a delay of three weeks a second start was made, and on this occasion there was no hindrance at the border. My original intention had been to make for Broken Hill, in Northern Rhodesia, and then to go by road to the southern end of Lake Tanganyika and proceed by lake steamer to Uvira. This plan proved impracticable without transport of my own, and the circuitous route via Elizabethville, Kamina, Kabalo and Albertville had to be taken as the only alternative. The ideal conveyance would have been a safari van, but this was beyond my means, and I could only look with envy and longing on the resources of people like Attilio Gatti, who toured the Congo with two-ton trucks, convoys of caravans, commodious tents and every convenience that could be desired.

A delay of an entire week was enforced at Elizabethville, where every hotel was filled up. Fortunately, after completing one full round of the town in search of accommodation, my plight was observed by an army officer who kindly made arrangements for me to spend the night on a camp bed set up on the veranda of his room at the Leopold II, where I could obtain a room to myself on the following day. Such delays had not been anticipated, and in order to preserve my money, I had to forgo all forms of entertainment and to refuse any offer of drinks. Even so, my enforced stay at the most expensive hotel in Elizabethville depleted my reserve of Belgian francs to such an extent that, for the first of many times, it became a matter of deciding whether to carry on or turn back.

It was disturbing to look at a map, with so little distance covered and the vastly greater amount of travel still to be done. Without labouring the point too much, it was a case not only of an outlandish ambition, but of attempting to accomplish too much with the cash and facilities available to me. Many were the times I should have taken stock of my resources, but if I had ever stopped to consider my position in relation to the hard facts of ordinary living, I should have seen that I hadn't a chance.

Instead, I blundered on, mindful only of the mountains which, I knew, would reward me, though when, or in what manner, there could be no telling. It is so easy now to look back and see the right or wrong, the sense or folly of any act, but at the time there was nothing in my make-up but brute obstinacy. I had come to appreciate beauty in nature, and I knew much about the reward for effort which follows at the end of a hard climb.

Many things I knew, but in some respects I was unschooled and still very much of a boy struggling forlornly with the problems of a man's world about which I knew too little. Some will say that I was running away from reality, but might it be that reality was just what I was searching for.

The route from Elizabethville to Kisenyi, at the north end of Lake Kivu, was already known to me, but in the reverse direction, for I had travelled this way from the Sudan to Southern Rhodesia. But whereas everything had gone smoothly and effortlessly on the previous occasion, there was now one delay after another to contend with. At Costermansville [1] there was the final delay, when the one and only lake steamer broke down and temporary accommodation had to be sought until a steam barge could be brought into service.

There were the usual compensations, however, and I found a kindred soul in a Dane, a grey, tousle-haired veteran who was travelling with a portable welding plant and " looking for somewhere to settle." He had taken a look at Kenya, the Rhodesias, Moçambique, Angola and the Congo, and of these he favoured Angola. We talked through the whole of the night until the early hours of the morning, and for all his store of experience, I felt sorry for him because, at his age, he had no home to turn to, nor any country to call his own. He had been in Ethiopia for several years until forced to leave when the Italians entered. Then he had undertaken what must have been an epic journey to the Southern Sudan and Uganda by motor-cycle and sidecar.

When the overcrowded steam barge eventually made its way with much fuss to Goma, which is the port serving Kisenyi, my dormant enthusiasm was awakened by a re-acquaintance with the mountains. For a while Nyiragongo appeared directly ahead, seemingly at the water's edge and providing an admirable navigational aid. Then, as clouds swept over, its great bulk receded into the distance, and as it did so, the less inspiring mass of Nyamlagira came into view. Karisimbi and Mikeno, which under favourable conditions may also be seen from the lake, remained lost to sight, and I amused myself by trying to imagine their outline and position in the area of thickest cloud. Mikeno has been described as the " Matterhorn of Africa," and that is how I was thinking of it when abruptly the clouds

[1] By decree of King Baudouin of the Belgians, the name of this administrative township has since reverted to its old name of Bukavu.

swirled and lifted, revealing both Mikeno and Karisimbi just where I had imagined them to be. Then, as suddenly as the clouds had lifted, they closed in again, and there was the rumbling of thunder in the air. My diary reveals my observations, but makes no mention of the most vivid impression of all—that of my own puniness in face of the task which confronted me.

Goma and Kisenyi form a single town in embryo, and midway between them runs the western boundary of Ruanda, which prior to the first world war was a German colonial possession but which now constitutes a mandated territory under Belgian trusteeship. Goma hill rises to the north-west, acting as a distinctive landmark, and there are higher hills standing as a background to Kisenyi. Some of these grassed, wooded prominences run into long headlands which jut into the lake. A number of islands, of which Idjwi is the largest, are visible from Kisenyi on a clear day, and from any of the surrounding hills there is a wider vista than ever of the lake and its islands and headlands, the volcanoes, and of Kisenyi itself, which nestles half hidden among avenues of palm and eucalyptus. Native villages, also partially obscured by trees and banana plantations, send up small spirals of smoke from fires that seem to burn endlessly.

On a clear day, the bell-like dome of Karisimbi can be seen: its native name means " the white shell," for its summit is often cloaked with a sprinkling of hail or sleet. The gaunt crag of Mikeno stands out in sharp contrast, and this, the smaller of the two mountains, gains appreciably in effect because of its austere outline. Karisimbi has the greater height and bulk, but Mikeno is the more splendid, more awe-inspiring, more challenging. Whenever those two giants of the Virunga range are visible from Kisenyi, then Nyiragongo and Nyamlagira should also be in view, for they are nearer and do not create so much bad weather in the vicinity.

This, as I have described it, was the Kivu region as it appeared to me before setting out on my Virunga adventure, and it lived splendidly up to the Africa of my dreams. This was the Africa which had drawn me, and I loved it not only for its mountains and sparklingly clear lake, but also because the indigenous Africans still lived their own lives there, and the fauna and flora of the mountain area had not changed through the centuries which have marked elsewhere the abandonment of simplicity and the development of ugliness and noise.

My first task in this delightful setting was to contact the Conservateur who, I hoped, would be at his residence at Rumangabo, about 32 miles from Kisenyi along the Goma to Rutshuru road. It was equally likely that this official would be out on tour, but to have sent a letter of inquiry would have taken too long, and in any case he might not have been able to read or speak a word of English. Various sorts of vehicles appeared to be making occasional journeys between Goma and Rutshuru, but I wanted if possible to reach Rumangabo and return to Kisenyi without hiring a car specially for the purpose.

After several promises of transport, and as many disappointments, I decided to walk, though I was told that I would be mad to do so because it would mean going by night along a tortuous road hemmed in by thick forests which are the haunts of elephants and several of the carnivores, including lion and leopard. I was saved from the consequences of my decision by a last-minute offer of a lift by two tourists who had made the crossing of Lake Tanganyika with me and were at the time making their way to the game reserve at Ruindi Camp. This welcome offer did not, however, preclude the hazardous return journey under similar conditions. I was taking the first throw of the dice in my gamble, but by now I was prepared to do anything rather than remain idle.

On the way to Rumangabo, I was surprised to notice the number of elephant droppings in the roadway. Since then I have on several occasions noticed that, where roads are constructed through game country, some species of mammals prefer to make use of these thoroughfares, especially at night when there is normally no traffic about. Elephants in particular find graded roadways easier to negotiate than dense bush, and being inveterate travellers, they need to cross the roads frequently when going from one place to another. It follows that clearings, roads and pathways are equally convenient to them as places in which to meet the calls of nature, and so their droppings are found at these points rather than in thick bush. Some of the larger carnivores also choose to travel along roadways, and I have often observed the spoor of noctunal carnivores following dirt roads for considerable distances.

The road between Goma and Rutshuru cuts through an extensive bed of lava, for the entire area was, until quite recent times, an active volcanic zone where not a blade of grass grew. Now there is thick forest and undergrowth, particularly to the west, and with the regrowth of flora there has been the return of a mammalian population.

I had to keep a sharp lookout for the small signpost which I knew to be obscurely placed on the west side of the road, for Rumangabo is not a town or even a village, but only the Park official's residence. When eventually we came upon the signpost I asked my companions to wait until I had made certain that the Conservateur was at home and not out on trek, for if he was away I would have had to go to Rutshuru and seek accommodation there.

So, sprinting up the gravel drive, I rounded a bend and came to a halt before a white man of slender build who stood supervising the work of a gang of Africans. The man, realising at once who his visitor was (for he had learned by " bush telegraph " of my arrival at Kisenyi), came forward with hand extended in greeting.

" Ah! Commandant van Cools? "

" Yes."

" You *do* speak English? "

" A leetle."

With a feeling of intense relief, I ran back to the waiting car, bade farewell, and returned with the Commandant along the drive and up the hill. The recently appointed Conservateur was living temporarily in a rather dilapidated wooden bungalow which had served his predecessor, Colonel Hoier, as home for many years. It was the construction of a new house for himself that the Conservateur had been supervising until my arrival that day.

In the Commandant's new block of offices on the hilltop we talked and scanned maps, sorted out and packed a tent, ropes, blankets and the other paraphernalia of mountain travel. The Commandant entered into the spirit of the thing with an enthusiasm which astonished and pleased me, and I wondered for a while if it was his intention to accompany me.

Fortunately my arrival had coincided with pay day, which meant that all the natives from outlying districts had gathered at Rumangabo, and that arrangements could be made at once which would cover my whole Congo expedition.

Commandant van Cools was of the opinion that the two live volcanoes, Nyiragongo and Nyamlagira, should be tackled first, and it was agreed to send all equipment on to the District Commissioner's hut at Kibati and have guides and porters assembled so that a start could be made in three days' time. Permission was given to use the D.C.'s hut while I was in the vicinity of Nyiragongo.

After the climbs of Nyiragongo and Nyamlagira it would be necessary to find some means of transporting all the equipment to the Conservateur's hut at Kibumba, in the Mikeno sector of the Albert National Park, from which I planned to leave with a fresh team of men for the group Mikeno, Karisimbi, Vishoke.[1]

A tent would be needed on Nyiragongo but not on Nyamlagira, where there is a hut at Mushumangabo, at 6,600 ft. The tent would be needed again on Vishoke, but for the ascents of Mikeno and Karisimbi I could make use of the Kabara and Lukumi huts of the Institut des Parcs Nationaux. The native chief of each area concerned was instructed to give every assistance and provide a reliable guide in each sector of operations. The only real drawback was that I could not go on to Sabinio, Mgahinga and Muhavura from the Mikeno sector. This trio would have to be approached from the Uganda side.

When all preliminary arrangements had been made, we strolled across the hill for lunch in the old wooden bungalow. The Commandant's English was not good, but we contrived to make ourselves understood about all important matters, and we had so much in common that no fine mastery of language was called for. All the same, I was at this stage so entirely dependent upon the goodwill of the Park official that I could not but be glad of what English, he had, even though he had acquired it while languishing in a German prisoner-of-war camp for several years. Indeed until he met an American officer during his last few months of captivity, he had been unable to speak a word of English.

From the hilltop at Rumangabo, we were able to look together on Nyiragongo and Nyamlagira where they stand out boldly from the lava plain. Storm clouds hid Karisimbi from view, and we had only a fleeting glimpse of Mikeno. On a clear day, the Commandant told me, the three volcanoes bordering on Uganda could be seen distinctly.

To the north-west there was the high Kabasha escarpment leading to the Ituri forest, Ruwenzori, and the lakes Edward, George and Albert. A small lake in the distance (Lake Tshuki, I believe) sparkled like a jewel whenever the sun's intermittent rays touched its surface. The lives of the scattered African community moved on serenely in the woods and grass-

[1] The Conservateur failed to notice that my permit did not cover this mountain, and I did not draw his attention to the fact. In self-defence I must say that I was unaware at the time whether instructions had been given for Vishoke to be included or excluded from my itinerary, for when he addressed the Africans the Conservateur spoke, at least in part, in Kiswahili. However, my intentions were strictly dishonourable, for it was already in my thoughts to bribe the natives if necessary, or take any action open to me rather than be thwarted by a failure to reach this one mountain.

lands, and a multitude of wild animals kept to their own little fastnesses, silent and unobtrusive.

Frankly, I envied the Conservateur, but I realised that he had gained no more than a fair return for all that he had suffered in the past. This was confirmed when he confided to me how all this freedom and beauty contrasted with the brutality of a prison camp. At times, he told me, he relived the horrors of war and found it difficult to believe in the reality of the beauty of Rumangabo. I knew from this that a worthy successor had been found to carry on the good work of Colonel Hoier.

It was 3 o'clock in the afternoon when I left Rumangabo with a small pack on my back. The weather was changeable, but with fair going I hoped to accomplish the worst part of my journey along the lonely forest road by nightfall. The presence of many wild beasts on both sides of me did not cause me any undue anxiety, for I agreed with the Conservateur's summing up that if wild animals were as dangerous as most people imagine, there would be no indigenous peoples remaining in the game areas of Africa.

Forests are usually quiet, but at this time the shrill noise of crickets was so unbearably loud that I was compelled to turn my head from side to side in order to gain some slight relief for each ear-drum in turn.

No more than a mile had been covered when a torrential downpour drove me to seek cover in the thick undergrowth bordering the road. Intrigued, I went unnecessarily deep into the forest, following a tiny rivulet, and as I advanced, the crickets for many yards around stopped chirping. The silence acted as a warning to other wild denizens of the immediate neighbourhood, for suddenly there was a violent disturbance of the closed canopy above, and the entire forest seemed to be filled with motion and sound. Just as suddenly there was complete silence again, and after remaining motionless for a while I retraced my steps to the road, where I was just in time to see a fully grown dog-faced baboon (*Papio papio doguera*) lope leisurely across on all fours. I continued along the road, quite pleased to have solved the mystery of the disturbance. Only a slight rain was falling.

I had scarcely settled into my stride again when a sound which was not like that of any forest creature came to my ears. A car? Surely not; but, if so, would it be travelling in my direction? I hardly dared to hope so, and carried on walking without ever glancing ahead or to the rear. A half-minute or so of suspense and then a car drew up at my side, and when I turned to look, room was already being made for me by an African, while the driver was clearing a way for me amongst an odd assortment of safari equipment and live chickens. It proved to be the District Commissioner for Rutshuru Province, and his destination was not only Kisenyi, but the hotel at which I was staying before leaving for the mountains.

The following few days were a whirl of excited preparations, with sleep almost out of the question. Now my thoughts could be given full rein, whereas hitherto there had been the persistent fear of reaching as far as Kisenyi only to find some insuperable bar to further progress. There was food to be bought, and water—for I had been forewarned that there would be no drinking water available in the Mikeno sector. This seemed unbelievable in view of the heavy rains in this area, but fortunately I had the sense to heed the warning and take with me a supply of bottled soda water. Most of my food was in tins, but several items, including a tin-opener, had been left behind purposely, as I intended to acquire them at the farthest point of my travels. This was a mistake, for the stores at Goma and Kisenyi were no longer filled, as they were in war-time, with the ceaseless flow of supplies which the United States sent in exchange for raw materials.

As zero hour approached, I was still without a tin opener and without a chance of getting one. It was a ridiculous state of affairs. Improvise? Of course I could, but all my life I had put up with makeshifts and substitutes, and inwardly I rebelled against them. I wanted, at this time, a tin opener—not a mallet and sheath knife. A multitude of people have their longings, great or small, and without them there would be no struggle for improvement. My longing was for a tin opener. I was furious about it,

IV. *The Cooking Pots*

IT WAS Saturday, June 1, when I left in a hired car for the D.C.'s hut at Kibati, about 17 miles due north from Kisenyi. Here there was a modest brick building, entirely empty, in a clearing to the west of the Goma-to-Rutshuru road. Small groups of native huts were dotted about the grasslands, but there was nothing in the immediate vicinity that deserved the name of village.

All my equipment, apart from the provisions which I had brought with me that morning, was piled outside the hut, and a horde of chattering natives formed themselves into a single line with their backs to Nyiragongo. I had specified eight, but there must have been nearer eighty. There appeared to be no leader amongst them, but one fellow, more forward than the rest, showed insolence from the beginning, and I made it clear to him that I did not want him. His unwillingness to leave made me think afterwards that, despite his insolent behaviour, he may have been the appointed leader of the party and that I may have offended, without meaning to, the local system of chieftainship and authority. The others certainly seemed cowed by the man. In any case his demands were quite outrageous and his manner so intolerable that I was pleased to be finally rid of him. Only when he had been literally driven from the scene was it possible to deal at all efficiently with the sorting and distributing of loads, but the incident left me with a feeling of unpleasantness, for I had never before experienced any trouble with native porters in Africa.

In my selection of men for any similar undertaking, I have always aimed at a working sufficiency, so that each man has a duty to perform and no one is overburdened in any way. The strongest physical specimens are not necessarily the best for porterage or climbing: it is generally the character of the individual which determines his ability to keep going in a crisis and to couple resourcefulness with vigour. To the uninitiated, all

Africans of one race look alike, but it is possible, if one makes a study of it, to distinguish at a glance the underlying character of any African. Arrogance is a trait to avoid, and fortunately it cannot be concealed by the pigmentation of the skin.

It appeared from a distance that Nyiragongo would call for three men armed with pangas [1] to go ahead and open up a path through the undergrowth. These men would be kept hard at work over the lower slopes, and could not be expected to carry any loads. The man chosen to be guide had to know the route, and by virtue of his status would keep me company and carry only a light haversack containing a few necessaries and a camera.

Eventually ten men set out with me in single file over the intervening plain to the base of the mountain. Our object was to establish a camp at about 9,500 ft. from which the climb to the summit could be carried out early on the following morning. It would depend upon what climbing we did in the crater summit as to whether a second night would be spent on the volcano before returning to Kibati. The number of men proved to be two or three too many, but this was the first of the mountains on my itinerary, so that conditions were more or less unknown to me and it was better, I felt, to be on the safe side.

I had neither watch nor compass, so that my only knowledge of time and direction had to be based on observations of the sun and the known points of the landscape. The points of sunrise and sunset would be noted carefully at each camping site, and from acquaintance with local times of dusk and dawn, I was able to estimate the hours between with a fair amount of accuracy.

Our start had been delayed as a result of the early morning preparations, but once on the way we covered ground rapidly. Beyond the flatness of Kibati, the impressive dome of Nyiragongo appeared above and beyond the extinct crater of Shaheru. Baruta, almost a mountain in itself, but attached to the northern extremity of the elongated mountain mass, was hidden from sight by the enormous bulk of the active crater. Two old crater cones lay between Shaheru and the gently rising slope of Nyamlagira. The farther we went, the more I became aware of the extreme scarcity of standing water in this volcanic region. The soil here is thin and the rock, being porous, allows water to percolate instead of forming into channels and becoming rivers.

We continued our approach from the south until we entered the thick

[1] A type of knife with a short wooden handle and curved blade, used widely in Central Africa.

forest of the lower slopes, whereupon we veered to the north-west before heading directly north again. The sky, which had become overcast, held the threat of rain, and before many minutes had passed, we could hear raindrops pattering on the leaves overhead. It is a strange feeling, passing under a storm without getting wet or uncomfortable, but this feeling did not last long. In a short time the rain had started to come through, and soon we were ankle deep in mud as we pushed our way through briars.

On only two occasions did we break out of the undergrowth and see the surrounding country. On the first occasion, Karisimbi showed up in the distance with Lake Kivu, clear and calm and dotted with islands, far away to the south. On the second occasion, we overlooked the Shaheru crater, now overgrown with a rich variety of small vegetation; but there was no time to go down to it.

There was still a light rain falling when we reached the camping site at about 9,500 ft., and the ground was sodden, with briars encroaching everywhere. The weather cleared shortly after our arrival, but the wood we gathered was so wet that it could only be coaxed into flame with the utmost difficulty. Then, while our clothes were drying and a meal was being prepared, I set about a few ordinary arm exercises. I next went through a routine series of exercises with the chest expanders which I find ideal for use on mountains, where space for equipment is limited and most of the hard effort of climbing is concentrated in the legs.

The reaction upon my porters, gathered round the fire, was totally unexpected. They had never before seen a white man perform in this manner, and the chest expanders with their bright coils of metal expanding and contracting were completely new to them, and something to wonder at. In a buzz of excited comment, they saw me go through a variety of exercises until, without a thought for the consequences, I handed the expanders to the biggest, brawniest of the men, who seemed to think it would be child's play to follow my example. Not for one minute did he doubt his ability to pull the springs to the full extent of his arms by any method that the tall, gangling *bwana* had demonstrated, and he grasped the wooden hand-grips eagerly and confidently after I'd shown him how to do the simple across-the-chest exercise. He pulled and strained, with muscles bulging, but try as he might, he could not extend the springs for more than a few inches.

By now the spectators of this surprising display were in fits of laughter and there was much good-natured backchat. It did not require an intimate knowledge of their language to know that they were ragging their crest-fallen comrade unmercifully, and he, seeing a chance to retaliate, handed the expanders round, but each in turn failed, as the first had done, to pull the coiled springs to anything like their fullest extent. Finally they were handed back to me and I continued with my routine, going through each of the exercises 12 times.

It was a small event in itself, but to these simple souls, whose lives follow an almost changeless pattern, here was a chance for endless gossip, and I would see them afterwards going through all the motions with imaginary chest expanders, laughing and gesticulating. Without a doubt my prestige had soared immensely!

As I sat by the open camp fire long after darkness had fallen I was rewarded by a memorable sight. A dull red pall of vapour could be seen rising from the crater and forming a cloud above the summit. It billowed and swirled in endless motion under the effects of a gusty north wind, now rising, now spreading out. The air was chill, but the sight above me lent a warmth that could almost be felt.

We started on the climb to the summit very early in the morning. It proved to be excessively tiring as the gradient was consistently steep, although not difficult. The forest ended abruptly within a short distance of our camp among the briars, and thereafter the ascent continued over bare, jagged lava. As we neared the top we lost our protection from the wind, which swept down with increasing force until our arrival at the uppermost part of the crater rim, where we were met by the full fury of its blast. Up there we had difficulty in standing erect.

Huddled together for warmth, we peered into the deep recesses of the volcano. Within the floor of the crater, far below and surrounded by almost vertical walls of insecure lava, there is a vertical round vent at the bottom of which, at an unknown depth, lies a pool of molten lava. An intermittent sound, like wild waves breaking on a rocky shore, came from this boiling lava pool, followed by successive puffs of vapour. It was an awe-inspiring sight, and I thought later how fantastic the view would be at night, with the red glow of the heat visible. It would be extremely dangerous to reach the crater rim after dark, and no one has ever done so to my knowledge, but the sight would be an unparalleled one.

At present, the bubbling cauldron of lava deep down in Nyiragongo acts as a safety valve, but this has not prevented the area between this volcano and Lake Kivu, particularly in the south-western sector, from becoming the centre of accessory activity since the eruption in 1905 of the Kanamaharagi cone, nearly 10 miles north-east of Nyiragongo. In 1912 an eruption which built up the Rumoka volcano between Nyiragongo and Sake,[1] is said also to have caused volcanic activity on the bed of Lake Kivu.[2]

A new fissure was opened up between Nyiragongo and Rumoka during an eruption which began on the night of March 1-2, 1948, after preliminary earth tremors had been felt in the area. The rate of flow of lava was much greater than from Nyamlagira during its 1938-39 eruption and within eight days a stream many hundreds of yards wide had reached a point south of the Goma-to-Sake road. This first lava flow halted about one and a half miles from Lake Kivu, but on March 10, a second flow began to issue from a new centre of activity near the eastern limit of the extinct Shove crater. A few days later a broader stream of lava, burning up everything in its path, reached the northern shores of Lake Kivu and poured into the water over an area half a mile in extent. Clouds of steam were generated and the water for some distance away was heated to a high temperature.

From this it might be assumed that the ascent of a volcano of latent energy is a fairly dangerous undertaking, but this is not really so. An eruption may take place at short notice, but normally there will be warning signals and plenty of time in which to take avoiding action.

What was decidedly foolish of me on this occasion, and an outright, indefensible courting of disaster, was to go down alone to the crater platform. I dared not take any of the natives with me, for there was no one reliable enough or at all experienced in roped climbing. However, there are times when impetuosity drives one to unguarded action, and again there are times when release from boredom and stagnation depend upon such impulsive decisions. At least I took the precaution, slight as it was, of fastening a rope to my waist and instructing the more intelligent of the fellows to belay it to a convenient crag of lava and then release and belay again according to my progress down the vertical wall. There was only a modicum of safety in these precautions, and what I could not guard

---

[1] Pronounced *Sakki*.

[2] It is significant of the volcanic nature of this region that there are no crocodiles or hippopotami in the lake, though remains of the former have been found near its shores, suggesting that crocodiles may have lived in the lake at some time in the past. It is possible that the chemical properties of the water may have changed as a result of volcanic activity, and that crocodiles, and perhaps hippos, have left the lake comparatively recently. I find it difficult to believe, however, that Lake Kivu could have been a suitable habitat for crocodiles at any time, or for hippos for that matter, though a few may have lived there at various periods of history.

against in any way was a crumbling of the lava, which at all parts of the wall was frighteningly insecure.

The step over the side was like a step into Dante's inferno, and the lower I went, the greater became this depressing difference from the world above. At times I had to glance upwards to reassure myself about the belay, but equally often I looked at the black faces peering over the crater rim in order to allay my own flagging confidence. Never have I been so dependent upon poor natives, and this incident probably had the effect in later years of making me realise afresh that all men of whatever race or colour are fully qualified human beings with no inferiority apart from their present stations in life.

From the farthest extremity to which my ropes—two of which had been joined together—would permit me to go, I went ropeless. I have seen it stated that the vertical wall leading to the platform containing the main crater of Nyiragongo is 800 ft. in depth, but in fact it is nowhere near this figure. I should not like to commit myself to an estimate of my own, for I did not make any accurate check at the time, and to-day I could only hazard a wild guess.

Once on the platform, there was no longer a view of the vertical chimney from which the activity of Nyiragongo arises, but it was possible to observe more clearly the intermittent " breathings " of vapour and to sense the rumbling explosions which released each puff of sulphurous fumes.

It suddenly struck me that if there was a veering or backing of the wind to a new quarter, the fumes would be sent straight at me. The thought was not a comforting one, and I panicked and started to climb out of the crater as quickly as I could. The ascent was comparatively easy, especially as I could guide the ropes and give signalled instructions for any slackness to be taken up. All the same, it left little time for contemplation, and I expended a good deal of nervous energy before helping hands and broad smiles greeted me at the top.

Like many adventures, difficulties and dangers, this one looked better after its safe accomplishment. I would not go again into that crater alone, and neither would I boast of having done so once. If we reflect, there is scant cause for self-satisfaction, let alone boasting, in the performance of any sort of feat, for usually the spur is fear, braggadocio, or down-right inability to reason.

The men who had been left behind had already struck camp when we reached there, and after a brief pause for food and drink we continued with a descent that was altogether too hurried, and somewhat marred for me by a rascal who went to great lengths to sort out for himself the lightest load. He further annoyed me with requests for food, clothing, cigarettes, and more money than the others on the grounds that he was a "policeman." Apart from fraying my temper, he upset the other porters with insinuations that they were to be paid less than the standard amount. Upon arrival at Kibati I had the satisfaction of sending this defaulter away with his bare dues, much to the delight of the more willing and capable workers, each of whom received an extra award of money and cigarettes. The most intelligent of the porters was retained to meet my needs while at Kibati and arrange for a few picked men to go on with us to Mushumangabo and the top of Nyamlagira.

This, the most accessible of the Virunga volcanoes, has nothing to offer from the purely mountaineering aspect, but it was important to me as an eighth part of my eight-peak scheme, and it served also to strengthen my limbs and give me a closer acquaintance with the area and its inhabitants. Therefore I will not include a description of the climb, but will limit myself to the following few details of general interest.

The last eruption of Nyamlagira took place in 1938. For several years prior to this, the huge, shallow crater had contained a pool of incandescent lava which gradually welled up, filling a section of the crater and eventually overflowing through a depression in the western rim. Colonel Hoier happened to be on the spot when the actual eruption began, on January 28, 1938, his arrival at the crater edge coinciding with violent tremors which shook the whole mountain and caused the collapse of the central cone. Shortly afterwards tremendous explosions heralded the formation of a new crater, now known as Shambena, on the south-western flank at a height of nearly 7,380 ft. A shower of ashes together with columns of steam burst out of the new cone and a flow of molten lava, subsiding in the main crater, poured out from fissures lower down. With inexorable force, the lava forced its path along a trail of devastation, burning up the forest on its way, to reach Lake Kivu in December of the same year. This lava stream crusted over at one period and continued thereafter in subterranean channels to its culmination in Sake Bay. Gradually the upheaval dwindled in its intensity until finally the volcano settled once more to its quiescent state.

Big game, though not in large numbers, is to be found on the volcano, for there is a water-filled crater below Mushumangabo, and while I was in the Mikeno sector in 1946, the present Conservateur and his assistant went on a tour of investigation during which they were obstructed by a herd of elephants. These congregated in the pathway at a point where there was no possible deviation.

Trees growing on the mountain and the plain below attain considerable size, but, as the soil is shallow, their roots spread along the surface instead of seeking depth, with the result that they are easily dislodged by the passage of elephants.

With the ascents of Nyiragongo and Nyamlagira accomplished, I returned to Kibati with the object of spending a single night there before moving on to the Mikeno sector by porterage; but in this I was defeated, for the natives could not be persuaded to cross over into what was to them foreign territory. There was faint hope of any transport materialising, but I told them—by constant repetition of a few known words of the native language and much gesturing—that a careful watch was to be kept and any passing transport was to be diverted from the main road to me at the D.C.'s bungalow.

Mikeno and Karisimbi could be seen distinctly from Kibati when the atmosphere cleared in the evenings, but they appeared very remote, and with porterage out of the question, it seemed that I should be marooned and would have to return to Kisenyi and set out again from there, though the expense of a specially hired car would be an unexpected drain on my resources.

In the meantime, there was much to occupy my time and thoughts, and one night in particular was unforgettable. There were frequent stabbings of lightning from two sides, but the sky held its own light from countless visible stars, and there was a small crescent moon coming up. Scorpio, one of my favourite constellations, was wholly visible, and the Southern Cross, which can be of the greatest significance to wanderers from the northern hemisphere, was also in sight. The Plough, inverted, had its " handle " obscured. The tremendous bulk of Nyiragongo loomed darkly, thrown into relief by starlight, moonlight, and its own red glow from above, which was offset to the south by a prevailing north wind.

Many times that night I left the warmth indoors to follow the progress of each heavenly body, and at one stage I was rewarded by a sight which remains for ever in my memory. The Plough moved in its orbit until it was poised squarely above the glowing summit of the volcano, and it all looked like a steaming Christmas pudding being poured from a huge pot.

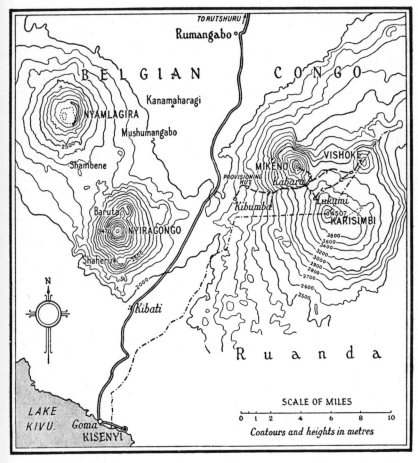

*The first and second sectors of the Virunga Mountains,
showing five of the peaks*

This impression was heightened by the red glow from Nyiragongo's expansive crater, which gave the effect of lighted brandy. As though this were not enough, occasional meteors hurtled across the sky like sparks thrown from the same giant cauldron. "Cooking Pots" is indeed an appropriate term when applied to the Nyiragongo sector of the Virunga volcanoes.

45

I retired to bed in a perplexed state of mind—so near to enjoyment and yet disturbed by my dependence upon fate, benign or otherwise. If only there could be an assurance that our strongest desires, so long as they are merited and fought for, will be brought to fulfilment! But there is no assurance—or we do not know how to heed it—and I fretted away the hours, dreading the thought of returning with a mission uncompleted.

My suspense was short-lived, for during breakfast on the following morning my native factotum came with the news, readily understood, that a lorry had arrived in the neighbourhood. Soon there came the sound of a heavy vehicle apparently passing on the Goma to Rutshuru road; then there was uncertainty as to which direction it was going in. At one time it was out of hearing in the distance, and it seemed certain that my instructions had not been understood or could not be obeyed. Then to my intense relief, an empty lorry driven by an Indian came bumping over the narrow, rutted track to the hut. The driver, who could speak a few words of English, was bound for Rutshuru but was willing to go out of his way in order to take me and my equipment as far as Kibumba, where I would be in the heart of the volcanic region and at the core of my adventure.

V. *An Expedition Sets Forth*

THE CONSERVATEUR'S bungalow at Kibumba was to serve me as a base camp before setting out for the trio of mountains in the vicinity, and it had been arranged that a messenger should be sent to notify Commandant van Cools after my return, whereupon a lorry would be dispatched from Rumangabo to take me on to Rutshuru, from whence I hoped to find transport to Kabale, in the Western Province of Uganda.

Remote places have always appealed to me, and at Kibumba I enjoyed a wonderful feeling of detachment from the man-made ugliness against which I had always revolted. There was a native village nearby, through which I had passed on my way by lorry, but this took nothing from the sense of detachment, for it blended perfectly with the scene as a whole. The cultivated plots of land, with their terracings and unplanned contours, were mottled with all shades of green, and with the white of pyrethrum, but nature never offends, even when vivid reds, blues and yellows appear together in the landscape. There was so much beauty in the surroundings, and so deep a silence, that my eyes and ears, from long abuse, seemed hardly able to appreciate it fully.

The Conservateur's bungalow was a brick building with its main entrance facing south ; it commanded a view of Nyiragongo and its subsidiaries, Shaheru and Baruta. A trim lawn was bordered with flowers, and beyond was a hillock covered with strawberries. The main room, with its large fireplace, was separated from the single bedroom by an antechamber with an interior stone archway. The furnishings of the bungalow consisted of a table, chairs and two beds. A small storeroom was fitted with a wash-basin, to which water was supplied from a rusty tank containing a little water that was so polluted as to be unfit for anything but washing.

I walked in the direction of Nyiragongo and Nyamlagira for a few hundred yards, and could turn and see the towering white dome of Kari-simbi and, though less often visible, the sheer rock summit of Mikeno. From this aspect Mikeno appeared to be quite unclimbable.

Within a few minutes of my arrival at Kibumba, two " Captains " (so they term themselves hereabouts) came to pay their respects. One was a tall, fine-looking fellow who acted with great courtesy and had the good sense to speak slowly and with studied deliberation on finding that I had practically no knowledge of Kiswahili, which is the language common to the natives of these parts. The other was a gloomy individual who appeared to be entirely lacking in humour (which most of them have in good measure). Doggedness appeared to be his chief quality. He looked under-nourished and seemed not to possess any of the attributes of a good climber. So much depended upon having a thoroughly trustworthy and resourceful leader for the coming expedition that the thought of having to put up with the morose Captain was not at all comforting.

They made it clear by words and signs that a sufficient number of porters would be ready for an early start on the following morning. In the meantime, I gathered, there was milk available, and to meet whatever demand there might be for this drink, a large herd of cows was driven on to the lawn. The hind legs of one beast were haltered with a bark rope and a quantity of extremely unhygienic milk came forth. It pays not to be too squeamish at times, but the methods used were so dirty that I thought it best to turn my back upon the proceedings, on the principle that what the eye does not see the heart does not grieve over.

Late in the afternoon, I glanced in the direction of Nyiragongo and saw a mass of white cloud building up from cumulus to cumulo-nimbus, and for one brief spell its towering form looked amazingly like the summit of Mikeno. The same overhang on the south face was shown and the inclined north face with its central vertical band was there in detail. This was no flight of imagination on my part, for the natives who were with me at the time recognised the striking likeness too, clapping their hands and looking first to the cloud and then Mikeno as they did so.

As night drew on, I sat at ease in a chair, watching the gathering storm and its vivid accompaniment of lightning. Only one thing troubled me at the time, and that was the thought of being so dependent upon that surly individual with his unprepossessing build and countenance—if he should be the one to go as guide to the mountains. In one sense, of course, I was alone, but in fact there was little that I could accomplish without the co-operation of all my helpers, from the humblest porter to the guide, who would need to be not only a capable leader but also a man who could be relied upon to climb with me, sharing my risks without being able to share with me the driving enthusiasm which had brought me this far.

Before settling down to sleep I prayed, not knowing that more important than prayer was trust.

By morning the storm had worked itself out, and with the first light of dawn there was a violent commotion outside which proved to be the arrival of a collection of men, which, with all respect to them, could only be called a dishevelled mob. These were the men who were to go with me, some to open up a trail through the forest and some to act as porters. The two Captains were there, the one supervising quietly and efficiently and the other taking a more active part. At this stage, with departure imminent, it was a simple matter to determine the true state of affairs, and my worst fears were realised. The dignified " Captain " was in fact the local Chief, and he was, rather out of courtesy than anything else, ensuring that all my needs were met. Really there was no need to ask if he would be going with us, for he was dressed in what was obviously his best clothing, which consisted of a military style jacket, a khanza,[1] a dark neckerchief and a hat.

The gloomy individual, whose face had not as yet shown the flicker of a smile, wore a greatcoat several sizes too big for him and wrongly buttoned, so that one side " rode high " while the other reached nearly to the ground. What he wore underneath could not be seen, but his hat was most noticeable, adding many inches to his stature. He was an official guide, in part employment, and he was to be in charge of the native porters. My disappointment was keen, for I had taken an instant liking to the Chief, and still regarded the dour Kabanza—for that was his name—as a potential trouble maker. I was apprehensive—immensely excited at the prospect of heading for gorilla country and getting to grips with the mountains, but doubtful as to the abilities of Kabanza as a guide and leader of men.

With the aid of a map (though Africans are notoriously bad map readers) I explained to Kabanza and his underlings that from the Kabara hut of the Institut we would go on to Vishoke and then make for the Lukumi hut at 11,750 ft. on Karisimbi, and after climbing that mountain

[1] A garment reaching from the waist to the ankles. White is usually preferred, but in this instance the cloth was a dingy brown. This is understandable, for white is difficult to keep clean at the best of times, and even more so under the primitive conditions of native life, especially in an area such as this where there are no permanent streams.

would return to the Kabara hut and tackle Mikeno. With the names Mikeno, Karisimbi, Vishoke, Kibumba, Kabara, Lukumi and about a dozen words of Kiswahili at my command I reiterated my plan an unnecessary number of times. There were other things to be done, and Kabanza's expression, though it hardly changed, gave me to understand that I was wasting time with words. And so, quite unaware of the precise arrangements made by the Chief and Kabanza about food for the porters, I made off with as motley a band of fellows as ever headed for a mountaineering venture of such magnitude.

How the members of any Alpine or Himalayan expedition would have laughed to see our ragged start! But to me, this was all a very serious business, and whatever I might have lacked in elaborate equipment, I did not go short in the necessary sense of responsibility.

The trouble was there was no one to share this responsibility: it was all mine, and the extent of it had been made clear by the Conservateur at Rumangabo when he had warned me of the bitter cold that could be expected. His apprehension had been too real to ignore. Lives had been lost on previous expeditions, and he did not think much of our prospects. He had not told me as much, but I learnt afterwards that he would have wagered anything against our chance of success on Mikeno.

At the nearby village we passed between two long lines of poorly constructed huts of beehive pattern. Completely naked children stood pathetically where they were, or ran in bewilderment to their parents. Women, poorly clothed and with naked breasts, were giving suck to their young, or sorting millet seeds on straw mats which seemed to be their finest possessions. There is a habit amongst many Africans of keeping all unmarried females, beyond the age when puberty begins, out of sight whenever a stranger passes, so that the only women I saw seemed to be old hags, though many clutched lovable black mites who nestled close to these coarse, withered bodies which contrasted so startlingly with their own. These were the wives or mothers of the men who were going with me. Many of them were not old, but they had the appearance of age which only poverty can bring, and their breasts hung thin and wrinkled.

A few hundred yards beyond the village, we turned right and continued northwards until we came to a wooden shack where a supply of crushed millet, which was to be the porters' food, had been stored. This was a great relief to me, for until this time I had feared that they expected to live off my own limited supply of tinned foods. Here loads were distributed without fuss or comment while I took off all but a pair of khaki shorts. When all preparations had been completed, the Chief, who had come with us this far, came forward to bid farewell and to hand over the leadership to Kabanza.

We continued along a narrow, winding path which led in the direction of the saddle between Mikeno and Karisimbi, both of which were visible in the far distance. A few scattered dwellings were passed, and at one there was an elephant spoor within a few inches of a hut, so that it surprised me that the beast had not demolished the flimsy straw abode with the passage of its body. I pointed to the spoor and its nearness to the hut, and Kabanza smiled for the first time.

Soon we came to an old crater of typical shape, depressed on one side and elevated at the point opposite. Native children were tending cattle on the far side of a muddy pool to which further elephant spoors led, and several women washed clothes which they left to dry on exposed rocks. They had to come this far to do their washing, for there was no other pool of which I was aware in the whole vicinity. The presence of cattle in the same water did not seem at all incongruous, for water is so scarce here that it has to be shared by man and beast.

Turning left to skirt the pool, we began to climb steeply by a pathway thick with mud, and when this had been negotiated we encountered the forerunners of a particularly virulent type of stinging nettle that was to plague our way on several long treks to come. As we gained height, we came to the bamboo forest, where there were no nettles and the going was pleasant. Numerous signs of elephant and buffalo were to be seen, and it was possible to tell where herds had rested, trampling the undergrowth and scattering their droppings. They had obviously passed quite recently in some places, and yet we never heard a sound of any wild life, big or small. It gave us the impression that we were being watched, and though no eyes actually peered at us, there was the feeling that every wild beast of the forest for miles around knew of our presence. This was indeed so, for it is part of the African's strategy to keep up a loud, ceaseless chatter, thus giving warning of his approach and causing all likely adversaries, particularly elephants, to retreat, which they will do readily enough rather than stand to face human beings, whether black or white. Whereas I wished to go as stealthily as possible in the hope of obtaining glimpses and perhaps photographs of wild animals, Kabanza and his men obviously intended to clear every obstacle from their way, and to achieve this, noise was all-important. Only when they halted would they remain at all quiet.

There is something absolutely fascinating about bamboo forests. No-matter how hot the day, it is cool there. The light which filters through is a restful green and the silence, unbroken by extraneous noises, is intense. This green loveliness and utter silence gives to me an almost unendurable pleasure. It is not an easy pleasure to enjoy, for it usually means travelling to remote places.

Our progress through the bamboo zone, with two pairs of men working in relays to cut a path ahead, was astonishingly rapid. Each man was adroit in handling his carved panga, and usually a single blow was sufficient to fell a bamboo with a girth of about 12 inches. As each blow had to be made downwards at a considerable angle, there would have been a dangerous bed of spikes, with the chance of those following impaling their feet, if the stems were cut off too near the ground. Kabanza's men did not need to be warned of this, for they were thoroughly experienced and invariably contrived to leave a good 12 to 14 inches of stem protruding, thus lessening the danger.

We stopped for a quick lunch at the far extremity of the bamboo zone and then moved on through a forest of a totally different kind in which hagenias (*Hagenia abyssinica*) were prominent, many with their gnarled branches bearing a mass of epiphytes. The undergrowth was dense, and at times we were ankle-deep in mud. For this reason, I carried on barefooted, though the interminable nettles through which, when I was on the go, I could blunder without harm, caused me to hop painfully from one foot to the other while I stood awaiting the opening up of the path ahead.

The further we went, the more involved and laborious our progress became, until I began to doubt if the forest had an ending at all. Then, quite suddenly, we emerged into the small glade in which stands the Kabara hut of the Institut des Parcs Nationaux.

My first instinct was for rest, but it was not long before I was busying myself with a few chores, sweeping away thick dust and innumerable cobwebs. There were two small rooms for my use and one large apartment for the guide and porters. The few simple furnishings included three beds, a number of chairs and a table. One bed was ranged alongside a slow combustion stove, and here I decided to sleep, for already there was a decided nip in the air.

The Kabara hut, built completely of wood, stands at the foot of Mikeno in a small grass-covered, flower-sprinkled clearing, the margins of which are sharply defined. It is as though the small grasses and the tall forest have a complete understanding, neither of them encroaching upon the other, except for the few scattered bushes well beyond the boundaries of the forest. It is a delightful spot to those who have a liking for rugged mountain scenery. The smallness of the clearing and the nearness of the forest combine to give a suggestion of guarded remoteness. There is no suggestion of a world apart from mountains, forest and glade, and the creatures which, if undisturbed, inhabit these parts. At the Vishoke end of the clearing there is a water hole, and at the time of our arrival there were a great many buffalo tracks leading through thick mud to the little water that had remained standing. The entire area must have been a congregating place for vast numbers of the big ungulates (*Syncerus caffer*), for we found the soggy earth near the hut churned about by their hoofs.

Isolated to one side of the clearing, under the lee of Mikeno's steep, thickly forested south-eastern slope, lies the grave of Carl Akeley, the American naturalist who devoted his latter years of life to the creation of a sanctuary intended primarily for protection of gorillas in the Mikeno-Karisimbi-Vishoke area. As a result of his efforts, the first small area was set aside as a national park on April 21, 1925. A second expedition was undertaken by Carl Akeley in 1926, but on November 17 of that year he died, and in accordance with his request, was buried at the foot of Mikeno. His good work was carried on by others, and as an outcome of his second and last expedition, two important extensions were made to the original park.

The first of these, in 1927, took in the south-west slopes of Karisimbi and Vishoke, in the mandated territory of Ruanda. The second extension, in 1929, incorporated a large area between the north shore of Lake Kivu and the southern end of Lake Edward. The Albert National Park, as it was called in honour of Albert, King of the Belgians, was extended still farther to the north in 1934, and in the following year, the Upper and Middle Semliki plains together with the western slopes of Ruwenzori were added, thus establishing the park on its present basis with seven sectors, each noted for some botanical, zoological or geographical peculiarity and given the name of a prominent geographical feature. The total area to-day is nearly $2\frac{1}{2}$ million acres.

A simple concrete slab inscribed, " Carl Akeley. Died 1926," marks the naturalist-explorer's burial place. The slab was overgrown with encroaching vegetation, and my first impulse was to clear this away, but upon reflection I decided to leave the site entirely undisturbed, thinking that a man so much in love with nature would wish his grave to be left to the natural forces which rule in this wild region.

At Kabara I came to know my men better. Kabanza, at first sight a trouble maker, was slow to smile, but I found he was neither morose nor sulky, and it transpired that, being uncertain of my character, he had at first sought refuge behind an excessive reserve. He did not, poor fellow, wish to overstep the bounds of familiarity, and it was not until our first day had passed that he realised from my own aloofness that there could be no fear of this happening. He was of no more than medium height, and noticeably spindle-legged, but he was no weakling. In fact his capacity for endurance and his unflagging energy came as a surprise to me, for there was nothing about his appearance to suggest these attributes.

His face was boot-polish black and crowned with the usual short, crinkly hair of the Congolese. His lips were not typically negroid, but his whole mouth pouted out, and it was probably for this reason that he did not smile frequently. Two deep lines ran from a broad nose to rather high cheek bones, relieving an often expressionless countenance which nevertheless held a depth of character that was quite outstanding. His individuality was most marked, as was his gift for leadership, which was remarkable in view of the communal life he led with the men over whom he held authority.

Most important of all was the fact that he was ambitious and had the essential courage and ability of a born climber. He was keen to go up Mikeno and did not seem at all frightened by the prospect. I like to think (and have good reason for doing so) that he would have moved heaven and earth for me. We did not converse much, and it suited me that he only opened conversation when it was necessary to do so, and that on such occasions he limited himself as much as possible to the words which I could understand.

I am not ashamed to admit that my first impression of Kabanza had been totally at variance with the true character of the man. There was nothing mean or petty about him, and instead of bringing me trouble, he helped me to the greatest satisfaction of my life.

Sometimes he wore a shapeless, nondescript hat, but on other occasions he appeared in the uniform hat of the Albert National Park. This was shaped like a tarboosh, and when he felt like it he would jam it on top of his other hat, which had a brim, with striking effect. Earlier in its life his official headgear had sported, in brass lettering, the initials of the Albert National Park, but the A had become detached and the N deranged: only the P remained upright, in its original position. His clothing consisted of a belted khaki tunic and knee-length shorts, while at times he would wear his more than ample overcoat, of which he seemed inordinately proud, perhaps because of its eight flashy, brass buttons. He was thus better dressed than the others, as befitted his station.

Ruhindura was my next most reliable man when it came to climbing, and he was to accompany me on Mikeno and Karisimbi, but not Vishoke. He was more stockily built than Kabanza, broader and bigger boned. His usual garb was a tunic similar to Kabanza's, but instead of shorts he wore a simple loin-cloth. He had an intelligent face and was a thoroughly nice fellow in every respect.

Boranze was another, and good looking in his way. He was always smiling and cheerful, but inclined to keep to himself.

Bunane, who had attached himself to me from the beginning, became my personal servant, always to hand with camera, clothing, ropes and other items of equipment for which there might be need. After our expedition to the mountains, where he put in much good work, he promoted himself to the position of house boy at Kibumba, after which time he sought seclusion and rest from all labour. He was a dull-witted fellow but entirely likeable and so inoffensive that it was altogether beyond me to complain. He was swarthy and must have been as strong as an ox in his prime, though when I knew him he was past his best and inclined to portliness. His vest, which buttoned at the front, could not conceal his large umbilical hernia, which jutted out beneath the lowest button.

Of the remainder, there was one who wore a knitted woollen cap with a tassel, and another who was of true pygmy stock. He looked much older than any of the others, but he had an abundance of energy in his wiry frame, and always appeared cheery and self-confident. His name was Kaimba and he was on the full-time staff of the Parc, although I did not learn this until later.

They were certainly a motley crowd, but there was never a sign of disrespect from one of them, and it is quite true to say that each played a part in which he was entirely indispensable. In this I do not attach any credit to myself, for Kabanza, had he wished, could have overburdened the party with any number of men in excess of the round dozen which proved the ideal number.

VI. *At the Forest's Edge*

WE DID not delay unnecessarily at Kabara, but pushed on next day to the dense forest beyond the small clearing. The only map in my possession was of no use in this region, and I was forced to rely entirely upon Kabanza for guidance. He in turn made frequent reference to old Kaimba, who appeared to know this particular part of the forest better than the others. Usually Kaimba was in the lead with one of his team, making quick, decisive slashes with his panga and seldom falling back to take a rest.

His tiny head, with its clusters of curly grey hair, was filled with forest lore and I never ceased to marvel at this energetic little worker who could have repudiated ten years of his life of hard living and yet remained the oldest member of the expedition.

It will be taking the sequence of events out of their order, but it is fitting to tell at this point of an incident which took place when the time came for paying the men after our return to Kibumba. Always while in the mountains I did not fail to keep a benevolent eye on Kaimba, so that his absence on this occasion was noticed at once. He was at the village, I was told, and did not expect payment from me because he would be receiving his usual wages as a Park official. Such utter unselfishness and lack of desire for gain astounded me, and an envelope containing exactly as much as the others had received was sent to Kaimba, who, being a gentleman by nature, duly hastened to thank me for this consideration.

Now, and in later years, as I come to look back on these things, the little African will be remembered amongst the finest characters of any colour or station in life I have ever met.

Some idea of the type of going encountered on the way to Vishoke will be gained from the fact that our outward trail was entirely overgrown by the time of our return a few days later. Indeed it seemed that the dense vegetation reasserted itself almost immediately after our laborious passage through it. Every yard of the way had to be hacked out with the pangas which, strangely enough, had blades so blunt that a finger could be drawn along them quite heavily without harm. Yet, when wielded with precision, they could be made to cut with the accuracy of a surgeon's scalpel.

Trees of various sizes, bamboo, thorn bushes, nettles, wild celery and a myriad other obstacles beset our way, and only once did we see the 12,370 ft. crater summit of Vishoke. Yet, save for one false move, Kabanza and his men made unerringly for the base of the mountain. Map reading was completely beyond them and there was no sun visible for most of the time, so that even if they had been accustomed to doing so, they could not have found their way by it. It is said that they leave distinct marks on the trunks of trees as they go along, but on no occasion did they stop to point out or even look for any old blazed trails, and only once or twice did I see a man make a deliberate cut in a tree trunk unless he wished to fell the tree. It is almost certain that when this was done it was meant to assist our almost immediate return and was not intended as an indication of the way for years to come. The reason for their amazing pathfinding capabilities is almost as difficult to account for as the migratory sense of birds. Perhaps it lies mostly in generations of adaptation to a forest environment.

As we emerged from the forest, quite suddenly as at Kabara, we walked into a different world. The upper reaches of Vishoke could not be seen, but continuing almost to the base of the mountain was an open tract of marshland. Water was underfoot at every step, for the whole area is level and nothing but a sponge: no clearly defined channels have as yet been formed through the porous rock with its thin layer of soil. " Old man's beard " lichen (*Usnea*) draped every tree in dank streamers, many of them several feet in length. The ethereal atmosphere was enhanced by a slight mist and a silence which no words can describe. The men, who usually talked without ceasing, moved forward with no sound other than that of the squelching of their feet.

There was nowhere to set up the tent except on the water-logged flats, where there was not a single square yard in which jagged lava did not protrude, but after a lot of contriving it was erected with one flysheet spanning a rivulet. For a covering on which to put my groundsheets and sleeping bag, the men collected moss and long streamers of coarse, sodden lichen. Then, for themselves, they erected a crude shelter of branches with lichen laid on top.

There was a good deal of excitement shortly afterwards when I distributed articles of clothing, including shirts, shorts, jackets, pullovers and blankets. Unbeknown to me, Bunane was away gathering firewood at the time, and his absence was not noticed. When he returned with his arms filled with wet branches, he did not utter a word of complaint, but his expression told of a betrayal of faith, and although I took from my own spare clothing in an effort to recompense him, I do not think he ever understood what a sacrifice I made. He had, in his opinion, been palmed off with something inferior as an afterthought, and what must have hurt him more than everything else was the fact that he had been working while the others were lazing and being rewarded for their inactivity.

Bunane's deep injury brought home to me the underlying significance of money and wealth, which are far from being the same. Money has value only when it can be spent or when it can bring security by being saved. To these men, at their homes in Kibumba, many miles from the nearest store, it has little value. While they are in the mountains it does not even give security and it would only be a burden to them. Clothing, on the other hand, is real wealth at all times, for it provides warmth without which there can be no life. Bunane knew all this, but he would have reasoned it out more simply.

In the brief interval between late afternoon and the gathering of dusk into night, there is often a total clearing of the atmosphere even on the worst of days in this mountain region, so that Mikeno showed itself for a very few minutes in its most formidable pose as it towered above the forest through which we had passed. As seen from the base of Vishoke, its steep central crag leans to the left—that is, to the south—in an intriguing manner, and from this side the chances of climbing it would be remote indeed, for there is a considerable overhang. The north face would present no difficulties but for an encircling band of rock which forms a sheer wall.

I could see every rock, and judge its angle of inclination, but after I had taken a single photograph and made a quick outline sketch, the gloom prevented any further detailed observations. This aspect of the mountain is rather frightening and yet, to a mountaineer, compelling. Certainly Mikeno was the most formidable task yet to confront me as a lone climber, and perhaps, if the cold had not become so intense as to make me seek refuge in the tent, I might have decided after more mature reflection that the prospects were too slender for success.

Mary L. Jobe Akeley covers the history of Mikeno in *Congo Eden*, in which she tells how, during 1926, Dr. Dercheid reached a point less than 200 ft. from the summit and " 1,000 ft. higher than anyone had previously reached. He was stopped by heavy storm clouds and the lateness of the hour." Three missionaries were the next to try, and fail, though one of them succeeded in climbing to within 100 ft. of the summit before being driven down by a hail storm. The first successful attempt was in August 1927 by Père Van Hoef and his companions. King Albert of the Belgians, an enthusiastic mountaineer, cherished the ambition to climb the mountain, but failed to do so. To quote again from Mrs. Akeley's book: " It is generally agreed that two of the greatest difficulties encountered in the climb of Mikeno are the quantities of deep moss on the sloping rocks which will not bear the weight of a man and the extreme friability of the cliffs, where often only precarious hand and footholds can be obtained. Certainly to me from whatever location I had viewed the peak, Mikeno possessed all the characteristics of a formidable mountain."

I retired to bed that night with thoughts of gaunt Mikeno and of my chances of climbing it with no one but Africans to accompany me. There was plenty of time in which to think, for the conditions were too unpleasant for sleep. The jagged lava permitted no freedom to turn, and the cold and wet penetrated everywhere.

The first streak of dawn found us all about our various duties, and after a light meal of bread and cheese (it would have been toast and cheese, and a hot cup of tea, but for the impossibility of making a fire) I set off to climb Vishoke with Kabanza, Ruhindura and Boranze. A deep cleft ran to the left of our route over the lower slopes of the mountain, and we could hear water falling from a considerable height, but we could not see it because of a mass of vegetation. Often we had to crouch low and worm our way through a tangle of briars after a narrow pathway had been cut. It was a hard and wearisome climb, though not a difficult one, and I was forced to wear boots and a thick khaki shirt as a protection against the thorns.

Beyond the briars we could make better progress, and after an unceasing upward toil we reached a circular basin which had probably been a subsidiary vent at the time of Vishoke's volcanic activity. Water ran away through a southerly gap, falling almost sheer to the base of the mountain. It seemed more strange than ever that there should be no definite water-course near our camp, but there was no time to do more than think about such things. The overriding object was to reach the top of eight mountain summits, and it had become obvious before now that minor excursions and the spooring of animals could not be undertaken while climbing remained the first objective. Further exploratory travels, much as I would have liked to make them, would have required more time, and consequently more money and equipment, than I could afford. Although always hopeful of a distant glimpse of gorillas, I was already resigned to the practical certainty of not coming upon them.

The summit of Vishoke contains an almost circular crater lake surrounded by a steep amphitheatre overgrown with vegetation, among which giant lobelias and senecios abound. I had hoped for a view of the country to the north, and perhaps a glimpse of Sabinio, Mgahinga and Muhavura, but by the time we had reached the top, the sky had become overcast, with clouds that were being driven helter-skelter under the changing wind. Kabanga seemed in a hurry to leave, so we started down almost at once and went as quickly as our legs would take us to a cup of warming tea and something to eat.

It was shortly after noon when we broke camp and left this cheerless spot, heading in the direction of the Lukumi hut on Karisimbi. The views of mountain scenery on this day's march were almost overpowering, and at times I found myself longing, for the first and only time, for a companion to whom I could speak freely. I wanted to say, "Look there, and there. Have you ever seen greater loveliness?" Or I merely wished to ask for confirmation, to make sure that the fairyland of Kivu and its wonderful volcanoes really existed as they appeared to me on that day.

At all other times I took delight in the companionship of the fine black men who were with me. The barrier of language did not prevent us from accomplishing what we set out to do. Each word that passed between us had to be heavy with meaning. We could not indulge in bickerings or snarls or any unpleasantness whatever, and there was no chance of any clash of personalities. My greatest moments have been spent in the company of illiterate Africans with whom I have felt that common bond which exists wherever nature holds sway, or where there is danger of any kind. It was only this once that I yearned momentarily for companionship other than that which I had.

Karisimbi itself, seen from its northern approaches, is divided into four sharply defined zones. There is the densely forested region in which wandering troops of gorillas make their temporary homes; a more open park-like area of grassland bearing clumps of trees and briars; an Alpine zone of moss and lichen where immortelles and other small flowers inter-mingle with giant lobelias and senecios, and finally there is the impressive bell-like dome of barren silt and rock, streaked at times with a white coating of hail.

The Lukumi hut, similar in every way to the Kabara hut, is situated at 11,800 ft. on the north-west slope facing across the heavily forested saddle to Mikeno. It stands clear of the forest limit on a gentle slope well covered with short grasses, lichen and moss, and liberally sprinkled with alchemilla and immortelles. Lobelias and arborescent groundsels (senecios) do not grow in profusion here, but a few scattered specimens are of exceptional size—the latter growing to almost twice the height of Kabanza, as shown by a photograph that was taken in this vicinity. Blackberries, which are relished by gorillas, grow a few yards behind the hut, and I had visions of fresh fruit for lunch, but unfortunately the berries do not have a chance to ripen before they are taken either by birds or gorillas.

A buffalo skull with horns attached was found near the hut, and it has been suggested that the beast was killed at this considerable altitude by a lion, which would be quite unusual, for these large carnivores are not accustomed to going high. I rather lean to the view that a leopard was responsible, for these smaller predators are more used to extreme conditions in forests and at high altitudes. The skull, I observed, was small, with horns more like those of the dwarf buffalo (*Syncerus caffer nanus*), though they probably belonged to an immature specimen of a race of the ordinary savannah buffalo that is becoming stunted in size as a result of an environ-ment which is not altogether favourable but which affords much greater security from man and predatory animals than open, low-lying savannahs. Leopards have been known to tackle young buffaloes, and such courageous killers would not hesitate to pick off a small mature specimen under condi-tions favourable to themselves.

Kabanza and Boranze set out with me at very early morning on the day after our arrival at Lukumi. Karisimbi would test our fitness more than anything else, for it is the highest of the Virunga volcanoes but is entirely clear of forest above the Lukumi hut and has not become sufficiently eroded to offer more than a hard, slogging ascent.

There had been a sharp frost during the night and the sun had not yet begun to clear the ground of it. Both men had put on their warmest clothing, but their teeth chattered and they looked thoroughly uncomfortable until the effort of climbing and the first rays from a rising sun brought zest to them.

My condition, which had given cause for alarm during the descent from Vishoke, had improved with a night's rest, and I wore only a shirt and shorts, with boots and warm clothing packed in a haversack for use if necessary. At first it was essential for me to go fast and step boldly in order to keep the blood circulating to my feet, and Kabanza and Boranze had difficulty in keeping up with me. Kabanza in particular was labouring and I was worried about him. He kept stopping, and for the greater part of an hour he remained very much under the effect of the cold and altitude.

The clarity of the early morning continued until, as usual, clouds assembled over Mgahinga and were driven in our direction by a north-east wind from which we were sheltered; we were climbing well over to the west and at times protected by long gullies which are not visible from afar. Bad weather at this time of year seems to build up with Vishoke as its centre, and it was obvious that early morning conditions of cloudlessness and good visibility would not prevail for long, and that we had been wise in making an early start.

The soul-stirring view on this morning remains vivid in my mind. That is one of the main reasons why we undergo the attendant hardships of climbing—to gain a wealth of memories that will stand us in good stead during later years, and to which we may unconsciously refer when surrounded by ugliness. We are aware, too, that old age, instead of being a kindly experience, is likely to overwhelm us if we do not garner a fair crop of memories in our youth.

I had seen the Virunga mountains separately or in groups of two or three, but now for the first time I was able to see them all from one vantage point. To my right, as I turned with my back towards Karisimbi for a true appraisal of the scene, Sabinio, Mgahinga and Muhavura could be seen with their peaks jutting above masses of gathering cumulus that lay below on the Uganda side. Directly ahead of me loomed the gaunt pillar of rock in which Mikeno terminates. So remarkably clear was the atmosphere that it seemed possible to reach out a hand and touch the mountain. Another deceptive impression was that of height, for with its lesser bulk and more precipitous sides Mikeno seemed to tower to a greater height than Karisimbi, though its altitude is less by 200 ft. or more. Beyond and to the left of Mikeno, the two live volcanoes Nyamlagira and Nyiragongo stood with what looked like a brood of young: these were the smaller volcanic cones dotted around. Lake Kivu, considered by many as the most beautiful of all African lakes, formed part of the horizon on my left. Even the ripples could be seen on its surface, though at its nearest point it lay more than 20 miles away. The Kabara hut could be seen across the saddle, while almost directly at my feet was the forest through which we would have to pass on our way to it.

It is for views such as this that we climb. Only the grossest of men wish to be victors in a triumph over nature: the majority of high altitude mountaineers desire no more than to come to terms with nature in its many moods—and of course, with themselves.

We moved on, and as we did so there was a sudden change. A sharp wind chilled us and shortly afterwards we were shrouded in a dank mist which seemed to take Mikeno into the distance until it could not be seen at all. From the Alpine zone of moss and lichen, where ice pellets remained frozen in the shelter of the several gullies, we climbed to a denuded patch of wet, slippery silt, which I recognised as the upper zone that I had observed from the foot of Vishoke on the previous day. Kabanza, who had continued to alarm me and had given me cause to fear that his condition on this mountain would be used as an excuse for not wanting to go with me on Mikeno, had improved, though the effect of altitude had given his face a strange pallor. Serried slabs of disintegrating rock lay to our right as we covered the final stage without stopping for more than a few seconds at a time.

For the first occasion on any mountain I had taken a small flagon of brandy with me and this I shared with Kabanza and Boranze who showed a pathetic gratitude for this small gesture. Then we linked hands and went down from our second mountain in two days.

While the three of us had been climbing Karisimbi the others, except for Bunane who had remained at Lukumi to await our return, had been going on with all the equipment across the forested saddle to Kabara.

Instructions had also been given for a team of men to open up a path on the lower slopes of Mikeno so that no avoidable obstacles should confront the climbing party when it made its attempt. All our efforts, in spite of our several deficiencies, seemed splendidly co-ordinated, so that there was every reason to feel pleased at the result so far and to look with quiet confidence towards the prospects which had opened up. A feeling of well-being and of goodwill towards others settled over me—fortunately indeed, for upon arrival at the Lukumi hut we found Bunane fast asleep in front of a dead stove, with the result that thoughts of a hot drink before pushing on any farther had to go unfulfilled.

A wearisome trudge over the route which had been opened up for us across the saddle led eventually to Kabara. Here, as proof of the way ordinary little annoyances have a habit of crowding together, I had difficulty with the stove, which smoked profusely: then an egg, of alarmingly explosive nature, burst full in my face. After this, the entire contents of a tin of vegetables went to waste and the toast was dropped into a heap of fine ashes. The only satisfaction I had was that my instructions to open up the lower slopes of Mikeno had been obeyed, as I saw for myself during a stroll with Kabanza to the Vishoke end of the clearing, from whence the trail leading to Mikeno's barren summit begins.

VII. *Mikeno Becomes "Mine"*

I WAS too excited by my nearness to Mikeno, and too filled with thoughts to sleep much that night. Then, in the late hours, a slight patter of rain disturbed me, and my apprehension increased as it broke into a down-pour. When dawn came it was still raining and the sky was so overcast that I had to tell Kabanza what he already knew—that the assault on Mikeno must await more favourable conditions.

After breakfast I set about a few menial tasks; although it was no longer raining I knew that the day was already too far advanced to think of setting off for the mountain.

Suddenly a growing sound of shuffling activity and subdued voices attracted my attention and I went to the door, not knowing what to expect, but fearing the worst. Lined up outside the door, to my intense dismay, was the entire outfit with Kabanza standing to one side and obviously waiting to hold parley with me.

This was desertion! There could be no other meaning to what was happening. I thought back to the pain Kabanza had obviously endured on Karisimbi the day before. The obvious conclusion was that he had in-fluenced the others to refuse to go on and they, in the cold, bleak discomfort of the mountains, detached from their womenfolk and homes, had been only too eager to turn back.

Instead of smiling as usual, they looked sullen and resentful—or so I imagined, for my perception had become blurred because of my fears. I was ready to forget my previous high estimate of their qualities because I was afraid, and fear can so easily degrade a human being until he is little better than an animal. Behind my fears all along had been the knowledge that these Africans were without the driving force of ambition which spurred me on. They were working for money whereas I was activated by a blind idealism. Looking at events in this light, who could be surprised that they should wish to turn back, and who could blame them?

65

Kabanza spoke slowly and with great deliberation. The only two words
that were immediately distinguishable to me seemed to confirm my worst
fears. The use of *kwenda* (go) and *Kibumba* (the base camp from which we
had started) were sufficient to uphold my gloomy forebodings.

So this was the end. There was to be no Mikeno and no eight peaks.
My vision seemed to cloud over, and I propped myself against the
doorway for support. I could think of nothing better to say, and so I gave
the Arabic equivalent of " Tell me again," at the same time making a
circular motion with my right hand, indicating " go over it again."[1]

Kabanza, intelligent enough to grasp my meaning, repeated his message.

A sense of utter frustration bore down on me, but after what seemed an
eternity of time a glimmer of hope appeared.

" Tell me again, Kabanza. Again and again." And I accompanied my
words with the previous circular gesture of the hand.

Kabanza went on repeating his message, for we had both learnt that
constant repetition helped to make the meaning of any short conversation
clear. With each repetition the light of hope flickered more brightly until
eventually, with the aid of more signs and the introduction of the word
mongereer,[2] the full truth dawned upon me.

This was no desertion. The poor fellows were running short of food,
and Kabanza was suggesting that two men be sent back to Kibumba to
pick up further supplies. My relief was unbounded and of course I gave
my consent without hesitation. Marco and Bereberaho were chosen for
the purpose.

Except for the anxiety which it had caused, the enforced delay did good
by compelling us to rest, though the afternoon gave an opportunity of
reconnoitring the lower slopes of Mikeno, and five of us went to 12,000 ft
before returning. As a result of this reconnaissance we were able to make
the path through the forest more definite and easier to negotiate, and
our needs for the full-scale attempt could be assessed. For my part I was
determined to try and climb the whole way without boots, which I now
looked upon as inessential and a hindrance up to at least 15,000 ft.

After our return to the hut, I saw Kabanza, stripped of all his clothing,
take a splash bath from the water that had collected in a round, iron bin,
and I followed suit. It was my first proper wash since leaving for the

---

[1] There are several Arabic words in Kiswahili, and therefore I often made use of a few
simple Arabic words and phrases during conversations of this kind.

[2] Food.

mountains. Also I had not shaved since departing from Kisenyi and I now sported the beginning of a luxuriant beard.

During the early hours of darkness, I could hear Kabanza and his men in a merry mood, singing to the accompaniment of their own clapping. The sound fascinated me because it was so primitive and in keeping with the occasion. No musical instrument was needed by these men, for they were the simplest of beings living under the simplest of conditions. The rhythm, with its monotony, was so compelling that I went to see for myself how they were spending their time. I found them gathered nearly naked in a group round a blazing log fire. These were the same men whom I had misjudged earlier in the day, and I felt pleased and reassured by their obvious happiness. I admired them for their splendid comradeiness and recollected that on no occasion had a sullen word been spoken by any one of them. A deep emotion filled me, partly with sorrow and sympathy but also with gratitude. Their clapping increased when they saw me taking an interest in their entertainment, and as I left them I gave an appreciative clap which seemed to add still further to their delight.

This small incident is worth recording because it gives an indication of our mutual understanding and the manner in which we gained respect for one another by means of action and without recourse to speech.

Only a few drops of rain fell during the night, so that at very early morning, after my usual pre-climbing meal of toast and cheese followed by a cup of hot tea, I set out with Kabanza, Ruhindura and Bunane for the still obscured heights of Mikeno. A pair of khaki shorts and shirt were my only garb, but in a small haversack carried by Bunane were more elaborate clothes together with ordinary climbing boots and rope-soled shoes. Ruhindura carried my camera and Kabanza the climbing ropes.

The entire camp was abroad to speed our ragged little party on its way, and we lost no time in making for the beginning of the steep forest trail, which by now had become well defined and clear of undergrowth. Bunane was armed with a panga, but it was seldom needed. In our anxiety to make use of the early morning cloudlessness and generally fair conditions, we pressed on without ever pausing, our only difficulty being the slipperiness of the sodden ground. Clouds would almost certainly come up later in the day, and there would be thick mist and drizzle, if nothing worse, to contend with while negotiating the bare rocks above. I do not think there can ever be a cloudless, rainless day on Mikeno.

Weather conditions during our reconnaissance of the previous day had been most unsatisfactory for photography, but now, when there was no time to spare for it, we had some magnificent views of surrounding peaks and it was possible to gauge our progress very roughly in relation to some of them. At one stage, catching sight of the Lukumi hut on Karisimbi, I was able to think, " Now we have reached the height of Lukumi ": on another occasion I imagined that we had climbed at least as far as the summit of Vishoke. Sabinio looked a grand sight with its jagged summit ridge exposed above masses of cloud, and it gave the impression that it might be a difficult mountain to climb. Nyiragongo and Nyamlagira were to be seen in the opposite direction, and at one time there was a view extending to some of the small islands north of Idjwi, on Lake Kivu.

While under the protection of thick forest and a tangle of undergrowth the weather did not concern us and we could not always tell if rain was falling or merely if accumulated water was dripping from leaves and branches above. When at length we emerged fully into the open, we found conditions above far from pleasant, and the saturated moss proved treacherous underfoot. As we went higher into the Alpine zone, we could see tall lobelias growing from sparsely covered, almost vertical rock faces their stems making an abrupt upward curve after growing outward sufficiently far to clear the rocks. In this, nature had taken into account all the factors involved and made an astonishingly accurate estimate of the exact requirements for survival.

A narrow, rapidly eroding spur (which had been the returning point of our reconnaissance) had been reduced in bulk by recent landslides, and there was evidence of other landslides on the large southern shoulder of the mountain. Here, on a grass-covered ridge above the forest limit, were two distinct trails which almost certainly had been made by herds of buffalo, signs of which we had encountered at a similar height along our own route. A small peak (the hard core of a once-active subsidiary cone) stood like a sharp fang in the north. It marks, I would say, the real stronghold of the mountain gorillas in this sector.[1]

A continuation of our eastern spur led us to the beginning of the rock section, where our first real difficulties were encountered, though we could have made things easy for ourselves by using a ladder which had been carried this far and left secured by some previous expedition. (It seemed

[1] Should the opportunity occur, I would like to explore this region with the object of climbing the crag and making investigations of the gorillas hereabouts. The forest is exceptionally dense at this point, and the crag would be difficult both to reach and climb.

Vishoke seen through trees draped with 'old man's beard' lichen (Usnea) on Karisimbi

Crater Lake on Vishoke: most remote of the eight Virunga Mountains

Summit of Mikeno

Northern shore of Lake Kivu, between Goma and Kisenyi

a pity that it should be there, and I was tempted to remove it, but did not do so.) Bunane remained in a rock recess, for he was too old to go any farther. He was given my warm clothing, with instructions—which he did not need—to wear it if he became too cold while awaiting our return. I felt able to continue without boots or rope-soled shoes, and so these were left with him too. The camera would have remained behind also, but Kabanza looked aghast at the idea, probably because he had visions of being photographed in triumph at the summit. Certainly his enthusiasm was remarkable for a black man and there was no doubt that he was now fired by an ambition to reach the top.

Ignoring the ladder, we found a way up to the right, on a pitch that was difficult and dangerous without the use of pitons, which we did not carry. We had investigated to the left without success, for the rock band in that direction begins to take on an overhang which probably continues right around to the south-west. We could not hope to explore further round that day without robbing ourselves of the chance of going any higher.

Thin wisps of cloud began to assemble above and drive towards us, and a light drizzle warned us of worse to come. In cities, to which we were unaccustomed, we would have been lost, but not on this mountain, or in the forests below. Whenever it was essential to do so, we used our ropes, though at times we climbed too fast to observe the finer points of mountaineering technique and, of course, we lacked any real co-ordination because of our language difficulties. It would have dismayed most mountaineers to see us stubbing bare toes into moss-covered rocks, with the bearded leader going through mist and rain with no covering but a pair of old shorts and a torn shirt. Nothing was either prim or proper about our methods. To a sceptical eye we may have looked more like a troop of baboons than men, but that is the way I like to be on mountains.

Despite these rough and ready methods, I kept an eye on the welfare of Kabanza and Ruhindura, both of whom showed tremendous natural ability and a surprising willingness to brave any obstacle. This was especially true of Kabanza, whose knobbly knees and slightly bowed legs had previously made me doubt him. He was not by any means a strong man, but he had reserves of power that sprang more from his tenacity than anything else. Kabanza impressed me more than ever on this day. He had by now become thoroughly acclimatised, and did not suffer any ill effects from altitude, as he had done on Karisimbi.

The only really frightening incident, which might have had serious if not fatal consequences, fell to my lot during a long traverse to the right on a particularly treacherous section across a ridge running down to the rock band in the north-east. The rock at this point had a thin covering of moss, and looked secure, but the entire mass to which I was clinging with my right hand came away without any warning, so that I could only make a hasty, instinctive clutch elsewhere. There was no time for thought and my hand made for the largest object within reach, which happened to be the rotting stem of a senecio. As a permanent hold this was useless, but before breaking away, it gave a momentary respite during which I regained my balance and searched for a more secure hold. Luckily, the rock on which I struggled for my next handhold proved less friable, enabling me to move at last to safety.

I had been warned of the great danger of the mountain, and shouting back to the others, I did my best to point out the danger to them, but they had noticed my predicament and were aware that every further handhold and foothold in this section had to be tested before trusting their full weight to it.

There were several shorter traverses to be made, and the way seemed always to lead upwards and to the right, upwards and to the right. My only fear, apart from my worry about the two splendid men who were with me, was to fail—and this nearly happened almost within sight of the summit, or what I fondly imagined was the summit though it turned out to be no more than the approach to the summit ridge.

Our progress up a steep wall of rock was balked by an overhang and no way offered to either left or right. Perhaps it was this same obstacle which had confounded others in their attempts to climb the mountain, and it may have been here that the late King of the Belgians turned back. There was little time to take note of my reactions, but I remember feeling horribly frustrated and very unwilling to retreat, thinking that to do so would only lead to other retreats and ultimate failure. This, of all moments in my life, seemed an eternity of fear and indecision. Then gradually it dawned upon me that since no possible way existed from where we were, there was no alternative but to go down and to seek a fresh route from the beginning of this baffling sector.

Going down was made doubly unpleasant by the awaiting uncertainty but from below it was seen that there was the chance of a route to the right. Kabanza, with a whoop of joy, led the way, and sure enough was a case once more of traversing to the right, after which we climbed up to a mound topped with slippery silt and littered with slabs of thin slate, a piece of which I took as evidence of having reached this far.

From this mound, we came to a crag of disintegrating rock. This was still not the top, for a knife-thin ridge led to a slightly higher point, and we wormed our way up to this. By now the visibility was limited to a few yards, and again it seemed that we must be at the very highest point, but Kabanza grabbed one of my arms and pointed to the left where a still higher peak could be observed when the curtain of mist thinned and lifted momentarily. We hurried forward, conscious of the bitter cold and wind, the mist and driving rain, but heedless of them. Then, without a word, but expressing more than words could tell, we joined hands. We had no thoughts, at that moment, of colour or social standing, for we were just three men on a mountain summit who had achieved an equal purpose. Standing on the summit of barren old Mikeno, we experienced as one that terrific elation which makes mountaineering so worth while.

This simple gesture—a white man linking hands with the two black men—was so spontaneous, that Kabanza and Ruhindura beamed with pleasure.

What were my actual thoughts at this, the time of triumph? To be quite truthful, a high mountain summit is too cold and exposed for thought. All I can recall is a sense of deep satisfaction. There was still the descent to be made, and not until camp had been regained in safety would any clear thoughts assemble and bring their delayed reward.

As usual, I collected a piece of rock from the summit. By now I had five pieces—and three to come.

Kabanza, who had made light of the camera as a burden, insisted upon being photographed with Ruhindura, despite the unfavourable conditions. The two men were barely visible at a range of only a few yards when the exposure was made, but this had become a most necessary ritual, without which no ascent would have been justified in the eyes of Kabanza and his men.

After this we hurried down in rapidly deteriorating weather, slipping, sliding, struggling for purchase on the treacherous moss-covered rocks. On one steep incline of loose stones, where we had thought it unnecessary to rope up, Ruhindura slipped and would have continued to glissade down on his bared buttocks if Kabanza had not been near to grab him in time and pull him to safety. My nerves became overwrought, and in addition

I began to worry about Bunane, secretly hoping that he would have made his own way across the intervening ridges and down through the forest. He must have been tempted many times to do so, but, poor stout fellow, he had remained where we had left him. He looked a pathetic sight, his whole body being convulsed with spasmodic shivers, a few of which he contrived for extra effect.

It was possible to glissade through the mud of the lower slopes, and as dusk was gathering, with heavy rain, we staggered more than walked over the clearing to the welcome sanctuary of our camp, our bodies spent with fatigue.

Our success caused a buzz of excited conversation which lasted well into the night. It was as though our stature had increased, and instead of being a small ragged band of men we had grown into an army. To me, above and beyond all physical weariness, there came a sense of quiet elation. The myriad aches and pains from my scratched and torn body might have belonged to someone else. On this day, which was a Sunday, I had taken part in a minor conquest, not of a mountain but of myself. Hereafter, while in the vicinity, I would be able to look on Mikeno with calm satisfaction instead of unrequited longing, comforted by the thought that I had struggled to its summit against all obstacles. In later days, no matter where I should wander, there would be rich thoughts of the mountain to sustain, fortify, strengthen. I had known bitterness and defeat? They would come again, and I would fight back. A home had been lost? I would lose another, and in time regain one. This is what Mikeno meant to me at the time,[1] and what it will always mean, save for the weak moments when I forget the mountain and lose faith with myself.

[1] There is no false sentimentality in these words, for they have been taken with only slight modification from my diary, which was written up daily from the day of my departure to the day of my return.

VIII. *Last Days in the Mikeno Sector*

OUR LAST night at Kabara was memorable for a sound which disturbed me in the early hours of morning when all was quiet and not a glimmer of light showed. My confused excitement and tiredness combined to rob me of any proper sleep, and the best I could do was to doze fitfully from time to time. During one of these sluggish periods of half-sleep, I was brought to full consciousness by a slight rocking motion and a coarse, rasping sound. A chill sweat broke from me, for I had not the strength of mind or body with which to combat fear. I sat bolt upright in bed, no doubt making a noise as I did so, for there was a sudden scampering outside which told plainly the cause of the disturbance—buffaloes had been using the hut as a rubbing post. In the morning we saw their spoor leading to and from one corner of the hut, and several hairs wedged between the splinters of wood. In the calm light of day, it was a pleasure to know that our presence had not debarred the wild life from its rightful access to this clearing in the forest.

Before leaving Kabara, I set up my camera for a group photograph that was to include myself. This meant that, as none of the men was capable of making an exposure, the camera had to be propped on a chair and its automatic delay setting brought into action. The necessary preparations and my hasty dash to join the group, followed by the audible click of the shutter, created a great impression and provided a topic of conversation for long afterwards.

Never was a more diversified group arranged in front of a camera. Kabanza stood in typical posture on the extreme left at the rear, his arms at his side and his shoulders slightly hunched. He wore both hats, one pulled down over the other, and a belted tunic and shorts. Bunane, with one muscular arm half raised, knelt before him in a sackcloth and the waistcoat from which he seemed inseparable. Boranze squatted with folded arms on my left and Ruhindura was similarly disposed on my right. Kaimba, unobtrusive as ever, was half hidden behind Boranze, his little wrinkled face bespeckled with grey, downy hairs. Despite their quaint apparel, the deep pigmentation of their skin and their obvious poverty, they had proved themselves worthy of this mountain setting in which Mikeno stands supreme. What more need be said?

Our trail back to Kibumba had become largely overgrown again, although it had been used by the men who had returned for food. Pangas were needed almost as much as before and our progress could be little faster than on the outward journey. Kaimba—who by his appearance and agility always reminded me of a black and white colobus monkey—was again tireless in clearing a way, and usually the others followed at slight intervals, jabbering ceaselessly.

What did they talk about? Very often their main topic was myself and the way I ate, the things I ate, the long strides I took, walking or climbing, and my exercises with the chest expanders. Their conversational powers, like those of most Africans, were extraordinary in view of their circumscribed lives and limited experiences, and I have no doubt that for as long as they live they will be able to talk endlessly of all that happened during our expedition to the central group of Virunga mountains.

We came to our journey's end in the late afternoon, the party disbanding here and there, leaving only those who carried my personal belongings to go on with me to the Kibumba hut. Bunane had been chosen to attend my further needs while remaining at Kibumba, and the others knew that they were to assemble early on the following morning for their pay. Our adventure together was drawing to an end, for they would not be able to go on with me to the three mountains bordering on Uganda.

All my equipment which had not been required on the mountains had remained behind, unguarded in the open hut at Kibumba, and it was found exactly as it was left—a tribute in itself to the entire honesty of the Africans of this region. I could not help drawing a contrast with Johannesburg where timorous citizens sleep behind barred windows and dare not leave a car unattended unless every door and window is shut and locked.

By now, with the second phase of my undertaking completed, the signs of a reaction setting in were a warning that rest was required after this period of intense activity. My throat became so sore that I could only speak in a whisper, and at night my sleep was broken by nightmares in which I lay alone and dying. My condition was indeed alarming, for

I had no medicines available, and to make matters worse, my supply of soda water had run out and there was no bread left.

A tremendous hubbub was expected to announce the arrival of Kabanza and his men for pay, but I was pleasantly surprised to find them all assembled and waiting quietly by the time I had breakfasted. Calling Kabanza and his Chief inside, I explained to them how much each man was entitled to receive in strict accordance with the standard rate of pay as fixed by the governing authorities, and how much they would in fact receive as additional payment. In this I wished to be entirely fair by rewarding them amply for their splendid services without overstepping the boundaries of generosity and tending to cause any corruption. The Chief and Kabanza showed their satisfaction with these arrangements, so I took my roll of notes together with a slip of paper bearing the names, and calling each in turn paid them as follows:

KABANZA—Captain and guide on Vishoke, Karisimzi and
    Mikeno   100 francs
               (and an additional blue tunic, woollen vests and blankets)
RUHINDURA—who climbed with me on Vishoke and
    Mikeno   60 francs
                   (also a pair of khaki shorts and a tunic)
BORANZE—who accompanied me on Vishohe and Karisimbi 60 francs
KAIMBA—Park official   40 francs
BIRARA, BATISTA, SEMIRYANGO, MARCO, HARAKANDI,
    BAREBERAHO, BUSHU—porters   40 francs
CHIEF AT KIBUMBA (whose name I never managed to inter-
    pret)   60 francs
BUNANE   60 francs
                         (and retained at 5 francs per day)

Cigarettes and remaining odd articles of clothing were distributed without favour amongst the porters, who showed great delight, but no more than Kabanza who now possessed a complete blue suit with a change of tunic.

As a final gesture to Kabanza, I shook hands with him in front of the others as they were drawn up in a single line. Then, with a wave of farewell, I parted from the loyal band of people who had helped me to the greatest achievement of my life.

A note was sent by native runner to the Conservateur, telling him of my return from the mountains, and while awaiting his arrival, I looked forward to a few days' rest under the benevolent eye of Bunane. Kabanza turned up on each of the following days, during which he went with me for walks in all directions for a radius of several miles. On these occasions, knowing himself to be no longer acting in the capacity of official guide, he remained discreetly in the rear, so that whenever I wished to make conversation with him I had to do so over my shoulder.

It was Saturday, June 16, when the Conservateur arrived with his assistant, Hubert, and one of his first questions was to ask if we had been successful on Mikeno. On being told that the three of us had been to the very top, both men showed evident surprise: in fact I do not think they had ever entertained the thought that I would succeed in climbing this most difficult of the Virunga mountains without the assistance of skilled European mountaineers.

From Kibumba I was transported with my appreciably reduced belongings to Commandant van Cools' residence at Rumangabo before being taken on to Rutshuru, from whence I hoped to find other transport for the journey to Kabale, in Uganda. When it came to paying my various fees for entry into the Nyiragongo and Mikeno sectors of the Albert National Park and for the use of the Institut's huts, etc., it was discovered that my permit had not included permission to climb Vishoke. The wording of my permit was at first reading a little ambiguous, and the Commandant had quite excusably been misled into thinking that it was valid for all three mountains instead of only two in the Mikeno sector. I had depended upon an oversight of this nature, but that it had come about so easily was almost unbelievable. My only part had been to refrain from pointing out the truth, but in this I was entirely to blame, and it is with no little trepidation that I record my artifice (deceit, surely, would be too strong a word to use). I had been guilty of a certain wrong, but who, backed by an ambition as overpowering as mine, would have remained so unswervingly righteous as to point out an error and thereby frustrate his own plans?

If any consolation were required, it could be found in the realisation that my real pact had been with the gorillas, elephants, buffaloes and other wild beasts of the area, and with these I was not in any way at variance. The laws of nature are so simple and easy to obey if we do but heed them: it is the laws made by man which prove irksome and bring about rebellion.

IX. *The Changing Scene*

M Y TRIUMPH on Mikeno still retained its glory, but there remained three more mountains to be climbed to complete the achievement. The ascent of Muhuvura, Mgahinga and Sabinio had still to be accomplished, but first I had to get there. How? Secretly I had hoped to be permitted to approach them from Belgian territory, and even to climb them with Kabanza and his men, but this proved altogether out of the question. Therefore I had elected to go on to Rutshuru in preference to Kisenyi, thinking that by doing so I would be nearer to Kabale, the administrative centre for Kigezi District, Western Province of Uganda, in which the three easternmost of the Virunga mountains are situated.

But at Rutshuru I met with a recurrence of my transport problems, and finding it impossible to make my way by Indian lorry or any other means into Uganda, I had no alternative but to return against my will to Kisenyi. From here it would be possible, if the worst came to the worst, to retrace my steps to Rhodesia without completing my original plans.

Again it seemed that I had set a goal that was altogether beyond attainment, and a greater despair than ever gripped me. I was becoming excessively wearied by my efforts, so that this new setback was seen as a final catastrophe instead of merely as a temporary obstacle. I sensed where the greater happiness lay, and tried desperately to shake off my ambitions. What did it matter, even to myself, if the eight mountains were climbed or not? What significance could there be in such an act? As for Everest, would it matter in the least if it remained unclimbed for ever?

But that is the irony of life. We can, after a while, perceive the makings of happiness, but by then there is a long road behind us, pitted with our mistakes and marred most of all by the follies born of our ignorance. If we are alone, we know that the road which we are taking is the road we must pursue to the end. If we are with others, we may be diverted from

77

our original course, but the new path may just as easily lead to disaster, for there are bad influences at work as well as good.

Although incapable of reasoning for myself, I was aware by some instinct that I could not go back voluntarily. The mountains might offer nothing but hardship, numbing coldness, misery or even death, but I had already committed myself and retreat was impossible.

Eventually, after several vexations, I found a seat in a postal van which took me in cramped discomfort to Ruhengeri, where there is a customs post, and after passing the lakes Luhondo and Bulera I left Belgian territory with a feeling of pleasure at once more being on my way, but with an underlying regret at having to leave Ruanda.

Being solely preoccupied with mountains, I had not travelled with the eyes of a political observer. Even so, I managed to draw a few conclusions, all of which show Belgian rule in a favourable light. Never once had I encountered a sign of perverse officialdom, or met with anything but obliging friendliness from Government authorities and everyone else. I had seen no drunkenness amongst whites or blacks, nor any indications of ill treatment on the one hand or of insolence on the other. It would be misleading to point to Kabanza and his men as an example of native behaviour, for it has been my experience that the best of Africans are to be found in the calming, ennobling atmosphere of remote, high mountains, where they have not as yet been corrupted by money or demoralised by the breakdown of traditional tribal living. Of the Albert National Park and its administration I am as qualified as any to judge, and I do not hesitate to say that its control could not be bettered by any other ruling power in Africa, for the Belgians are best fitted, by reason of their technical qualifications and also because of a necessary streak of sentimentality, as guardians of wild fauna and flora on this immense scale.

The road from Ruhengeri joins the Rutshuru-to-Kabale road near Nyakabanda, a few miles east of the Uganda customs post at Kisoro. Beyond this intersection there is a finely graded climb which reaches right up to the bamboo forest at 8,000 ft. before descending to Kabale at nearly 6,000 ft. This provides one of the most picturesque drives in Africa, but I was in no position to enjoy the scenery on this occasion, for the forward driving compartment, in which I was cramped between the Indian driver and piles of mail and additional baggage, was almost directly above the furiously boiling engine.

After arranging for accommodation at the White Horse Hotel, Kabale,

I was relieved to find that permission had been granted for me to climb the three local volcanoes (I had written for the necessary authorisation from Kisenyi on June 1, before setting out for Nyiragongo) and it was suggested that I should call at the District Commissioner's Office, where they would be interested to hear how my ascent of Mikeno had gone. It pleased me to do this, and especially to know that Mikeno had an equal reputation here as in the Congo.

Arrangements now went with a swing. The Uganda slopes of Sabinio are a gorilla sanctuary,[1] but no restrictions were placed in my way. On the contrary, every assistance was given, to the extent of granting me permission to make use of the Government rest house at Kisoro. Also, a short note was typed out for presentation to the Gombolola [2] Chief at Nyalusiza, who was requested to provide me with accommodation near the mountains. No tent would be needed, and guides and porters would be available on the spot.

On the spur of the moment, a new and exciting plan sprang to my mind, and I made inquiries as to the feasibility of spending a week or two at Lake Bunyoni when I had finished climbing. This was readily agreed to, and it was further suggested that I should include a week at Lake Mutanda. This lake, it was said, was more remote and even more beautiful than Lake Bunyoni, which I had seen previously and knew to be one of the most beautiful of all African lakes. Therefore the arrangement was made that I should go from Sabinio, the last of my mountains, to Kisoro and then on by native porterage to the north end of Lake Mutanda, where the Government rest house would be at my disposal. Afterwards I could go on, again by porterage if I wished, to Lake Bunyoni, where similar accommodation would be available for my use.

What glorious prospects had opened up—a hard mountaineering campaign followed by a period of rest in the tranquil atmosphere of two unspoilt lake regions. There was no need for deliberation. Of course I would go on from the mountains to the lakes.

There were no longer any crippling transport difficulties to contend with. Indian traders were sending out their lorries regularly between Kabale and the Congo border, and in the opposite direction as far as Kampala. It was only a question of time before one of these lorries would be making the journey to Kisoro, so I held myself in readiness and on June 25

[1] Proclaimed 1930. Area 17 sq. miles. For the protection of gorillas only.
[2] Sub-county. A District is divided into Counties (Sazas), sub-Counties (Gombolola) and Parishes (Mulukas).

left with the barest of essentials for what remained of my undertaking. A short rest from climbing had restored my energies and I was in fine fettle, my face bearded, the soles of my feet hardened. Only a constant gnawing pain in my stomach gave rise to any suspicion of trouble.

I had not planned it so, but it appeared likely that the single month of June would see my programme of eight climbs completed.

Of the three mountains which remained to be climbed, Sabinio was still represented by a large question mark. From what I had read about this mountain, and from first hand information, it was either (a) a fairly easy ascent, or (b) a difficult one requiring ropes. The mystery attached to it could only be resolved by actual encounter. Certainly it had looked a grand mountain as I had seen it from Ruanda, and of all African mountains, only Mikeno has intrigued me more.

At Kisoro, events moved swiftly, due in great measure to the Portuguese customs officer, Mr. de Sousa, who within a few minutes of my arrival despatched a note by native runner, informing the Gombolola Chief of my arrival. With corresponding alacrity, the Chief came in person to assure me of his utmost help, which included placing a house of his own and a hut at my disposal. He could not speak English, but with the customs officer acting as interpreter it was provisionally arranged that I should remain for one night at Kisoro and make for Nyalusiza at early morning with two porters who would be provided. A guide, and more porters if necessary, would await me at Nyalusiza where, after climbing Muhavura, I would spend the following night. The ascent of Mgahinga would also be undertaken from Nyalusiza, but the remaining mountain, Sabinio, would have to be reached from Ntebeko, unmarked on most maps, but several miles to the west. It would be a strenuous programme if carried out in this manner, without the use of tents at intervening points, but no more so than the series of climbs I had already made in Belgian mandated territory.

My new-found friend, the customs officer, suggested an afternoon visit to a mission station near Lake Mulehe, but we were neither of us prepared for what we found upon arrival there. The White Fathers had struck wolfram deposits in sufficient quantity for the pegging of a claim, and the hillsides were rent with numerous excavations. The talk was entirely of wolfram and its present market value, except when a blessing was offered before we sat down to tea.

A surprise of a different kind confronted me on our way back at sundown. I had not expected to set eyes on Mikeno again, but at a bend in the road it could be seen with its cathedral peak silhouetted against a reddened sky. I have noted down in my diary that I felt the mountain to be so close to me that I wanted to put out my hands and stroke its sheer sides. Here was the real house of God, lasting, incorruptible, divine. This sentiment may not be understandable to all, but it was true to me on this evening in June.

Once again I sensed that supreme elation, not of a conqueror but of a privileged human being who has been permitted to worship at this shrine mountain. I never speak of having *conquered* Mikeno—we simply climbed the mountain. Personally I felt that the only one to be conquered was myself. Previously I must have held a certain amount of fear when looking at Mikeno from nearby, but having climbed it I no longer feared it. I had been intimate with it after the manner of a lover, and, as with a lover, the last barrier of reserve had been removed.

Mikeno has not been climbed since, to my knowledge, but it will be climbed time and again in the future. Even so, I shall always look upon this mountain as " MINE," and I believe that no other climber will ever have the same oneness with it. I think this because I climbed it in the simplest manner possible—barefooted every bit of the way, and groping through the mist and rain with only a pair of shorts and a ragged shirt as covering. Mikeno meant much to me—more than I can say.

Upon returning to the rest house at Kisoro I found to my pleasure that Tomasi Sebukweto, the Gombolola Chief, had sent a gift of chicken and eggs and had also provided a youth to cook for me. The Chief had selected this youngster because of his alleged knowledge of English, but this proved to be so slight as to be worse than no knowledge at all, for he did not possess the intelligence to go with it, and unlike Kabanza, he could not apprehend a single thought or need. As in Ruanda, Kiswahili is spoken by the indigenous Africans, but this well-intentioned if misguided fellow ignored my own few words of this language in his efforts to make use of his own very limited English vocabulary. Nor was he any more successful as a cook.

The rest house was shared on this occasion with a Greek recruiting officer for the mines of Ankole District, who was scouring the area for native labour. A pleasant evening was enlivened by his tales of travel and the extraordinary happenings which serve to show how much stranger is truth than fiction. My rôle was mostly that of listener, for I have never looked upon mountains as a topic of conversation amongst those who do not share an equal liking for high, remote places, and who fail to understand what underlies the notions of people who are drawn to them.

There was less pleasure for me when it came to turning in to bed: the night had to be spent in extreme discomfort without a mattress or any similar covering over the cold concrete floor which was no softer, though smoother, than the jagged lava on which I had slept at the base of Vishoke. It came as more of a relief than anything else when, long before daylight, I was summoned to arise by the lighting of a candle and the unmistakable request of my cook. Two porters awaited me, and after a few hurried preparations I went out to join them on our trek to Nyalusiza while it was still quite dark. No sound could be heard as we set off in a southerly direction with our trail illuminated by a single lantern. Cockerels had not yet begun to crow and dogs were still sleeping in neighbouring villages. The air was bleak and not a star was to be seen.

Two miles or so farther on, we turned to the south-west along a native path, and with the first glimmer of dawn, Muhavura could be distinguished ahead of us, and thereafter, in the gathering light of dawn, it stood out more and more boldly until the deep clefts in its north face showed up plainly under a strong side-lighting. Hereafter it was our infallible guide, as befits its name.[1]

At one time, while the early morning haze lingered in the east, partially obscuring the sun, I watched a strange cloud formation assemble over Muhavura. It came piling up from the Congo side, where there is thick forest, and settled like a huge hand over the summit. It billowed out and rolled under to the right, as though the fingers were being clenched. It hovered above the mountain for several minutes, parts of it dispersing only to reassemble in the original pattern. Despite the poor visibility, I obtained a photograph which, although not good, provides a reasonable picture of the strange formation.

Long, jagged gullies, running practically from top to bottom, have been cut on Muhavura by landslides started by water and, perhaps, the effects of frost. In the west, the mountain slopes evenly to a saddle which joins it to Mgahinga, the smallest of the eight Virunga volcanoes. Dense forest exists on the saddle and on Mgahinga, but Muhavura itself is devoid of true forest on its eastern and northern sides, and above the saddle in the west. Cloud is nearly always more prevalent on the diminutive Mgahinga

[1] Muhavura means, literally, " he who brings one back in the right path."

than on Muhavura, which stands like a towering colossus beside it, and more than once I have seen clouds totally obscuring the smaller mountain while the higher and broader mass of Muhavura has remained wholly visible. This appears strange from afar, without knowledge of the different indigenous growths which are entirely responsible for the apparent absurdity.

At Nyalusiza, which we reached after a trek of about five miles, I was greeted by Chief Tomasi, who had already impressed me as a thoroughly likable man of considerable character. A guide and porters were assembled beside a newly whitewashed building set on a concrete foundation with bricks sloping away from it. Several square wooden beams, with their bases sunk in the concrete, supported a tiled roof. The doors, of stained wood, were neatly made in one piece, and the glassless windows were barred with hinged wooden shutters.

I was shown into two rooms, entirely unfurnished, but spotlessly clean, and it was clear I was being offered the choice of either as a living-room and bedroom. I made my selection, happy at the thought of such comparative luxury to follow at the end of a crowded day. Then, without further delay, I set off to cover the intervening distance of about five miles to the base of Muhavura, taking with me a guide and two fresh porters. I was pleased that no attempt was made to impose a greater number of porters upon me, than I needed, though many additional men were available if required. On this mountain there would be no need for a team of men to chop out a route with pangas, and the Chief seemed to realise that my methods called for no more helpers than would be actively employed. What he did not know was that my funds were too low for over-indulgence of any kind.

X. *The Domain of an African Gentleman*

THE PLAIN between Nyalusiza and the base of Muhavura is now thickly overgrown with grasses, but it was at one time an active volcanic region, pitted with small subsidiary vents, evidence of which is still noticeable though the vents themselves are now covered with small vegetation. Only a few trees grow singly or in small clusters and there are no streams of any importance. No doubt the area supported a large mammalian population between its final stage of active volcanism and the time when vegetation was able to reassert itself. To-day there are no longer any big game animals in the immediate vicinity, for the land has been populated by too many native pastoralists, though their presence is not readily noticeable from afar because their thatched huts are scattered in small groups and blend with the natural landscape so as to be inconspicuous, even from nearby.

At intervals along our route, we encountered these small habitations, and occasionally we came upon small numbers of men and women carrying loads of straw to their homes. Usually my guide and porters would engage them in conversation while still far away and the two parties would meet without stopping, their talk continuing uninterrupted while the distance between them grew steadily. For some minutes there would be no contact by sight, and yet the ringing voices would go on and on in ceaseless chatter until the last of many salutations and minor pleasantries would be trailed out. There were many instances of this, and from them I gathered that Africans have developed a tone of voice which carries unusually far, and that this is a result of many generations of having to depend upon unaided vocal powers for propagation of news and views.

When the mountain was reached, it became obvious that my physical condition even after a few days of comparative rest was not all that it should have been. However, I tried to conceal the fact from myself and drove

84

The third sector, showing the remaining three peaks

on and up in a battle that was more against my own fatigue than anything else. The climb itself entailed no difficulty whatever, but consisted of an annoyingly constant gradient, which needed to be taken in easy stages with frequent pauses. Instead, we plodded relentlessly on as though taking part in a private feud between white man and black in which the briefest of halts would have involved a loss of prestige.

An occasional magnificent view served to break the monotony, although there was always a certain amount of haze. One incomparable panorama was of six lakes which shone like jewels; Mutanda the brightest of them and the others Muanga, Bulera, Luhondo, Mugisha and Tshahafi. In a clearer atmosphere, Lake Bunyoni would also have been visible. If these lakes were jewels, then the countryside south-east of Kisoro was a bed from which jewels had been plucked from their clasps, for it was pockmarked with numerous small volcanic vents, most of them identical in shape and practically the same size. The rim of each was similarly high at one point and low at another, indicative of the way in which lava deposits had been built up from the centre of explosion.

Tall lobelias and senecios sprouted thinly over a large area of Muhavura's eastern slopes and at one point where conditions seemed most favourable there were some particularly fine specimens almost reminiscent of the extraordinary growths on Ruwenzori. Immortelles grew in profusion, larger and more plentiful than I have seen them anywhere else. At the summit there is a small crater lake, no more than 100 ft. in diameter and probably of no great depth at its centre. From this, and the general structure of the mountain, I would place its age as slightly greater than that of Karisimbi, but less than that of Sabinio and Mikeno. We drank from the cold, clear water and then went down on the long, tiring descent, after which we had the apparently endless trail back to Nyalusiza confronting us. For me, Muhavura holds the least appeal of any of the Virunga mountains.

I tried hard not to let my state of exhaustion be noticed, but it was too real to be concealed, and I half stumbled, half dragged myself to the eventual retreat of Chief Tomasi's dwelling at Nyalusiza. I was too utterly wearied to think, or if I did it was only to feel relief at not being faced with having to put up a tent. Assuredly I was not prepared for the many pleasant surprises that awaited me.

The floor of my chosen room, previously bare, had been covered with clean coir matting, and a curtain had been strung across the window, which faced west. A wooden bed with a support of intertwined ropes was ranged along one side of the room, and there was a chair and a table draped with a neat, printed tablecloth. These were the entire furnishings, and they were rough and even crude by normally accepted standards, but it was the thought and care behind the preparations which counted most with me. No European housewife could have been more fussy or could have provided better results with such limited means, and yet there had been no other guiding hand than that of a man of colour who had never glimpsed beyond the barrier which separates black from white in Africa.

Chief Tomasi stood in the doorway, smiling with pleasure because of the appreciation shown in my face for his own spontaneous charity. A bond of inalienable friendliness united us thenceforward.

A native, whom I discovered later to be the Chief's personal cook, entered with a large metal teapot which he placed on the table together with a cup and saucer. It was a strange brew with a smell strongly suggestive of mealies, but its taste was pleasant and I consumed one cup after another until there was none left.

The Gombolola Chief, following events with a paternal eye from a discreet distance, then came forward to conduct me into an adjoining room in which a medium-sized tin bath stood in the centre of the floor with a large bowl of water at its side. Tomasi Sebukweto bowed slightly and smiled, and then left me to the incalculable luxury of a stand-up bath with delightfully hot water. This was indeed a change, and my mind wandered back to the times when I had come down from Vishoke and Mikeno in much dirtier condition and had been forced to go to bed as I was, with feet and legs caked with mud.

Meanwhile a chicken, eggs, milk and mealies had been prepared, and after my bath they were served to me hot at the table. Again I drew a contrast with earlier occasions in the Congo when there had been no alternative but to set to and prepare my own meals because there had been no one skilled enough to cook for me. It was also a welcome change to be able to live off the land.

The green [1] mealies were deliciously sweet and tender, but the chicken provided me with a small but not insignificant dilemma. It was tough, excessively tough, but to have left it untouched would have offended the hospitality extended to me by the Chief, so out of respect for him I set about the main course.

At first I refused to give in, but in the end I had to admit defeat. No one was with me in the room, but I had a persistent feeling of being watched from outside. The chicken could not be eaten, but neither could it be left whole: nor could it be got rid of by any effective means at this stage. Courtesy demanded that at least half the meal should be disposed of, but by what means, when my teeth were so inadequate?

In desperation, I picked up a leg and gnawed without relish until, by

[1] This really refers to the covering leaves which, while still green, are a sign that the corn is young and succulent. The corn cobs are preferred by Europeans in this stage of immaturity, but Africans usually allow them to become fully grown and firm before cutting and eating them. By this time the covering leaves are yellow, or the colour of straw. Mealies, or corn on the cob, are generally boiled by Europeans, whereas Africans prefer them roasted.

amateurish sleight of hand, I could put it in my pocket. The same performance was carried through with a wing, and all the time I sensed that eyes were watching me. I also sensed a feeling of guilt, and this gave me the cunning of a murderer trying to secrete away a dead body. And like a murderer I made one fatal mistake. There should have been cleanly picked bones as evidence of a repast carried to its proper conclusion. Instead there was nothing but a few shreds of skin on my plate. Disregarding this finer point I stole out of doors and, while pretending to study the stars, hurled the contents of my pocket far and wide.

The result of this infamy was that no more chickens were sent to me as a gift, so it is doubtful if the subtlety of my act had fooled the Chief in any way. But he may have smiled to himself, for his next thoughtful deed was to send an English-speaking boy along—perhaps with the object of making explanations easier for me.

Chief Tomasi Sebukweto was a handsome man, with gentlemanly manners and a fine, dignified bearing that was well in keeping with his status as head of an important border region. Of rather more than average height and build, he was obviously a man of considerable strength, but this was tempered with an extraordinary charm. He was always polite and courteous, and while in my company his quietness matched my own.

He displayed neither servility nor arrogance. His mode of dress displayed his entire character at its true worth, for he contrived a perfect balance between European and African style by wearing a splendidly tailored grey jacket over a long, white robe. For special occasions, he wore a neatly folded, spotlessly clean handkerchief in the breast pocket of his jacket, and more than once he appeared with a red carnation in the buttonhole. His vanity was undeniable but not excessive, and because of it I presented him with a folding mirror before leaving.

Seldom have I been the recipient of such kindly hospitality as from this Uganda Chief who never once offended in his desire to please—unless he did so indirectly and unintentionally through the chicken. What is more, he was a model of decorum, and unobtrusiveness. He always retired discreetly once a gift had been made.

The lad who had been sent to act as interpreter was in his ordinary walk of life a clerk. His name was John Mbonigaba, and he looked undernourished, as perhaps he was, but after misjudging Kabanza by first appearances I refrained from making any further early assessment of climbing ability and stamina. His command of English was very limited, but he had the makings of an intelligent young man, and by methods to which I had become accustomed we were able to make all essential arrangements, and in addition I was provided with information which would not have come my way otherwise.

As evening drew on, a lamp was sent in to enable me to write up my diary before retiring to bed, but before this was done we made our plans for the following day. The forest on Mgahinga was said to be very thick, so that a team of four men armed with pangas would be necessary. A new guide would have to be employed on Mgahinga as well as Sabinio, for these two mountains fall within a different domain. Nevertheless, my guide of the previous day on Muhavura wished to stay with me in order to gain experience with the central and westernmost of the local volcanoes, neither of which he had as yet climbed. In particular he wished to claim the feat of having been to the top of Sabinio. He was so keen to remain with me for the two further climbs that he made no claim for payment. He was tall, slim, good looking and appeared to be about 30 years of age. He was quiet and reserved in manner and possessed more initiative and intelligence than most of his fellows. I had already taken a liking to Robeni and from this time I liked him all the more because of his willingness to set the mountains above considerations of time and money. Also, no doubt, I was flattered by his show of attachment to my own unpretentious efforts.

It was not until the following morning that I met Ndabateze, who was to be my guide on Mgahinga and Sabinio. He, too, was a worthy leader. Rather older than Robeni, he did not object to the presence of the less experienced man. It would enliven my account if I were to tell of bickerings and open arguments or of any untoward incidents, but the truth is that all the men were amicably disposed to one another at all times. As in the Congo, each one had his own job to do and he went about it willingly and without need for instructions. Neither Kabanza, Robeni nor Ndabateze ever gave a forceful command and it seemed throughout that the men under them required no more than a slender authority to control them. There is no credit due to myself for any outstanding qualities as a leader: rather there was a kindred spirit amongst us, which acted as a binding force and kept us free from the common afflictions to which larger expeditions are prone.

Instructions were given by Chief Tomasi for the bed, table and chair to be carried to Ntebeko, which I gathered to be several miles to the west and within striking distance of Sabinio. I did not even bother to wonder what would await me upon arrival at Ntebeko, for I felt that the Chief had this part of the organisation under his control and that he could be trusted implicitly.

Thinking to please the Chief, and not knowing that I would be returning to Nyalusiza, I offered to take his photograph before leaving. At this suggestion he beamed with delight, but he asked with great seriousness for time in which to change into his best clothes. The village itself, in which his house was situated, was no more than a few hundred yards away, but his change of clothing took the better part of an hour, with the consequence that we were later than I anticipated in setting out for Mgahinga.

Our party consisted of Ndabateze, Robeni, John Mbonigaba and six porters: Ndikumuzima, Ntawaluhunga, Rwihandagaza, Bizagwira, Kangabo and Ryaziga. I had always planned to keep to the absolute minimum, and thus it seemed to be an excessively large party for so small a mountain, but we were soon to find that every man would be needed. No one had set foot on the mountain for fully ten years, and Ndabateze and his men would have to hack out an entirely new trail.

As we headed for the western extremity of the saddle running between Muhavura and Mgahinga I had time to remember that three-quarters of my self-imposed task was already completed and there seemed every likelihood of complete success. Soon I would be at peace with the eight Virunga mountains and with myself, until a restless yearning should drive me on to further struggles in mountainous places. There was no telling at this stage if Everest remained the dominant factor, for I kept it deliberately from my thoughts, and intended doing so until Mgahinga and, finally, Sabinio had been climbed.

We made good time to the base of the saddle, where the plain was strewn with boulders washed down from a deep fissure which starts high up on Muhavura and cleaves the saddle near Mgahinga. There is an element of danger in this area, for avalanches of rock occur frequently, but it so happens that the short, sweet grasses and other herbage make the plain and the lower slopes of Muhavura a favoured pasturage. A risk has to be taken, and only a few days previously a cow had been killed by a fall of boulders. It took little imagination to visualise the change of scene from tranquil quietness, as we saw it, to sudden rumbling activity, a stampede and then death.

In this area, too, there had been the case of an old male gorilla who wandered down to cultivated plots in the Gombolola of Nyalusiza. Unfortunately for the animal there was an organised pig hunt in progress at the time, and he was speared by mistake in dense undergrowth some two miles outside the gorilla sanctuary. Leopards are still fairly common in the neighbourhood, though they are nocturnal and usually keep to the rocky mountain slopes to which they have retreated for safety.

Keeping the fissure to our left we started climbing, and almost immediately we were into thick forest, with three men slashing ceaselessly with their pangas, one concentrating his efforts directly ahead and the others cutting away the tangle of branches, roots and undergrowth to left and right. As soon as they tired, three other men took over, and in this manner we made surprisingly rapid progress.

Perhaps the fact that it was the smallest mountain of the group made me treat Mgahinga with too little respect, for I blundered along at times, receiving more than my normal due of cuts and scratches. On one occasion I stumbled and nearly fell over a tree root. " Sorry," said John Mbonigaba, who was immediately behind me. A trailing creeper wound itself tightly about my throat, and I was nearly swept off my feet. " Sorry," said John again.

It was always the same, with each man apparently feeling himself personally responsible for my wellbeing. But when I trod on a particularly vicious stinging nettle, dancing with pain as I did so, and a chorus of " Sorries " greeted me, I thought the whole thing was being taken a little too far. After all, I would persist in going about at all times with the very minimum of clothing. (This reaction, as a matter of fact, is typical of most Africans, and is to be taken lightly. In this respect they are somewhat akin to Byron's Jack Bunting, who " knew not what to say, and so he swore." These fellows didn't know what to say, and so they apologised.

The abruptness with which the forest belts begin and end is a fascinating peculiarity of equatorial Africa. There is, generally speaking, no gradual merging with the savannahs, but a clearly defined break, a cleavage. The best appreciation of a phenomenon of this nature can, in my opinion, be gained when overlooking a tropical forest from a considerable elevation, as from a mountain side. The great Ituri forest, for example, can be seen to no greater advantage than from the foothills north of Ruwenzori, and for a true appraisal of the " Neopolitan ice " effect of clear-cut vegetal zones, I can recommend the Virunga volcanoes.

The reason for this sharp distinction between high forest and savannah is that neither the forest nor the grassland can establish itself beyond its own boundary. Where trees predominate, there is a tangle of roots and a canopy of leaves through which little light can enter. Grasses cannot flourish under such conditions. On the other hand, the grasslands are burnt regularly and thus there is no chance for seedlings to take firm root before they are devastated by fire. Only freak intrusions of nature, or man, can break down the barrier between the two. Man does so by setting up habitations, in and around which the grasses are trampled and trees encouraged to grow. These effects are to be seen in varying degree wherever there are forests and savannahs in Africa, but the definition between the zones is perhaps strongest here and in West Africa because of the tropical intensity of growth.

Once we had gained the saddle top on Mgahinga, we came out of the closed forest to a clearing entirely devoid of trees, but well grassed. Here was an exception to the rule, as I stated it above, for there was no human population at hand to fire the grasses and keep back the forest. The explanation, I think, is that an original clearing had existed and had been kept open by the congregation of herds of large fauna. It was obvious from the numerous spoors that elephants and buffaloes occurred in big herds, using the clearing as a welcome retreat from the thick forest in which to disport and sun themselves, and incidentally trample the plant life and prevent its establishment.

What are big game animals doing in such numbers on a cold, excessively damp mountain? We may be sure that very few, if any, belong by choice to densely forested highlands. They are there, as on the Virunga mountains, because of persecution elsewhere. They have been driven from their favoured open savannahs and lightly forested savannahs at lower altitudes by encroaching civilisation, and have had no open lines of retreat except to the mountains. The larger antelopes, with the notable exception of the bongo (*Boocercus euryceros*) cannot survive away from open or fairly open pasturage, but the elephant and buffalo are highly adaptable creatures and consequently have been able to seek a natural sanctuary in high forests and mountains. Over the course of several centuries, they have adapted themselves to such an extent as to take on different characteristics, so that it has become necessary to distinguish between them in scientific nomenclature. Thus the elephant is separated as *Loxodonta africana* (savannah elephant) and *Loxodonta (africana) cyclotis* (dwarf or forest elephant). The common *Syncerus caffer*, or savannah buffalo, is represented in regions of high forest by a much smaller race which in West Africa is so inferior as to have gained the non-scientific name of bushcow instead of buffalo.

Looking beyond the clearing on the Congo side I could discern a lake, but could not be certain if it was Bulera or Luhondo. The two Uganda lakes, Mutanda and Mulehe, showed up more distinctly, and, turning back to the Congo, I caught a glimpse of Karisimbi with its dome completely covered with a fresh fall of hail. I peered apprehensively in the direction of Mikeno, but I am not sure if I saw it in dim outline or if the desire to do so played a trick with my imagination.

Beyond the clearing on the saddle, we came to a zone of thick bamboo which did not possess the ordinary attributes of this kind of forest. It harboured an extremely offensive stinging nettle, noticeably smaller than any I had hitherto met, but more vicious and harmful to the touch. It would conceal itself and then spring unsuspected from cover, stinging like an angry hornet. Fortunately there was not much of this unpleasantness to contend with, for we were able to leave the forest and to climb up the dried bed of a stream, preferring the steepness of its gradient in parts to the drawbacks elsewhere. At times of heavy rain, this watercourse would become a rushing, plunging torrent, but on this day there was only a thin trickle leading at one point to a small " bottomless " pool with no visible signs of egress.

Two diversions had to be made where precipitous, slippery falls barred our way, and at one of these there was leopard spoor to be observed in the soft earth at the entrance to a cave which no doubt was one of the lairs put to occasional use by leopards. Farther on, we came to droppings which were most likely those of a gorilla, for Ndabateze assured me that these animals lived in the vicinity. Some authorities have denied the presence of gorillas on this mountain, but they have apparently been wrong in their assumptions. However, Mgahinga is only a small mountain with little suitable vegetation, and probably it supports no more than a single troop at various times during periodic migrations between Mikeno and the easternmost part of their range, which covers approximately twenty miles in an east to west direction.

Getting back to the forest, we proceeded to a part in which huge rope-like vines hung down from the uppermost branches of the highest trees, which would be considered giants anywhere. Until this time I had ridiculed the existence of such stupendous forest growths as those familiar from Tarzan films, but here was proof of them. To convince myself of its strength, I suspended myself from one particularly robust liana and then persuaded a porter wearing only a loin cloth to swing from it while I photographed him. This caused a great deal of merriment, with the principal actor playing his part according to type, but not having the least idea as to what had prompted this strange jungle scene.

To reach the crater summit we followed the forest to its termination along a narrow ridge and then emerged into a zone of small vertical extent where rotting senecios and ferns grew in profusion from a carpeting of moss and alchemilla. I had expected to find a crater lake, but instead there was no more than a small pool at the western extremity, where there was also a grassy platform covering what may have been a circular vent in the days of Mgahinga's volcanic activity.

I had found this mountain of absorbing interest, and perhaps for this reason, or because I hoped for a break in the clouds through which to look once more on Mikeno, I remained longer than at any other mountain summit. Another consideration was that the men, who had worked hard without a pause on the ascent, wished for a rest. So we sat apart, they in a tight circle eating roasted mealies and *matoke* (plantains), while I ate my bread and cheese in the partial shelter of an arborescent groundsel. This was my second mountain in two days and I wondered, without caring, if the following day would provide a sort of hat-trick. There was no need to hurry, even if I had been anxious to accomplish the eight climbs before the end of June, which had three more days to run, and I was willing to go along at the pace set by Ndabateze.

It did not take us long to go down, and a short distance beyond the forest edge we were met by four natives carrying gourds of milk on their heads. Cattle were grazing nearby, and presumably the milk had been produced on the spot. Each of my men drank his fill, and when we were ready to move on I inquired about payment, only to be informed that instructions had been given for no charge to be made. This was just one more example of the goodwill of Chief Tomasi.

There was still a long way to go, and our trail meandered so much that at times we doubled back as though heading for the mountain instead of away from it. In places, the ground had only a slight covering of soil, through which outcrops of lava protruded, but elsewhere there were plantations containing mealies and millet of a growth which indicated a good deposit of highly fertile earth. Several hills had to be skirted, and occasionally we passed through villages in which we received cordial greetings, though the children were eager to scamper out of sight. Our march, coming as it did at the end of a day already crowded with activity, seemed endless, but at length we came to a hill surmounted by a cairn of stones, and this was our journey's end. Only a few inhabitants were settled in the area, and it appeared that Ntebeko was not so much a village as an outpost near the Belgian Congo frontier which received occasional visits from the Gombolola Chief and perhaps from a few European officials.

My house here was less pretentious than the one in which I stayed at Nyalusiza. It consisted merely of a typical wattle and daub hut of beehive shape enclosed by a bamboo palisade. Simple though it was, no pains had been spared to make it as attractive and comfortable as possible. The low entrance did not have a door, but a screen of split bamboo had been suspended to above half-way and could be made to cover the entire gap. The floor was of plain earth cemented with cow dung, but it was firmly stamped and clean. Cloth partitionings made a living-room, bathroom and bedroom, simple enough, but luxurious and welcome to me in this purely native area. Again there was tea, a hot bath and a meal, which consisted significantly enough of eggs and mealies, without any chicken.

While there was still sufficient daylight, I went outside and climbed the hill, and from there made an outline sketch of Sabinio and Mgahinga. As the sun was about to set, Sabinio was revealed more clearly than I had seen it before, the almost horizontal rays of light causing deep shadows which provided a sense of depth. The Uganda side of the mountain, facing northwards, was shown to be deeply cleft and irregular, and much more impressive than when observed from Kisoro or Nyalusiza. It stood out as a bold and magnificent mountain with a summit ridge, from this viewpoint, of five jagged peaks which give rise to the name Sabinio— " father with huge teeth."

That night, Sabinio retained for me its mystery, but whatever difficulties it confronted us with, I knew that we could not fail. I had my own confidence, inspired by Mikeno, to stand me in good stead, and of Ndabateze and Robeni there could be no doubt whatever. They would be lost on mountains elsewhere, but in their own native territory there was no one to beat them. They had been born and bred within sight of Muhavura, Mgahinga and Sabinio, and they were intimate with every nook and cranny on the Uganda side of these mountains. Every human inhabitant was known to them, at least by sight, and they also knew what to expect of every species of wild beast that was likely to be encountered. Their knowledge of the landscape and every element in it was complete. In this, I feel, lies the unerring accuracy with which they find their way about in an area which would confuse any white man. Although there may be thousands of trees, seemingly alike as bamboo, yet they are able to distinguish between them, and recognise each outcrop of rocks as a definite landmark. There is no need for street names or signposts to the well-trodden dirt trails or to the indistinct footpaths leading from them in a maze of directions, for they have scampered about them as naked children. Pathfinding, even on the mountains themselves, gives little trouble to men like Ndabateze and Robeni; they have only to pass a way once in order to know that way forever.

Ndabateze, lithe and in the prime of his manhood, never caused me to think of him as strongly as I had thought of Kabanza, but that was only because he never gave me the same apprehensions or, on the other hand, the same buoyant expectancy, and there was the added reason that we were not together long enough for the formation of any strong attachment. Ndabateze did not by any means lack character, but his was not a forceful personality.

Robeni, too, was quiet and unassuming, and I have already described him as good looking. In appearance he reminded me strongly of Boranze, who had been with me in the Mikeno sector and who was similarly good looking or even handsome in his own way, and equally restrained and unaspiring. In white men who are notable for their looks, there is usually more than a trace of vanity, conceit, hauteur and other despicable traits. With these men it was different, and I wondered why. Could it be that the high mountains restrained them and gave them a touch of humility?

XI. *Sabinio—the Eighth Peak*

SABINIO, as I could see, had a lot of forest on its lower and middle slopes, but I decided to reduce the number of men by two, more for reasons of economy than anything else. We set off in single file at the first sign of daylight, covering in very quick time the three miles separating us from the foothills at the western extremity of this mountain. Despite the earliness of the hour and the cold, I started off and remained without any encumbrances other than the same shorts and shirt that had been put to hard use on seven other climbs and were by this time distinctly shabby and torn. Robeni went ahead with my camera, following Ndabateze, and John Mbonigaba kept close behind me with a haversack containing the usual items of clothing and climbing gear in case of need.

Although our start had been an early one, we were not alone on the mountain, for we met a number of men, including a very old, bent fellow, carrying loads of bamboo to their huts which must have been a considerable distance away. This was amazing industry for people who are normally accused of dilatoriness and indolence. We could see, as we passed from ordinary forest to the fringes of the bamboo zone, where they had "nibbled" at its edges, but no matter how much they cut away, they would make little impression upon a forest of such dimensions. Africans in their primitive state do not destroy either fauna or flora beyond repair. It is only white men with their excess of greed who do this.

By the time the sun had appeared at full strength, we were into the thickest bamboo that grows on any of the Virunga mountains, but our progress remained surprisingly rapid because of the expertness of Ndabateze's men with their pangas. A level clearing was reached, and beyond it we passed into what, because of the sudden and complete change that was involved, appeared to be a totally different world. It was an area of new growth in which the bamboo stems grew so closely together that, crowded

97

from the life-giving sun, they grew pale and slender to a height which could not be estimated because of the closed canopy which gave a semblance of endlessness.

Here we walked through a pale green wilderness which shut out the sun and its heat so completely that to me it seemed as though we had stepped out of a sunlit room into one with drawn curtains. Because so little of the sun's rays filtered through from above, the air remained delightfully cool, and underfoot there was a thick, springy mass of soft mosses, entirely free of nettles and thorns. While we advanced, there was no sound save that of steel blades chopping once or twice against each hollow bamboo stem. Then, whenever a change-over took place and our advance was halted for a brief interval, the forest would lapse into profound silence.

The grace and delicacy of the tall bamboo, the feeling of softness and yet of dependable security underfoot, the pale, restful light, the utter silence, which I did not consider oppressive—these were sensations of a few precious minutes that will last for a lifetime. The fascination of this bamboo forest was so compelling that at the time I could entertain no feeling or thought that was not delightful.

Only once was the silence broken by others than ourselves. This was when we heard a scrambling and a crashing ahead and to our right, when we were at nearly 10,000 ft. Gorillas! There was no mistaking the sound or the closeness of it, and the atmosphere became electric. My first thought was for my camera, which I took from Robeni and prepared hurriedly for use. For only a few seconds there were indications of intense activity after which the sound [1] dwindled and then ceased abruptly. We stood quite still, and the forest lapsed into complete silence.

I waved Ndabateze onward in the direction from which the sound had come, but he only smiled, without showing any disrespect, and I came to know after brief reflection what he had realised instinctively and at once—that with our noisy and laborious progress we could not hope to come upon the gorillas in their dense, natural habitat. Men could not pass through without clearing a trail, and gorillas could not make their way

[1] For the sake of accurate record, the only sound distinguished was that of obviously heavy bodies passing through the dense bamboo by sheer force of weight. There were no weird chest-thumpings, nor any vocal sounds. As a mere assumption, based on the intensity of noise and its sudden cessation, I would say that the troop was made up of a small number of grown animals. Young ones could hardly have been whisked away with such speed and without any vocal hastening.

at speed without breaking down all obstacles, but this they could easily do.

There had been no sign of fear on the part of Ndabateze and his men. They were well versed in the ways of nature, and so it was obvious to them that the troop of gorillas was carrying out evasive action as fast as they could. As these men knew, there are few dangers to be faced in the wilds by those who keep to themselves and obey the normal rules of safety. It is an almost infallible rule that all wild beasts will escape rather than attack. The few exceptions are (1) in the case of a wounded animal or one carrying festering sores (this includes the so-called rogue elephants which are almost invariably driven to desperation by old wounds or disease) and (2) animals which fear for themselves or their young as a result of real or imagined molestation. Man-eating lions are a case apart, but they will not as a rule turn to human flesh while sufficient of their normal food is available.

Having at various times stood close to practically every species of big game in Africa, and always unarmed, I have come to look upon them as friends, or at least as companions in otherwise lonely places, and it is perhaps for this reason that I have never met with any injury from them. When the open spaces in Africa no longer contain any wild fauna, then I shall have no more desire to roam there.

A great deal of uncertainty surrounds the past and present status of the gorilla in Uganda. The discovery of *G.g.beringei* in the vicinity of Karisimbi came more than half a century after the West African species was made known to science, and it was not until a quarter of a century later (1929) that the mountain gorilla was acknowledged as a resident in Uganda and added to the Protectorate's list of completely protected animals. Its presence in the territory was not suspected at all until 1919, and for several years after this it was thought to be no more than an occasional or seasonal visitor from the Congo side of the Virunga mountains. It is still not known for certain if gorillas are permanently established on Sabinio. It is my belief that they are, and that they may be more numerous there than has been hitherto supposed. My own experiences lead me to these conclusions, and especially the fact that Sabinio appears to possess a greater area of young, succulent bamboo than any other mountain in either the eastern or central group of the Virungas.

Later we saw the dung of gorillas near a large tree immediately outside the upper limit of the bamboo zone, and a little further on I photographed a typical nest [1] built in a fork made by the lowest branches of a tree. This, presumably, was where the troop had rested during the previous night. Very recent elephant and buffalo droppings indicated the passage of small herds not long before, and at one point to the right of our trail there was leopard spoor in damp mud. Perhaps one of these courageous little killers was keeping watch over the troop of gorillas, hoping that perhaps there would be an immature specimen straying within pouncing distance; or perhaps " Spots" was hunting higher up the mountain, or just moving away from our line of approach. Whatever was happening, the thought of being with these creatures of the wilds and sharing with them the adventure of an uncertain existence gave a pleasurable thrill to every minute.

Other species of *ungulata* occurring on this mountain are bushbuck (*Tragelaphus scriptus*), red forest duiker (*Cephalophus natalensis kivuensis*), bushpig (*Potamochoerus porcus*) and elephant. Several reptiles, including the black-lipped cobra (*Naja melanoleuca*) and green tree viper (*Atheris nitschei*) occur, but we never encountered any.

Every yard of our advance had to be hacked out until the ordinary forest as well as the bamboo zone had been cleared, and all this time there was never a sign of the peaks for which we were heading. Here at last I thought, is some slight error of judgment to bring these fellows and their sense of direction within the bounds of ordinary human fallibility But far from it; instead, we made a decisive swing to the left which took us beyond the tree line and there, directly ahead of us, could be seen the serried peaks of Sabinio's summit ridge.

We gained a grassy knoll from where the various forest growths could be observed, and the places where each zone ended abruptly, giving way to growth of a different kind. It gave the strong impression of a giant hand at work, planting each type of forest and crop of smaller vegetation with extreme precision and following contours to the best of advantage.

We carried on over soft moss and warm grasses on which it was delightful to tread with bare feet. Rocks began to predominate, but something was missing, and I became aware that for some reason or other Sabinio has no profuse growth of senecios, lobelias, immortelles and other allied flora Eventually, we emerged to the first peak, and here all but Ndabateze Robeni, and John Mbonigaba remained. So, too, do most climbers on

[1] Apart from the beds, made as described by Mr. Ionides on page 26, gorillas are known occasionally to construct rough forms or " nests " with grass, leaves and twigs. These crude structures are mainly for the protection of young animals whose chief enemy is the leopard Otherwise gorillas are too heavily built to be arboreal in the true sense of the word.

this mountain, for Ndabateze informed me that he had guided 15 parties on the mountain but only three had ventured beyond this point to the fourth and highest peak of all.

At last I had uncovered a part of the mystery surrounding this mountain, for it appears that some parties have claimed a total ascent when in fact they have only reached the first peak of the long summit ridge. This undoubtedly gives rise to the difference of opinion as to whether Sabinio presents any real difficulty or not.

From this first peak, or " tooth," our way led down to a thin, curving ridge, and I saw in this another solution of the mystery, for I remembered reading an account of a full ascent which had been made by straddling along the crest of this sharp ridge—a practical but most ungainly method and one that is not at all in accordance with acknowledged mountaineering technique.

We tackled the obstacle from the right direction but not in an orthodox manner, and the least said about it the better. A traverse was made a few yards below the ridge on the Uganda side, where there is a precipitous drop of many hundreds of feet leading to thick forest. For a while I was apprehensive about taking John Mbonigaba with us, but he was most keen to go the whole way, and, as a matter of fact, he turned out to be a surprisingly active and good little climber. I had no such qualms about Ndabateze, who knew the mountain well, or Robeni, who inspired full confidence with his quiet, calm approach and his obvious love for all mountains.

I have always held a secret pride in the fact that no accident or injury of any sort ever befell a single man who has been with me while climbing and trekking in Africa—but perhaps instead of being proud I should be thankful.

By the time we had gained the second peak, the inevitable swirls of thin cloud were gathering, and before long we knew we would be enveloped in an unbroken pall of watery vapour through which we would be unable to see from one peak to another. I was just in time to observe that the third peak from the west partially shields the fourth and highest peak from observers on the Uganda side. Therefore I had gained the impression while sketching the mountain from my viewpoint at Nyalusiza that the third peak was the highest. This illusion is increased by the fact that, from below, the fourth peak may appear as a part of the third peak, whereas from a suitable vantage point on the mountain itself it can be seen in its true perspective, set some distance behind and rising slightly higher.

Between the second and third peak, along a connecting ridge where a semi-circular formation of bare rocks protruded, we came upon a cleanly picked bone, and at the same time an awful stench was borne in our direction by the wind. A few yards farther on we had to stride over the remains of a klipspringer (*Oreotragus oreotragus*) which had been killed and eaten by a leopard. That an antelope could have climbed this far, even under the tremendous impetus of fear, seemed unbelievable, but it had of course passed along the crest of the ridge where we had made our traverse. Most likely it had been killed at the third peak for which we were heading, and had been dragged back to this point to be eaten. At the time I thought that this must have established a clear height record for any form of antelope in Africa, but I have since been informed by Lt.-Col. Hoier that in July 1931 he found part of a skeleton on top of Karisimbi. It was very old and may have been red forest duiker (*Cephalophus natalensis kivuensis*) though it was judged, from a piece of the skull, to be klipspringer.

Swiftly eddying clouds blotted first one peak and then another from view, and by the time we had moved from the third peak to the ultimate summit there was very limited visibility in any direction. This was to be my supreme moment, and yet I cannot faithfully record any emotion that was strong enough to dispel the feeling of anxiety, strain and cold which gripped me.

I shall always refuse to believe those who claim a multitude of deep, philosophical thoughts on a bleak, inhospitable mountain top. It is only a turning point that has been reached, and like all turning points it has neither beginning nor end.

There was only one immediate reward to be gained, and for that I stooped to pick a small piece of rock from the highest point. At Ntebeko there were seven more pieces, making a total of eight. An ambition had been realised and the gateway to a further ambition had been opened, though I gave no real thought to Everest at this time.

After making our way from peak to peak and across the traverse back to the waiting men, we stopped for something to eat. Then we pressed on with such speed through the forest that I could feel the effect of the decreasing height in my ear drums in the same way as when one descends rapidly in the air. Creepers, trailers, roots and other insidious growths which had not appeared to congest the trail on our way up now appeared in great profusion, twining themselves round our ankles or lying in wait to trip us. Once I was held firmly round the neck by a vine which hung down and twirled itself with astonishing intricacy into a stranglehold from which I had to use both hands to release myself.

Evening was drawing on as we arrived back at Ntebeko, where a refreshing hot drink awaited us and I was able to sit by a log fire and gaze at the mountains as a fond father might look on one of his own children. For only a few minutes I was able to discern the dim outline of Mikeno in the distance beyond Sabinio, and I literally feasted my eyes on the mountain, realising to the full that each glimpse might be the last.

I remained peering into the gathering gloom until only Sabinio could be seen. I looked on this, too, with extraordinary affection. Apart from providing the culminating point for a crowded three days of activity, it had given just the required degree of difficulty and danger to conclude satisfactorily a glorious adventure which included an aggregate ascent of more than 100,000 ft. of mountain altitude in a single month. In addition, it had presented a wealth of variety and had brought me close to the interesting fauna and flora which will always be associated in my mind with this mountain in particular. Of all African mountains, only Mikeno has intrigued me more.

Here, at this time, and not at the summit or during the later stages of our hurried descent, there came the reward for effort which could be delayed but not altogether denied, and I enjoyed a delightfully mixed feeling of happiness, tiredness and dirtiness.

At early morning a runner arrived with a message to the effect that Chief Tomasi sent his respects but regretted that he had been summoned to an important meeting at Kisoro and could not therefore be at Nyalusiza to await my return. All was prepared for me and I was at liberty to retain my room as long as I wished.

The four men who had acted as carriers between Nyalusiza and Ntebeko prepared to set off with me on the return journey. Their names were typical of the area; Nzabarantumye, Bakundinka, Bakina and Mahano. Ndabateze was remaining behind for a while with some of his men who wished to make calls on their friends and relatives while the chance offered. Robeni and John Mbonigaba were to go with me, the latter dressed as usual in khaki shorts with shirt, shoes and stockings to match, and a brown felt hat which he always doffed before addressing me.

When all was ready, we turned our backs on Ntebeko and walked due east, into the rising sun. The still damp but warming grass gave a pleasing thrill at every stride, for we did not follow any worn paths for a while and as usual I wore nothing that could take away from the full joy of an occasion such as this. Our direct route took us through fields of peas, beans and mealies where women with naked babies tied to their backs hoed the soil. Later we passed through villages entirely fenced around with bamboo, and there would be the usual protracted interchange of greetings between my men and the idle villagers.

It is difficult to describe my feelings on this day, for they were so intense as to be unforgettable and yet so intimate as to be impossible to communicate. Perhaps, more than at any time, I felt self-satisfaction. By this I do not infer a strident egotism born of physical conquest, but a quiet glow of inner well-being derived from a way of living that was near to nature and far from the wranglings of a social system which is daily at war with nature and with itself. Only the stupid and the ignorant will say that my joy was a shallow one resulting from a temporary escapism, for there is never any escape from oneself or the consequences of one's actions. It is not men who go to high mountains who seek escape, but the people who never remove themselves from a crowded and noisy atmosphere of work and play.

Away to the north, Lake Mutanda could at times be seen with its calm surface shimmering through gaps in surrounding hills, but in the opposite direction a solid blanketing of grey cloud lay from peak to peak of the three Virunga mountains. The unevenly serrated summit ridge of Sabinio was never once revealed to us, and all we could see of Muhavura was its base. Mgahinga, with its dense forest, was entirely lost to view. It was as though the mountains had granted us so much and would grant no more.

John Mbonigaba took off his hat and said, quite simply and sincerely, " God has been kind to us."

The day was Saturday, June 29, 1946.

The journey from Ntebeko to Nyalusiza did not take as long as I anticipated, so that I decided to stay only long enough to await the men who had been left behind at Ntebeko. Then payment was made, according to status and the service rendered, at a rate approximately equivalent to that which held good in the Congo, though payment was in East African currency instead of francs. The total complement of men was made up as follows:

MUHAVURA:	*Guide* : Robeni.
	Porters : Selumveli, Seluhago.
MGAHINGA:	*Guide* : Ndabateze, accompanied by Robeni.
	Porters, etc. : Ndikumuzima, Ntawaluhunga, Ryaziga, Rwihandagaza, Bizagwira, Kangabo.
SABINIO:	*Guide:* Ndabateze, accompanied by Robeni.
	Porters, etc.: Ntawaluhunga, Rwihandagaza, Bizagwira, Kangabo.
Interpreter:	John Mbonigaba.
Cook:	Rubumba.
Porters:	(Kisoro to Nyalusiza, and return journey): Ntilivamunda, Munyabalenzi.
Porters:	(Nyalusiza to Ntebeko, and return journey): Nzabarantumye, Bakundinka, Bakina, Mahano.

There appeared to be entire satisfaction all round with the payments received, and I bade farewell to as staunch a band of men as any of their counterparts in the Congo.

Then I took with me Ntilivamunda and Munyabalenzi, who had been earmarked for the purpose, and made for Kisoro and the beginning of a restful interlude away from the mountains.

XII. *First Lakeland Interlude*

OR MY stay at the north end of Lake Mutanda, I had been provided with a letter of introduction to the Gombolola Chief of Mushungera, which appeared on my map as a promontory with no European settlement nearer than Kabale, except for the customs post at Kisoro.

My personal effects had been limited to the contents of a single kit-bag and two haversacks, so Chief Tomasi sensibly provided me with two small *totos* [1] to act as carriers. They were confident little fellows who, after the manner of their elders, balanced their loads on a circle of twisted and matted leaves worn on the head. An elderly man kept us company, but I could not tell if he was with us officially as a guide or if he was making the journey independently.

The totos, I had been told, would only be able to go as far as the southern end of the lake, but I had not been able to gather if any arrangements had been made for my journey beyond this point, or whether it would be accomplished on foot or by canoe.

Everything was uncertain, but I saw no cause for apprehension. A great deal had been carried out successfully under similar conditions in the past, and there was no longer my driving ambition to give rise to anxiety or plague me with worry. There was, as a result of the uncertainty, a strong element of surprise, and I knew that life itself would not be so intriguing if one could predict future happenings with certainty.

Our trail meandered between delightfully green hills until we came to a gap which permitted a view to the south. (It was through this break in the hills that I had caught glimpses of the lake while trekking between Ntebeko and Nyalusiza.) Here there was an open expanse of swamp fringed with rushes and papyrus, but elsewhere the hills continued right down to the lake edge. The man went with both totos to the top of a hillock and began hallooing to the neighbouring hills, which echoed back

---

[1] Youngsters, beyond the age of childhood.

his cries. Then a relay of sounds was started, each hill springing to life with halloos that were taken up and passed on. After several minutes there was silence, and I sat down to await the outcome of what had apparently been a series of requests for a canoe.

A long interval followed, and when I was beginning to doubt the efficacy of this system of broadcast I was motioned to follow, and we all went down to the lake shore. Half an hour passed, and the same doubts were reasserting themselves when a canoe pulled into the small bay to which we had gone. It was very crudely fashioned from a solid tree trunk, and was obviously in the final stages of decay. Many cracks were visible, and though some of them had been inexpertly stoppered there was a deep, continuous pool of water along the scalloped bottom which was increased by sudden gushes and trickles from all directions. The frail craft was paddled by a single man of much more than middle age, but how it was made to progress in a straight line was something to marvel at, for the bow was out of line with the stern by at least a yard.

There was no question of rejecting this craft, so a bed of reeds was laid on the waterlogged bottom, but despite this attempt at comfort, I was forced to sit in a pool of water, and could only hope that my equipment would survive.

We had six miles to cover, and I knew how suddenly these Central African lakes can be whipped into a frenzy under peculiar weather conditions, so I kept a close watch on the nearest piece of land in case of an emergency. The water, fortunately, was splendidly calm, but it was soon obvious that we would never make our destination, even if the fine weather lasted all through the day and into the night.

Occasionally I took over a spare paddle, but my attempts to speed our progress only resulted in a more pronounced circling motion and so I returned to the more urgent task of baling.

Our unpremeditated course took us close to an islet, but I could only notice briefly three crowned cranes (*Balearica regulorum gibbericeps*) feeding in the fringing marsh. At any other time their golden crests and glorious plumage would have claimed my undivided attention. What might have been a desperate plight was saved by the chance approach of another, and better, canoe which seemed capable of a much higher speed. There was an interchange of words and then both craft were taken shoreward, and I guessed from this move that an arrangement had been made which in our present straits could only benefit us.

Any slight lateral movement would have been sufficient to upset the narrow, unstable craft, but we made the difficult transfer after wedging the canoes alongside each other in a mass of high reeds lining the shore. The leaky craft was abandoned—perhaps for all time—and thereafter we made better progress with both men paddling, or with one paddling and the other making an effort to steer.

It was now possible to take more interest in my surroundings, and when two more crowned cranes appeared on a narrow headland I could give them the attention they deserved. There appeared to be many birds, with the African darter, or snakebird (*Anhinga r. rufa*) most prominent, but there were very few ducks.

Only the slight ripples caused by our passage disturbed the deep, calm waters, for there was scarcely a breath of wind blowing, and I could look down and see the delicate wisps of cirrus cloud reflected in extreme detail. As we went farther north a number of islands came into view, looking green and peaceful, but most of them too small to be inhabited.

It was late in the afternoon when we drew to the shore near the tip of a narrow promontory and made our way up the grassy slope to what I knew at once to be the Government rest camp. The single, square building was of mud, left in its natural colour on the outside, but whitewashed inside, and the roof was heavily thatched. There was only one room, with a dirt floor, and it was entirely empty but for a bed of rushes and bamboo raised about 2 ft. 6 in. from the ground on six Y-shaped pieces of wood. In front was a shallow pit for a fire, and well clear of the hut in the background were trees which continued along the promontory. It was a pleasant spot, but entirely deserted, and when the two men left in their canoe I felt extremely lonely. There was no Tomasi Sebukweto, or any other African chief, to come forward with a friendly greeting,[1] and I realised with a start how much the presence of a black man had come to mean, even if no open conversations could be held between us.

My first need was for warmth and so I set about gathering wood and soon had a fire burning. It may have been the smoke from this which attracted attention, for within a few minutes a native appeared, clad only in a dingy loin cloth. With scarcely a word (for he soon became aware of my very limited knowledge of his language) he settled in and began to make himself useful.

I had thought at first that he was empty-headed, but as if from thin air,

[1] This was not to be expected, for no warning of my coming had been given.

he produced a large stalk of plantains and proceeded to cook some for me in the hot ashes of the fire. These, known locally as " matoke," are a cooking banana, almost identical with the tropical fruit that is better known to Europeans, but they remain green and are quite uneatable in the raw state. Their size varies, but the larger ones are considerably longer, fatter and more curved than the ordinary banana. It may not be generally true, but on all my travels in Central Africa I have found that either plantains or mealies serve as the staple food, but one always predominates to the almost total exclusion of the other, so that Africans who live on plantains do not produce significant crops of mealies, or vice versa. Millet, on the other hand, which is a loose grain and therefore cannot be compared as a handy, easily prepared food, forms an additional crop in many parts of Africa.

The cooked plantains were handed to me covered with ashes (for the skins had been stripped away before thrusting them into the fire) but I had by now become inured to rough and ready living, and no longer objected to a fundamental earthiness. Wherever water is available for washing, I have found that Africans make ready use of it, and under the most primitive conditions they deserve admiration for their cleanliness. Never once, in the Congo or Uganda, did I find any Africans with an offensive body odour. This is only acquired, I think, where fats and oils are used as natural embrocations.

I found the roasted plantains most unappetising, and apart from being almost tasteless they clung to the roof of my mouth to such an extent that I could hardly swallow them, no matter how little I took at each bite. On later occasions I had them boiled, and when properly served they were every bit as good as potatoes and very similar in taste. Thereafter they were used as a substitute for potatoes, which were unprocurable, and I had them with eggs, fish, sausages or anything else which happened to be available. I even tried them as a sweet with jam, though in this form they were not a success.

My cook, if he deserved such a title, disappeared when our meal was finished, but he came back an hour or so later with logs for the fire and a straw mat on which he squatted and smoked a pipe. We remained facing one another across the fire, he wrapped in thought, or vacancy, and I keeping constant watch on the stars. Fireflies whirled among the trees, and there was the deep croaking of frogs and the deeper grunt of hippopotami. There was nothing whatever beyond these few simple things, and yet I felt no lack of anything. Others may gain a vast amount of pleasure and even contentment by listening to swing music, or by congregating in dance halls and at cocktail parties. Civilisation cannot remain in a state of quiescence: there must always be change. But surely, through all our striving, we have lost something which no artificiality can replace when we fail to retain a love and appreciation of the simplest, most fundamental things in life.

On this night, having no watch, I went to bed when Scorpio touched the horizon.

At early morning, a retinue of men arrived, one of them bearing a container of milk and some eggs, and another a chicken. At their head was a young man, hat in hand, who claimed to be a clerk in the nearby village of Mushungera. Stepping forward, he announced in a quaint mixture of Kiswahili and English that the Gombolola Chief was away for a few days but would visit me upon his return. In the meantime he sent his respects and these few gifts which the men had brought with them. In addition I was to be provided with a table and chair, and a cook.

The table and chair duly arrived and were put to good use, but the so-called cook was a worthless individual with no imagination and little ability. The rest-house attendant (for this was what he really was) who had already prepared a substantial breakfast, was therefore retained as cook and the new man was set to do the menial tasks.

I spent the rest of the morning swimming, and in the afternoon I made a few minor explorations about the promontory and on the hill beyond, which leads to the village of Mushungera. From here I could see a wide expanse of the lake. I noticed ten small islands scattered near the promontory, while there were probably as many more at remoter parts of the lake. I also got a glimpse of Muhavura, but the atmosphere was too hazy for Mgahinga or Sabinio to be discerned.

The entire setting was magnificent, and I remembered that in the D.C.'s office at Kabale the claim had been made that Mutanda was more than the equal of Bunyoni and Kivu, and that it was in fact the most beautiful of all African lakes. This is not an exaggerated claim.

At dusk, the clerk returned to inform me that his chief was still away but had again sent his respects and had given instructions that every possible provision was to be made for me. At the same time he offered to go with me on any expeditions I might wish to make in the surrounding territory. My Belgian map was brought out and we arranged to go on the following day to Kamena, shown as a prominence of 2,398 metres lying to the north-east of Mushungera and overlooking the Ruezaninda River, which emerges from a swamp at the north end of Lake Mutanda. What intrigued me most of all was the blank space directly north of Kamena marked " Forêt Impénétrable." This is the forest (impenetrable indeed) of Kayonza, the only home of gorillas in the Uganda Protectorate apart from the Virunga mountains, and perhaps their only permanent habitat in the territory.

I delighted in the prospect of making more than a " map acquaintance " with this practically untouched region which is fortunately devoid of roads, and that night I had the same pleasurable reverie by the fireside, though now the explorer in me had been stimulated and there was a new yearning in place of the previous contentment—a renewal of the desire to see beyond the next bend and look down from the next mountain height.

Otherwise the night held the same enchantment as before, with fireflies stabbing the gloom under the trees and frogs croaking in ceaseless chorus. Certain sounds are easily described on paper, but not that of the hippopotamus. This time I tried to identify it more accurately, for it is not a deep grunt so much as a hoarse bellow, very low down the scale: perhaps it can best be described as a combination of the two. It is a sound which needs to be heard, and the best time to hear it (often the only time) is at night.

There was one new sound—a joyous one—which I must mention. This was the musical chant of remote Africans living their quiet lives, which came to me on a soft breeze. I listened enthralled, for this was the real voice of old Africa, with humans and animals harmonising together.

After an early breakfast I prepared for the journey, and while doing so, my attention was drawn to a group of men drawn up outside. It was the Gombolola Chief and some of his headmen come to pay their respects. The Chief was introduced to me by his clerk. We did not shake hands, for it was not my custom to do so on meeting, though I would not fail to do so at the time of parting.

He was dressed in the usual mixture of European and African garb which proves so attractive and entirely correct for men who stand between the dignified poverty of their own dark, semi-naked people and the splendour of a foreign white race. He was courteous—as his race are without exception in this part of Africa—but he lacked the noble countenance and bearing of Chief Tomasi Sebukweto, and it was at once obvious that his people were poorer and not of such good physique as those living farther south, nearer the mountains. I made it clear that his hospitality and gifts were appreciated, and in turn he made it known that I had only to ask in order to receive. His English-speaking clerk had chosen two other men for our exploratory trek to Kamena, and we departed in company with the Chief, keeping with him until reaching his village on the hill, after which we carried on alone.

We covered fully 25 miles of hard going that day, from hill crest to hill crest, down into valleys and across rivers and swamps. Our general direction of travel was north-east, but our trail wound considerably, though never to avoid the heights. The whole district is a catchment area taking water to Lake Mutanda, and some of the low expanses looked very like dried lakes. From a hill marked on my map as Kasooni (height 2,260 metres, or approximately 7,420 ft.) I was able to look back and see Mutanda in three sections over its entire length, and for the first time I obtained a real impression of its extent. This time I made a more accurate tally of islands than on the previous day and reached a figure of 24, though it was difficult to be precise. Only the extreme south end has any area of low-lying ground bordering it, and at the south-western tip there is the outlet to the River Kako. From here I could also see the smaller Lake Mulehe.

Between Kasooni and the slightly higher Kamena, we crossed a swampy stream which originates in the high escarpment west of Kabale. In some of the larger swamps, I was told, the hippos took refuge during the day, whereas previously they had remained down at the lake. The cause of this change of behaviour was a chief who, being in possession of firearms, had persecuted the animals to such an extent that they had become wary and would only venture forth at night. The chief had been relieved of his high post as a result of this indiscriminate shooting, but it is doubtful if the lake's hippopotamus population will ever revert to their old habits, for the struggle to survive becomes daily more involved in an Africa which has awakened to the sound of firearms and machinery.

From the hill Kamena, when it was gained, I had a splendid view overlooking the Ruezaninda River and the impenetrable forest, which spans four ranges of hills as far as the eye can see. This is the Kayonza Forest of Kizezi District, but even in official reports it sometimes retains its other and more intriguing name of Impenetrable Forest.

The total population of its isolated colony of gorillas is unknown, for no investigation has been possible and the species both in this habitat and on the Virunga mountains is completely protected and may only be hunted under a Governor's Permit. Only one Permit has been issued during the last 20 years, and this, I believe, was for the Virunga habitat and not Kayonza. From skulls sent to the British Museum (Natural History) before this, Dr. Ernst Schwarz had been able to identify the Kayonza Forest gorillas with those of the Virunga mountains, though the two zones have widely differing vegetation and the gorillas of Kayonza are thought to live a more arboreal life.

It would be interesting to know how and when the latter came to be separated from the mountain-dwelling troops, for the two must surely be directly related. Perhaps a few troops, or even a single family, trekked away from the mountains while freedom of movement was not so restricted as now, and established themselves at a lower altitude in the forest nearly 25 miles away which they either sensed to be there or came upon purely by chance. The separation must have been comparatively recent, otherwise some subspecific differences would have been bred as a result of the change in environment and food. There have been many extraordinary migrations in the animal world, but this must be one of the most amazing of all.

There was no time to go any farther, so I contented myself with this distant view and secreted away for possible future fulfilment the desire to penetrate the Impenetrable Forest and to survey its gorilla population. Africa still offers scope for exploration, especially if this involves scientific investigation.

Our journey back to Mushungera was hurried, and a long, tiring, but thoroughly satisfying day ended with a swim and a meal, prepared for me by the rest-house attendant, promoted to cook, who proved a real " find " and served up some excellent dishes. Lake fish, as on this instance, were made more appetising with the addition of a little butter, tomato and leeks, and when served with the inevitable plantains made a tasty meal.

The cook had a tiny, shy *picannin* who came each morning with milk, sometimes quite naked and sometimes with a circlet of blue and white beads about her waist. Occasionally the same mite—she could have been no more than four years of age—brought me fresh vegetables in a small basket which she balanced expertly on her head, and always she would deposit her load just beyond my reach and then scamper to her father's side for protection. She would not permit herself to be photographed, and I failed at every attempt until I found her curled fast asleep by the log fire one afternoon. She was a most lovable little child, erect and like a black doll; very rarely she forgot her fear and joined me by the fire, busying herself as any other child would with make-believe.

The Chief's clerk was as strange as his mixture of English. Whenever he opened conversation with me he would begin with the words, " Dear Sir," as though at the start of a letter. He was a great help, and judging by his words and his willingness to serve he seemed to respect and like me. On one of our several excursions in the neighbourhood we walked down to the Ruezaninda River and followed it to the point where it discharges its water into the easternmost of two small bights at the north end of Lake Mutanda. The river at its mouth is set in a papyrus swamp, and in this season (the month was July) it was about 8 ft. wide between banks, though it obviously extends to much more than this in the rainy season, for the papyrus on either side showed distinct high-water marks. The narrow ribbon of water adds its water indirectly to the Nile, and it fascinated me to stand there and visualise other sources of the great river which I had been privileged to see, and then to picture it in its full magnificence at Pakwach, Juba, Khartoum and beyond.

On our way to and from the Ruenzaninda we saw where hippos had trampled crops on their daily migrations between the lake and its northern swamps. We also passed over wooden gratings set in the hillside to prevent their passage, and I reflected, as on many occasions before and since, how primitive Africans are able to meet every situation crudely but satisfactorily while entirely reliant upon themselves. Now, in parts of Africa where there is a white population at hand, they are no longer willing to meet their own needs with natural defences of this sort. Instead, they petition the white man, who goes with his guns and deals most effectively and permanently with the nuisance. And so, departing from their old tolerance of animals which of themselves are inoffensive, they indulge in or permit on their behalf a remorseless slaughter.

Another incident of this day was tinged with a similar pathetic dependence, for upon our return the clerk brought a boy, less than ten years of age, for treatment of a suppurating sore on his left leg. All I could do was clean the wound, apply ointment and a bandage, and give instructions for it to be kept clean. There were surprising repercussions on the following morning when, the news having spread, half the men and women of the village came for treatment, each one making suggestive grimaces of pain while pointing to the offending region. They all looked far from ill, but like small children, they could not bear the thought of being neglected.

They were, like all these people, likeable and honest, and neither I nor
my possessions were in the least danger from them. The only slight unpleasantness at Mushungera was that swarms of midges flew in whenever
a candle was lit in the rest house at night, so that I could never make up my
diary by candlelight: and the only misfortune to befall me was when my
supply of salt ran out.

This loss affected me more than the fact that I had not been able to
receive a single letter since leaving Southern Rhodesia. It will never
happen again, for this once was enough to prove how indispensable salt
is at practically every meal. There are substitutes for sugar, or it can be
dispensed with altogether, even though the palate is ordinarily accustomed
to it: rusks will serve admirably in place of bread, and plantains are just as
good as potatoes once the taste has been acquired: but there is no substitute for salt, and to do without it makes nothing but a sheer chore of
eating. However, the loss was made up for me by the Chief, who sent
along some coarse native salt which I was able to crush and use.

My last night at Mushungera was no less fascinating than the preceding
nights. The lake surface was unruffled, and a continuous procession of
clouds passing over the bright face of the moon was reflected in a multitude
of shadowy forms.

My cook had produced a musical instrument which was made simply
and effectively of six wires stretched over an oval piece of wood roughly
hollowed out to a depth of two or three inches. The corners were rounded
and it was about 3 ft. in length by 1 ft. in width. With this he played a few
native rhythms involving much repetition, but I was never bored by the
monotony because anything more involved would not have blended so
well with the African setting. Then, most touching of all, there came the
sound of massed voices, of men and women, chanting a haunting melody
which they had learnt in the mission schools. It was one they sang before
a journey, praying for a safe return home.

I had enjoyed every hour of my stay, but it made me wistful and sad
to recall the story confided to me by the clerk—which I had every reason to
believe—concerning the annexation of this delectable site by the Government. His father, he had told me, was established on this promontory
with his five wives when a Government official gave him notice to quit
and a rest house was set up for the occasional use of officials when on
tour. An insignificant happening of the past, maybe, but there are in Africa
to-day the seeds of revolt, and occurrences to which we may attach no

importance have been, like a canker, eating into the souls of Africans for centuries.

In the morning a canoe and four men waited at the lake edge, and I prepared to leave. All who expected payment for their various services had gathered in a line by the dead fire, and amongst them, to my delight and to the amusement of all present, was the tiny *picannin*, resplendent in her circlet of beads. She cupped both hands together and extended them to receive her due reward, and this time she did not turn to run, perhaps because of childlike curiosity, or perhaps because she sensed that her presence in a grown man's world was appreciated.

Lastly, I presented a small gift to the Chief, who had joined us. Then I walked down to the canoe and stepped into it, and as I did so the Chief hurried forward and pressed his knobbed walking-stick into my hand in one of the noblest gestures I have ever known. It made me feel certain of a warm welcome should I ever return, and there is no better feeling to take away on any departure.

The lake was wonderfully calm, and with four men paddling we made far better progress than on the way out. From my position in the canoe, I could see more clearly than ever before why Muhavura has been so named, for it was the mountain, standing out boldly in the south, which guided us to our destination as surely as a beacon guides a ship at sea.

One man stayed with the canoe while the others portered my belongings from the lake to Kisoro, and the first of two delightful lakeland episodes came to an end.

XIII. *Second Lakeland Interlude*

HIEF TOMASI, never failing, provided me with two porters for my safari on foot to Bufundi Camp, which is situated at the end of a long promontory jutting from the western shore of Lake Bunyoni. I wanted grown men, not boys, for this occasion, for we had at least 20 miles to cover, and all my belongings had to be carried.

I saw my last of Chief Tomasi just before leaving at an early hour. In fact it was a day of many farewells—to the Gombolola Chief and his delightful domain in the south-western tip of Kigezi District, and to Muhavura, Mgahinga and Sabinio, which stand like three tall sentinels, one (Muhavura) to act as guide, another (Mgahinga) to ensure a plentiful rainfall, and the third (Sabinio) to induce unobtrusively a measure of humility, which is one of the saving graces of mankind. It was also farewell to bamboo forests criss-crossed with elephant spoors, which we encountered, to my surprise, at the highest point of our trail.

Beyond the bamboo forest we descended to a valley in which crimson-tinted immortelles (*Helichrysum* sp.) and red-hot pokers or kniphofiae grew in profusion. Here, with a tremendous hullabaloo, we were " attacked " by a mob of about 20 young men, mostly naked except for loin cloths, and with faces and chests streaked with paint. They came whooping down from a hill, brandishing spears, bows and arrows and catapults. They were a hunting party, after animals, but it required only a little imagination to take one's thoughts back to earlier days—not very long ago—when they set out in similar nakedness and paint to hunt human quarry.

Beauty lay around us everywhere until, before leaving the valley, we came to a devastated area in which the bush and grass had been fired, perhaps by the hunting party as a means of driving out the duikers and other small animals which they were in search of. The scene of grey and black desolation was in sharp contrast to what we had left behind and what lay ahead.

117

Once, in trying not to deviate from the most direct route, we struck danger in the flames which were already near to left and right and soon had closed in behind us, blocking our line of retreat. We were forced to continue straight ahead, and in the end to run as fast as we could through billowing smoke. Brief as our danger was, I gained a sharp intimation of the terror which animals must undergo when subjected to ringfiring. In this method of hunting the victims are encircled by a wall of flames from which the only avenue of escape is blocked by dogs or nets, or by armed men.

As we neared the lake, we came upon a group of natives dragging the body of a leopard from a trap. The men scattered at our approach, thinking no doubt that I was an official come to investigate the killing and probably to reprimand the culprits. Eventually they returned somewhat hesitantly, and each one took a pinch of fine powder from a small box carried by one of them and scattered it over his left shoulder in exactly the same manner as superstitious white people will do with salt after spilling it.

Africans on the whole have a greater respect for the leopard than for any other animal, if only for the fact that it is the most ubiquitous of all the larger carnivores and has been responsible for more damage to humans and their livestock than any other wild animal. They have many superstitions regarding it, and there is much in their folklore and customs to show their veneration for the animal.

The skins may not be used by everyone, but are reserved for men of high rank, and with certain tribes those who have killed or come into contact with a leopard are required to be washed in medicine before speaking or eating. In some instances, the skins have also to be washed, and until this is done, the whole country may be considered in danger.

The trap which had been set for this leopard was a gigantic wooden structure set in a hillside. The mechanism consisted of a system of logs which, when the bait was taken, disturbed a large boulder suspended at a height of about 12 ft. The animal which I saw was still warm and must have been killed only a few minutes before my arrival. Death appeared to be due to a broken spine, but there was no sign of injury to the skin to show where the boulder had fallen.

Every now and again, as I walked along, I looked backwards. Each step was a step away from the mountains which had become " mine " because of my association with them. I had given to them and had taken from them.

That, surely, is the key to happiness, and the ultimate in life itself. We must give in order to receive. This is true, not only of the mountains, but of every walk of life. It is true of love. It is also true in relation to nature. Those who would gain most from the wild life of Africa must not go with a gun in their hands. They finish only with a corpse from which they hack a trophy, dripping with blood. What have they achieved, what good have they done, what have they *given* to life? They have taken all and given nothing. Theirs is a hollow victory, if it is a victory at all.

Despite my longing, and my many backward glances, I never saw the Virunga mountains again. Beyond the leopard trap, we came to a small stream which collected water from a few neighbouring hills and fed it into the lake. About two miles farther on we reached the Government rest camp at Bufundi. Here I was not as remote from the outer world as I had been at Mushungera. Kabale lay only six miles away, and in order to reach there I had only to take a canoe to a north-easterly bay and then to walk across the hills.

Like most lakes of its type—a drowned valley resulting from volcanic activity—Bunyoni is of great depth (exceeding 130 ft.) and is subject to violent storms which blow up with extreme suddenness. The native name means " lake of little birds," and in support of this there is an astonishing abundance of birds, including a species of raven which, during my stay at Bufundi, lived chiefly on my supply of soap. These birds acquired such a taste for it that they would wait at the water's edge while I washed, and then boldly take it from within my reach. At other times they sneaked into the rest house, never taking anything but soap.

Fishes are numerous and there are many otters. There are no crocodiles or hippopotami, but it is said that the elusive situntunga (*Limnotragus spekei*) inhabits the swamps at the southern end of the narrow, sinuous lake. Purple water-lilies, delicately tinted and with stems many yards long, add beauty to some of the numerous bays.

There are several islands, the largest being used as a leper settlement in which the community grows all its own food, and manufactures all bricks used in building living quarters, hospital and school rooms. The island's small church was built entirely by their own labours, bricks and all. Each new patient receives a small plot of land, but is necessarily segregated into one of two parts according to whether he or she is infectious or not.

On my visit to the settlement I was amused by the school children who sang delightfully: *"If the load be weary, never never mind it!"*—always adding the extra vowel to the pronoun. I went amongst these stricken people, some blinded, others with faces covered with unsightly nodules, and still others with hands and arms eaten away by the terrible scourge. With some I shook hands, and as I left, one poor old woman came forward with the stumps of her arms extended in an unaffected gesture of thanks. There is no praise too high for those who ease the lot of these sufferers, or for the black men and women who face their suffering with such fortitude.

Living was extremely cheap for me at Bufundi. Chickens cost 2d. each (though I never risked trying one, even at that price) and eggs were 1 cent each. Thirty cents (at ten cents to the penny) was all that was asked for two dozen green mealies. A good variety of vegetables was obtainable at equally low, controlled prices. Milk was delivered on the spot.

I made several excursions about the lake by canoe, and on one occasion used a large craft with 12 men to paddle it. They were a jovial lot, some of whom accompanied their actions with a variety of grunts and grimaces. More often than not, though, I would sit squeezed into a narrow, leaky craft, hardly daring to breathe for fear of capsizing it. Once, when in the centre of the lake, the canoe was slowed by the men trailing their broad paddles, and I saw one of them poise his hand and then plunge it into the water. When he brought it to the surface he revealed a struggling fish of a good size. I had never before seen one caught by this simple method.

I was loath to go, but there was the one remaining farewell to be made, and I left in a week's time when the chance came of a journey by road to Kampala. Thereafter I made my way by train to Nairobi, and then by road to Arusha. Here I was within easy reach of Moshi, and Mount Kilimanjaro, so I decided upon an alteration of plan. I had always claimed that I would never go one stride out of my way to climb Kilimanjaro, which has seen too many people on it to hold any appeal for me. However, it is the highest mountain in Africa, and with the thought of Everest uppermost I went along to see what could be done about a quick ascent.

I did not greatly enjoy the climb, which in places was no more than an easy saunter. I actually ran the half-mile along the level plain before the scree slope leading to the 19,455 ft. summit.

The rest of my journey back was by military convoy *via* Dodoma, Iringa, Mbeya, Mpika, Broken Hill and Salisbury, where I arrived on August 11. By this time I was in poor fettle and was forced to go into hospital where, on the day the major war criminals were being hanged in

Germany, an end was put to my internal maladies which had been the price I had to pay for living in tropical regions under very primitive conditions.

At this stage, my thoughts once again reverted to Mount Everest. I had put a great deal of enthusiasm into my lone undertaking to the eight Virunga mountains. I was at peace with the eight peaks, and therefore at peace with myself in relation to them. But the eight peaks were not sufficient in themselves for the real truth, the ultimate peace, the greater wisdom.

There are, needless to say, many other high dangerous, remote and magnificent mountains in the world besides Everest. But such is ambition: Everest it had to be.

XIV. *My Preparations for Everest*

THE ESTABLISHMENT of Everest [1] as the world's highest mountain took place just over one hundred years ago when a clerk of the Indian Trigonometrical Survey made a computation from the observations of several surveyors which set the height of the mountain clearly above that of any of its rivals in the Himalayas. The precise date of this first official computation is not known, but it was some time in 1852. The mountain had been observed before and had been plotted on maps, but it was thought to be smaller than some of its neighbouring peaks, and it was left without a name, being listed simply as Peak XV.

(The height arrived at in this first computation does not seem to be known for certain. Several figures have been reported, but there is obviously a great deal of confusion, and it is best not to quote them here.)

Having gained full recognition, it was not sufficient that the peak should remain nameless, and so it became known to the Western world as Mount Everest, after Sir George Everest who held the post of surveyor-general of India from 1830 until his retirement in 1843. There has been a good deal of criticism of this foreign name in recent years, but it should be realised that no Tibetan, Nepali or Chinese name was known until later, and no Indian name had been suggested before this time.

Triangulations undertaken at a later date set the height of the mountain at 29,002 ft., this figure representing the mean of six individual calculations obtained from different stations, the lowest being 28,990 ft. and the highest 29,026 ft. Figures ranging up to 29,200 ft. have been put forward in more recent years, but for my own use I have adopted 29,002 ft. because it is most widely accepted at the present day.

---

[1] I am aware that much of the ground I cover in this chapter will be familiar to all those who have made a study of Everest literature. But for the sake of completeness, and to place my own attempt in its context, I think it best to give a brief history of previous assaults on the mountain.

Brig.-Gen. the Hon. C. G. Bruce, who was to have a long association with the mountain, was probably the first man to think of an Everest reconnaissance. In 1907 he planned to go on an exploration of the northern approaches, with Arnold Mumm and T. G. Longstaff, M.D., as his companions, but Lord Morley, Secretary of State for India from 1905 to 1910, put a stop to these plans. Then, in 1909, Bruce actually obtained leave for himself and Longstaff to approach Everest by way of Nepal, but in this instance permission was withdrawn at the last moment. Two others, Kellas and Noel, were also frustrated in their efforts at an unofficial approach through Tibet. Col. C. G. Rawling was another who might have been first in he field of active exploration, but he was thwarted by the outbreak of war in 1914.

The idea of actually climbing the mountain did not originate until after the First World War although a secret reconnaissance was made by Captain Noel in 1913. Captain Percy Farrar, while President of the Alpine Club, took the initial step at a meeting of the Royal Geographical Society in London, but it was Sir Francis Younghusband, who succeeded Captain Farrar as President, who made the important decision to bring forward Everest as the main feature of his term of Presidency. It was he who inaugurated the Mount Everest Committee, made up of representatives of the Society and the Club.

Ultimately it was left to the official Reconnaissance Expedition of 1921, led by Lt.-Col. C. K. Howard-Bury, D.S.O., to break the seal of the mountain's isolation and open up the first of two distinct chapters of assault which were to be separated by a second world war.

The climbing party attached to the Reconnaissance Expedition included two names of particular note—Dr. A. M. Kellas and G. L. Mallory. The former, pre-eminent in the field of Himalayan exploration, died during the march through Tibet: his was the first of many lives to be lost in the search for the ultimate goal. George Leigh Mallory was destined to take part in two later expeditions, and to lose his life under mysterious circumstances during the second of these.

The reconnaissance party was equipped for climbing, but its main object was to establish the principal features of the mountain and find a possible climbing route. The mountain was reached in June, and it was seen at once that the north face presented an insuperable obstacle. After exploring the Rongbuk Valley and failing to find a route to the west, the expedition succeeded in tracing a likely line of attack from the east. Difficulty arose over finding the narrow passage, subsequently named the Lhakpa La, leading to the East Rongbuk Glacier, but after this obstacle had been overcome, the expedition made its way to a col on the main north ridge before returning. This was named the Chang La, or North Col, and the approach by way of it was obviously the only one available to an expedition from the Tibetan side.

Armed with information resulting from these preliminary investigations, the first real attempt was organised for the following year, 1922. This time, in fitting recompense for his disappointments of 1907 and 1909, Brig.-Gen. the Hon. C. G. Bruce was placed in command. Longstaff and Noel were others who were rewarded for their earlier attempts by being included. Mallory, Norton and Somervell headed the climbing party. Preparations were made on a grand scale, and eventually an expedition of 173 men, including 13 picked mountaineers from England, made the journey with 300 pack animals in support. A chain of camps was established on the mountain, and by May 20 the first party was ready to make its bid. A height of 27,000 ft. was reached before Mallory, Norton and Somervell were forced to retreat. A second attempt was launched, this time with the aid of oxygen—in use for the first time on Everest—but the added weight of 30 lb. nullified any advantage that may have been gained. A third attempt ended in disaster of the worst kind when a party of 14 porters, carrying supplies to an advance camp, was overwhelmed by an avalanche. Seven of the men lost their lives.

Disaster struck again when the next expedition went out in 1924. Bad weather was encountered below the North Col, and a retreat had to be made to the base camp. The weather cleared, and a high altitude camp was established from which Norton and Somervell set out for the summit. Norton, continuing alone beyond the point where Somervell had to stop, went to about 28,100 ft. before being forced to turn back after enduring all he could from the effects of altitude. Like Somervell, he was without oxygen, and, in my opinion, his performance ranks as one of the greatest of all time on Everest. Mallory and Irvine followed, both equipped with oxygen. N. E. Odell, the geologist of the party, going up from Camp V in support, caught a brief glimpse of the two men far above him as the mist cleared momentarily, and then Mallory and Irvine vanished, never to be seen again. Odell on his own and without oxygen, did all he could, climbing twice to 27,000 ft. His was a truly stouthearted effort, and it is one of the minor tragedies of Everest that he never had a place in any of the actual climbing parties to go beyond Camp VI.

What happened to Mallory and Irvine? Did they lose their lives going up or on the return? If on the return, then had they been successful or not?

It is doubtful whether we shall ever know. It may have been that their oxygen supplies gave out while they were on their way up, causing them to lose consciousness and fall down the mountainside. Many are inclined to think otherwise. They believe that the two men were on their way down when a slip by one of them, and an insecure belay, took them both to their doom. Certainly a descent from a difficult mountain, if undertaken without the aid of a fixed rope (by means of an abseil, that is), involves greater danger than an ascent. It is therefore most likely that Mallory and Irvine were on their way down—returning, but from where?

It is unlikely that any positive proof will ever come to hand.

Two other men, a young Gurkha and a Tibetan, also lost their lives in 1924, the former as a result of over-exposure and the latter from frostbite and pneumonia.

The kindly Dalai Lama, shaken by events, refused for some years to consent to any further attempt to climb the mountain. There was a lapse of nine years before the next expedition went out, in 1933, and on this occasion there was extremely bad weather to contend with. A brief chronology of this expedition, led by Hugh Ruttledge, reads as follows: Jan. 21, the main body left England; April 17, base camp was established; May 22, Camp V established; May 25, Camp V was evacuated due to bad weather; May 28, Camp V reoccupied; May 30, first attempt on the summit was made by Wyn Harris and Wager; June 1, second attempt by F. S. Smythe and E. E. Shipton; June 7, the expedition returned to base camp; June 15, Camp III re-occupied; June 21, Camp III was evacuated and the operation discontinued; July 2, expedition left base camp on return.

Wyn Harris and Wager, during their climb beyond Camp VI, found an ice-axe about 60 ft. below the crest of the north-east ridge, and this was identified as the one which had been used by Mallory in 1924. A good deal of significance has been attached to this find, but in fact it proves nothing.

In 1934, the unofficial attempt by a lone Yorkshireman, Maurice Wilson, led to his death. He seems to have been a very determined but totally in-experienced man, and something of a fanatic. His body was found next year by Eric Shipton, who led an expedition which ranked as no more than a reconnaissance, though it had the backing of the Mount Everest Committee and was no doubt organised with the object of reaching the summit if at all possible. H. W. Tilman was a member of the party, and so was Tenzing, a Sherpa who gained his first experience of the mountain in this year and of whom I shall write in detail later on.

The 1936 Everest Expedition was, in Eric Shipton's own words, " a bitter disappointment." Early monsoon conditions were met, and none of the climbing party succeeded in surmounting the North Col. The closed circuit oxygen apparatus with which the expedition was equipped could not be put to serious test.

No expedition, official or otherwise, was organised for the following year, but in 1938 a small party was sent out with Tilman in charge. Bad snow conditions were encountered beyond Camp V, and though oxygen of both open and closed circuit types were in use there was never much chance of reaching the summit on this occasion. No lives were lost, but two porters had a bad time and one of them suffered permanent paralysis. The party had intended to stay and investigate winter weather conditions, but did not do so.

This was the last of three occasions on which Frank Smythe, one of the finest of all Everest climbers, went to the mountain. Other members of the party were Eric Shipton, Peter Lloyd, N. E. Odell, Dr. C. B. M. Warren and Capt. P. R. Oliver.

The history of aerial surveys over Mount Everest does not concern us directly, but I will mention it for the sake of the complete story. The first flight over the summit was made on April 3, 1933, by the British Houston Everest Expedition, sponsored by Lady Houston and using two single-engined Westland biplanes, one of which was renamed the Houston-Westland. Organisation was under Air Commodore P. F. M. Fellows, D.S.O., and behind the idea from the beginning was Lt.-Col. L. V. Stewart Blacker, who flew as observer with the first pilot, Squadron-Leader the Marquess of Douglas and Clydesdale, A.F.M., M.P. The second pilot was Flight-Lieutenant D. F. McIntyre, who had with him Sidney Bonnet as cinematographer.

During the flight, Clydesdale's plane was endangered by a down-draught, and Bonnet lost consciousness after treading on and fracturing the oxygen feed pipe close to his mask. McIntyre, aware that something was amiss, and turning in his anxiety, pulled off the nose-piece from his own mask and was compelled to hold it in place for most of the return flight.

The flight was only partly successful, for the survey films were found to have little on them, and less still that was of value. So a second flight was undertaken, this time without full authority and in the knowledge that there was no insurance cover. The men who took part (Bonnet's place was taken by another observer, Fisher), were prepared to be condemned as insubordinate, but there were no repercussions of this kind, and their survey photographs made up splendidly for the previous lack of success. The summit was not flown over during this second flight, the pilots keeping to a course south of Everest.

Only two solo flights have been made over the summit. The first was by Col. R. L. Scott of the U.S.A.A.F., in 1942, and was officially authorised. The second was made without permission by a pilot of the R.A.F., Kenneth Neame, who took a Spitfire XIX on a private photographic flight over the summit in 1947.

These two solo flights are of recent occurrence, but I have included them at this point because I do not wish to return to aerial surveys over the mountain, which really have no connection with the aim of reaching the summit on foot.

This concludes a necessarily brief history of Everest from the time of its discovery on paper to the outbreak of war in 1939, and indeed until the termination of hostilities in 1946, for no climbing expeditions were undertaken during the eight years between 1938 and the end of open warfare in 1946. I have given the whole of this history because of its bearing on my own story, but in actual fact I did not know at the time of Maurice Wilson's brave but suicidal effort, undertaken without any previous experience of mountaineering. Knowledge of it would have made no difference to me, however, because Wilson's entire outlook, as well as his background, was very different from mine.

The problems confronting me were numerous, and would have proved insuperable if I had stopped just once to weigh up the possibilities of success or failure in an atmosphere of calm reasoning: but the power of past events robbed me of all ability to think clearly, and had the effect of blocking every avenue of retreat. In the less impassioned light of to-day I can see all this, but at the time I was blinded by the ambition which had held me in its grip during most of the war years, and perhaps most of all while I was trying deliberately, as on the Virunga mountains, to disregard it.

There is little use in self-analysis at this stage, for the plain truth is that I had pledged myself to the task of a lone attempt against Everest if I were successful on the Virunga mountains. I had been successful in that undertaking, even beyond my wildest dreams, and for this reason alone there could be no turning back, no sensible reflections, no thought but of advancing in the face of every difficulty and danger. In this way I was committed to an impossible task, though I do not say this with bitterness or regret, for what would human nature shrink to if favourable odds had always to be awaited?

The least of my problems—or so I thought in my ignorance—was that of obtaining permission to enter Tibet, which had been closed to all foreigners for several years. It would have been a waste of time to make application through normal channels: there was only one course open to me, and that was to rely upon getting into the forbidden territory unnoticed with a small party, in disguise if necessary, and to submit to the extra hardships and dangers involved.

Travel arrangements throughout would have to depend upon whatever was to hand, for there was the aftermath of war to consider, and because of this it was altogether out of the question to book a sea passage to India in advance. Every ship was booked to capacity for many months to come, and so I had to keep constant observation on the spot, in the hope of being able to take a berth in the event of a last-minute vacancy.

In my quest for information about the route through Sikkim and Tibet, and the actual mountaineering difficulties to be met with on Everest, I searched through books and Press cuttings, but in the end I had more or less to pioneer for myself, which is inevitably the case when anyone faces a problem alone for the first time. While not belittling the difficulties, I was not overawed by them, but in my assessment I was perhaps too busy with thoughts of the obstacles to be surmounted en route to consider how slender my chances would be if I should happen to reach the mountain.

Darjeeling would have to be my real starting point for Sikkim and Tibet, but how could I contact a suitable guide with Everest experience, and if I succeeded in finding one, would he be prepared to go with me into a closed territory which I had no permission to enter? How many porters could I afford to take, if any would go with me at all?

The problems of food and equipment resolved themselves into what I could afford and what I could find. Food would have to be limited to

Boranze (left) and Kabanza on Karisimbi, with giant groundsel in background

Mount Sabinio 'Father with huge teeth' and the thatched rondavel at Ntebeko used by the author

An insignificant little party moving through Tibet

Tenzing, the author and Ang Dowa (a self-taken photograph)

the barest necessities for a Spartan existence for one,[1] but equipment would have to be provided for others as well as myself.

There were two schools of thought regarding the use of oxygen on Everest, but I had no choice in the matter. Even so, I was (and still am) unswervingly opposed on principle to the use of any artificial aid until it becomes a necessity. To me, an ice-axe is a terrible burden unless there are steps to be cut or some other essential service to be rendered by the implement. Similarly, if I can climb in freedom and no great discomfort to 17,000 ft. (as I have done) without clinkered boots, or any boots at all, why should I wear the offending things below that height and rob myself of the simple delight of going barefooted? A similar reasoning applies to oxygen, with much greater emphasis, for it is a completely artificial aid which is both dispensable and foreign to the ordinary equipment of a mountaineer, who is usually a type of fellow who looks upon his efforts as something of a spiritual as well as a physical adventure.

Is oxygen dispensable at the high altitudes encountered in the Himalayas, and on Everest, the highest of them all? I think so, and in support of my belief would draw attention to a fact which is often overlooked, namely, the extreme adaptability of the human body. To place a small limit to its capabilities is about as senseless as suggesting an absolute maximum speed for any form of travel by land, sea or air. (Remember how the force of " g " was at one time spoken of as the deciding factor for speed in the air? No one makes mention of it nowadays, when even the speed of sound is not beyond the range of certain piloted aircraft). A few men have already demonstrated their ability to survive without oxygen while climbing at an altitude of nearly 28,000 ft. On this showing, it would be ridiculous to assert that no man could possibly reach 29,000 ft. or slightly more, under similar conditions.

I have never forsaken my belief that the mountain *could* be climbed without the use of oxygen. And I *wanted* it to be climbed that way, knowing that a successful climb with the aid of oxygen would only lead to a further series of attempts with the object of providing the first ascent without recourse to this artificial aid. The procession to Everest would then start again, and perhaps more lives would be lost, until men, by their own unaided efforts, stood on the summit of the highest mountain in the world.

There was at one time a feeling amongst purists that Everest should be

---

[1] Guides and porters could be expected to provide their own native foods, as in Africa —with suitable emolument, of course.

climbed once, and once only. Stated more bluntly, it was not the wish
of those most intimately connected with Everest that it should become
another English Channel, with all that is involved when constant relays of
contestants are in opposition to each other.

I thought much about oxygen, but of course I could not in any case
afford to equip myself with any costly apparatus and so my conclusions
did not really matter.

Other problems, of which I was equally aware, had to be faced, but
each was inseparable from my two basic difficulties—(1) of attempting
a task of such immensity with only 1-50th of the money that had been
spent on at least one previous Everest expedition, and (2) of bearing the
added burden of going unlawfully all the way through Tibet, and possibly
Sikkim. But most of all it was lack of money that was the crippling factor.
I could not, as I have already explained, book a passage to India by sea,
and neither could I afford to travel by air, and consequently it was impossible
to time my departure so as to be certain of arriving at the mountain in time
to make use of the short, critical period in which climbing is possible, and
which terminates with the onset of monsoon conditions. In fact, I could
plan nothing with absolute certainty because, to be perfectly candid, I had
only £250 left over from my Virunga expedition, and this would have to
suffice for the buying of all equipment and provisions, the entire journey
from Bulawayo to Darjeeling and back, and the intermediate journey with
guide and porters to and from Everest. Looked at in the cold logic of
distance, time and money, the venture was doomed to failure from the very
start, and by all the laws of common sense and ordinary achievement
I would do well if I reached as far as Darjeeling before finding myself
penniless. It might be thought that I could have saved on expenses by
working my passage between Africa and India, but this I already knew
to be out of the question on shipping lines which have to consider the
factors of colour-bar and prestige.

Africa proved a most unsuitable continent in which to gather together
equipment for high altitude mountaineering in the Himalayas, and circumstances were made worse by unsettled world conditions. The result was
that in the five or six months available between the return from my Virunga
expedition and leaving for Everest I was unable to buy any sleeping bags
of genuine eiderdown, and all I had in the end was one of goose down and
another with a canvas outer covering and a fleece lining. I had read about
the appalling cold on Everest, and should have known without the need

for actual experience that sleeping bags form the most important of all single items of equipment. This was the time for laying aside all plans for a lone attempt against Everest. Instead, I decided to take a chance with what I had, and hope that the porters in Darjeeling would have eiderdown sleeping-bags of their own, left to them as presents from previous Himalayan expeditions.

After much time and effort I was able to obtain a quantity of silvercloth fabric, used for making barrage balloons during the war, and from this two tents were constructed to my own designs. One was made large enough to take four people, 6 ft. 10 in. long and 4 ft. 1 in. high. Eighteen pegs were required, and the total weight, in a container of similar fabric, was 15½ lb., which was lighter than any hitherto used on Everest. A smaller tent was made, after the pattern of a simple hiking tent. This had no side walls and required only 12 pegs: its weight, with container, was 13½ lb. I intended to use both tents at camps low down, the large one being for the porters and the small one for myself. Thereafter only one tent would be used. The total cost was £20 15s.

An ice-axe and crampons were made specially for me by Fezzardi Angelo, an Italian internee at Gwelo, Southern Rhodesia, and a cotton climbing rope was made by hand at the same internment camp by another Italian, Tedesco. Each article was exceptionally well made, and as a nice gesture from the two craftsmen I received a small card bearing a mountain flower in one corner and the words, " With best wishes for a successful climbing."

The only climbing boots obtainable were not up to the desired standard, but were adequate. Balaclava helmets, warm mittens and gloves, snow goggles, etc., were not easy to acquire in Africa, with the consequence that I had to hunt through second-hand shops. It was a question of economy and improvisation throughout, and because of the need for strict secrecy there were few to share with me the burden of planning and preparation, so that I could not help but compare myself with a professional boxer who dispenses with a manager and has to act as his own matchmaker, trainer and manager, and then climb into the ring and fight.

Rusks were to act as a substitute for bread, and these, with cheese and chocolate, would serve as my main sustenance on the mountain, if I should reach that far. An innovation (or so I believe) was a supply of biltong, which is dried and salted meat of game, cut into strips. This is most nourishing, and ideal for eating while on the march. A Coleman instant-lighting stove was to provide a means for cooking, but I took no petrol or container, relying upon obtaining these, as well as most forms of tinned foods, in India. Kit-bags of ordinary military size (3 ft. by 1 ft. 6 in. diameter) I considered to be the best means for carrying all equipment and provisions.

XV. *The Lone Trail Out*

WHEN ALL was prepared, I left Bulawayo by train for the port of Beira, in Moçambique; the date of my departure was February 17, 1947.

Immediately upon arrival, I was driven all over Beira by a taxi-driver who had been hired to take me to the office of the nearest shipping agent. Knowing that I was unfamiliar with the town, he twisted and turned through a maze of side streets until his tactics became obvious, even to a stranger. A sharp rebuke kept him from further needless peregrinations, but the vastness of the registered fare only became obvious when I walked back to the railway station which was no more than two streets away.

An early disappointment awaited me at the shipping office, where I found to my chagrin that the S.S. *Karagola*, one of the few passenger-cargo vessels operating on the British-India line in immediate post-war days, had left for Mombasa earlier the same morning. What followed was a dreary trial, only worthy of record because a journey that would be very ordinary when undertaken by a properly financed expedition became, in my case, something of an adventure, with each move dependent upon a fresh throw of the dice. It was not a stimulating adventure, or one in which untrodden ground was covered, and to tell it in full, with each uneasy incident emphasised, would be out of place where there is so much to follow of real adventure in out-of-the-way places: but to omit all reference to the outward journey to Darjeeling would be to give an erroneous impression of the enterprise as a whole and of the constant striving that was called for.

Harbour facilities at Beira were so strained that cargo boats were often delayed, sometimes for months: but there was one, more fortunate than the rest, which had discharged its cargo and was due to proceed up the East Coast, calling at all ports on its way.

On one of my daily visits, I was introduced to the skipper, a fine Scotsman with a broad accent and an impressive head of thick white hair, parted centrally, and bushy black eyebrows.   He was taking one passenger on to Dar-es-Salaam, and had room for one more as far as Mombasa, which as the northernmost port of call for ships crossing from Africa to India could be of use to me, though just as easily I could be in worse plight there than at Beira.   I was persuaded to take the risk on learning that another B.I. passenger-cargo vessel, the *Isipingo*, would be overtaken in harbour at Dar-es-Salaam.   Also, I admired the look of the Scotsman and liked the name of his ship, though its appearance had nothing to recommend it.   The name—S.S. *Explorer*—seemed an apt one.

So I joined the *Explorer* on the evening of Friday, February 21, a bare 12 hours before its departure.   Final loading was carried out by lamplight, and I sat on deck until late, watching the bustling activity all round me, in company with my fellow passenger.   Powerful, splendidly built Africans, their ebony bodies glistening with sweat and coal dust, manoeuvred cranes into position, hoisting, traversing, lowering, while those on the ground assembled more crates.   They worked cheerfully and well on the dock, but they belonged more properly to the interior, and even as they busied themselves they chanted their own songs and beat a changeless rhythm with their flat hands on the thin sheet covering which protected the working parts of the crane.   Quite accidentally, one of the workers obstructed a Portuguese official who was about to board the ship.   The white man pushed the African, who was unaware until then of his trespass, to one side with unnecessary force and cursed him volubly.   Each African, when it was safe to do so, added his own comment, and the last to do so brought out a very emphatic " Simba! "—" Lion! " I wondered how long this attitude of white to black would prevail in Africa, and how much longer the retaliation would be but a single, explosive epithet.

The *Explorer*, which contented itself with a leisurely nine knots, had one claim to fame.   It had brought four of the special railway coaches from England to Cape Town for use during the Royal Tour which was to take place during my absence.   Otherwise it was the sort of ship which could well be called a " boat " without undue offence, and I wondered how many U-boat Commanders had balanced its worth against that of a torpedo and decided to let it go in peace.

Despite its nine knots, the *Explorer* succeeded in reaching Dar-es-Salaam before the *Isipingo* had left, but the latter had a full complement of passengers and I was left with no alternative but to remain with the *Explorer* as far as Mombasa, where it arrived after a voyage of just over seven days. Here again I was confronted with a major shipping problem, and after moving to a hotel I started once more on the dreary trudge from berth to berth of the harbour and from one shipping office to another in the full heat and humidity of the coast. The S.S. *Shirala*, also of the B.I. shipping line, was unexpectedly in No. 5 berth. All the vessels of this Line, by some turn of fate, were following in unusually close procession, and failure to gain accommodation on the *Shirala*, after failing with the *Karagola* and *Isipingo*, would mean failure in my attempt to reach India, let alone Everest, before the 1947 monsoon broke over the mountain. I would not have the money to try again in 1948, and was not prepared to give this a thought, for it was almost certain that official expeditions would be under way during the following year, thus putting an end to all hope for a lone expedition. It had to be now or never, and the realisation of this bore down on me until the burden was almost more than I could bear.

The *Shirala's* purser gave me no hope. The passenger list was full and there was no likelihood of a last-minute vacancy. I could call again in two days' time, when the ship was due to sail, but the only really sound advice was for me to return to my starting point and await my turn after entering my name on the long waiting list. I would have taken this advice but for the fact that I had struggled against adversity and similar long odds to reach the most remote of the Virunga mountains, and had succeeded. Only this, and a persistence which had engrained itself from childhood, drove me doggedly on when submission would have provided an easier course.

Nothing could be done on the following day, which was a Sunday, but on the Monday morning there was the first glimmer of hope when I was told to return later to the main shipping office. On the second occasion the *Shirala's* purser was there, and it was suggested that I should have my passport checked and stand by in readiness to go aboard, but at the same time I was warned not to build up any high hopes. Finally, with only one hour left for embarkation, it was announced that a passenger from Nairobi had failed to turn up and I could have his berth.

My passage to Bombay cost 845/- in East African currency, which was considerably more than I expected, but this was an expense which could not be avoided. To make up for it in some slight measure, I refused resolutely throughout the voyage of twelve days to join in any social round that was likely to involve drinking, though to make a social outcast of myself for a voyage of this duration was difficult enough, especially as there was nothing whatever to do but sit and relax—no deck games, no music, nothing.

And how was I to relax when fully aware that on the corresponding day to my departure from Mombasa, the 1936 Everest Expedition had left Darjeeling? I imagined myself as trailing more than 3,000 miles behind schedule, but there was nothing I could do to alter the situation. I was the impecunious child of my time, learning slowly that ambition, if it cannot be repressed, must subordinate itself to the amount of cash in hand. If there is rancour in this, it is because the days of travelling cheaply and freely about the world have disappeared in my time, and though my generation has seen the rise of hitch-hiking, this is a poor substitute because it affords no true freedom of movement or thought. Those who indulge in it are never really free, even though they are in search of freedom; and though they are striving to gain independence by breaking away from the fetters of their own poverty they are still in bondage, being utterly dependent upon money, though it happens to be the money of other people. There is something pitiable about our age.

The *Shirala* did not call at the Seychelles, and so my first sight of land was at Porbandar, where the ship stood out at sea to disembark Indian passengers bound for the northern provinces of their homeland. This provided my first glimpse of India, but the impression I gained was that it might have been a part of Egypt or Arabia. Behind the mud houses were low, barren hills, and to the north a sandy waste. There was little vegetation anywhere and no surface water or shade. Another call was made at Veraval, farther to the south, and on the following day, Saturday, March 15, the *Shirala* tied up at Bombay.

My first impressions of Bombay were of pavements and streets red with betel-nut spat out by addicts (sometimes from above) without regard to passers-by, and of hordes of birds which made the roofs of buildings white with their droppings. The Indian mynah (*Acridotheres tristis*) was familiar to me, for since its introduction to South Africa in the 1880's it has spread from Durban, where it is particularly numerous, right through Natal to the Transvaal.

Men lay on the pavements, some with blankets or sacks drawn over their bodies, but none bothering to seek shade. A wrinkled beggar woman slapped her bare hollow stomach and whined for food. One of several sacred bulls wandered into a shop and came out just as leisurely. A cab horse, little more than skin and bone, had collapsed in its traces opposite a branch of Lloyds Bank and could not be brought to its feet, though a small crowd gathered to pull, push and kick.

At the railway station I received conflicting information. Firstly, it was said that no train was due to leave for Calcutta during the day, then it was intimated that a train would be running but no accommodation was available on it. Finally, as though a decision had yet to be made, I was told to return within two hours. On this later occasion, after a whispered consultation behind the scenes, I was issued with a second-class ticket and impressed with the fact that a first-class ticket would have cost me twice as much. There had been a saving of Rs. 75, so . . . how about splitting the difference?

At times, looking out of my carriage window, I half imagined myself to be travelling through the Karoo of South Africa. There was the same flat, dry scrubland and the same heat. Only the train seemed different, being commendably free from roll because of the lines, which are of wider gauge than in South Africa. Also there was no suggestion of *apartheid*, for I shared my compartment with three Indians. No suggestion, that is, of the South African brand of *apartheid*, but at each wayside halt I saw water-carts being trundled along the platforms, and the cry of one pedlar was " Mussulman water," and of the other " Hindu water." It was notice-able too, that the three men sharing my compartment never spoke among themselves.

Another comparison could be drawn between this journey and the one which had taken me to the Virunga mountains of the Belgian Congo. In each instance there had been the frightening suspense, the same frus-trations and despondencies. Darjeeling was to be the equivalent of Rumangabo, where I had arrived alone and ill provided for. There I had met with every kindliness and assistance from the Conservateur, Comman-dant van Cools. Would there be a counterpart of the Commandant at Darjeeling to help me on my way? Then there was the memory of Kabanza fresh in my mind. Would there be a Kabanza, only under another name, to guide and be with me on Everest? The clickety-clack, clickety-clack of the train running over the rails seemed to say, " You fool, turn back. You fool, turn back."

A change had to be made at Calcutta, for Siliguri, and during the interval of awaiting my next train I jotted down my early impressions of the city. " The red stains of betel-nut and white of bird droppings as much in evidence here as in Bombay. There is the nauseating stench of urine everywhere, in the streets and in the buildings. A dead cat and a dead rat lie within inches of one another in a gutter, and nearby a dog tears at the carcase of a goat, possession of which is disputed by a flock of ravenous birds. Passengers overflow from buses and taxis, cluttering the running boards, clutching window ledges and door handles. At the rear of one bus there are three men clinging to a spare tyre. As people leave their places of employment to go home they form a solid mass, not only on the pavements but right across the main streets. There are many fine public buildings and private residences in Calcutta, but these are overwhelmed in the first impression by sights and smells of squalor, and of a population which must be greater than that of any city of comparable size in the world."

There was another change at Siliguri, this time to the narrow-gauge railway which leads from the open plain to the Terai forest and then climbs through innumerable close turns to Darjeeling, where I arrived in the late afternoon of Tuesday, March 13.

There was a thick, damp mist through which little could be seen, and consequently I was wholly willing to put my trust in a youngster who came forward with an offer to lead me to a " good hotel." He took me instead to a dismal boarding-house in a back street, but I did not protest. For one thing, I could not very well afford to stay at a luxury hotel, and furthermore, I wished to keep to myself as much as possible and not be drawn into conversations which would lead to added furtiveness and lying.

My room, utterly comfortless and cold, was bare of everything but a bed and wardrobe, but I settled in after assuring myself that if forced to remain in Darjeeling for more than a few days, I would move to better lodgings, if not to one of the high-class hotels. At times like these I sometimes feel a tinge of bitterness, but on this occasion I had no feeling but that of complete resignation. The lassitude remained as I retired to bed for the night, so that I could think of no opening gambit for the following day.

By some means I had to contact (1) a guide with an intimate knowledge of Tibet and the Tibetan language, (2) an accomplished climber with high altitude experience on Everest itself, and (3) a man with sufficient knowledge of animals to arrange a means of transport all the way from Darjeeling, through Sikkim and Tibet, to the mountain. It was a tall enough order as it stood, but it was also necessary to call for an extraordinary amount of idealism and a willingness to accept inordinate risks for very little remuneration.

The field of selection was practically limited to Sherpas; that is, to Nepalese of the Sola Khumbu region, for they have gained a reputation far above that of any other hill tribe for resourcefulness and endurance on Everest. This being so, was there any amongst them who could be expected to show the essential high idealism? It was most unlikely—a million to one chance, say. And yet—remember Kabanza? He, in his primitive way, was an idealist, a lover of mountains who climbed for the satisfaction of doing so rather than for what he would be paid at the end. On these grounds there was reason for hope, but the hope was such a slender one that I was not kept awake by it.

XVI. *Underground Activities*

N O IDEAS were formulated overnight, so I took an aimless walk when morning came. The weather was cold and dismal, permitting no view of the mountains, and I paid little heed to the cosmopolitan population other than to notice the Mongolian features of the several hill tribes, with their high cheek bones and oblique eyes. Only the day before I had been on the hot Indian plain, and now I walked as a stranger among people dressed in furs and greatcoats, gloves and fleece-lined boots, but they passed almost unnoticed. Usually observant, I had eyes for nothing but the purpose of my visit.

A photograph of a snow-capped range of mountains in a shop window was the first thing to attract my undivided attention. It was of the Kang-chenjunga group, and elsewhere was a photograph of Everest. I glanced at the name inscribed in white above the door, and because it was Paul (the name of Karma Paul I remembered from one of the Everest books which I had read) I entered the shop. After a few discreet inquiries I asked very casually if Karma Paul was a relative of the shopkeeper. I do not remember what answer was given, but Karma Paul was sent for from not far away, and I was introduced to a heavily built man, broad and short, of more than middle age, who looked at me with eyes heavy from sleeplessness. It was explained that a daughter had died, and according to the custom of his people, Karma Paul had spent the night without sleep. So, at his suggestion, it was arranged that we should meet in his own office at 2 o'clock in the afternoon.

Later in the morning, in an atmosphere which had cleared miraculously, I looked out from Observatory Hill and saw for the first time the line of snow-capped mountains dominated by Kangchenjunga. There was at the time a lot of low cloud forming a solid base, and above this the snow peaks towered in unobstructed view. The sky was a clear blue, forming a void above, and because of the layer of cloud below, there was no visible connection between the mountain peaks and the earth. All I could see to the north was a tremendous acreage of gleaming white snow, 45 miles distant and so high that for a while I thought it was the tops of huge, billowing cumulo-nimbus towering above alto-stratus. I found myself gasping with astonishment, almost unable to believe my eyes. Something impressive I had expected, but nothing on this vast scale.

This was my first glimpse into the heart of the Himalayas, and it was sobering to think that Everest, which was out of sight, topped the highest of these giant peaks by several hundred feet.

Promptly at 2 o'clock, I turned up at the arranged meeting place, a comfortable office just off the main street. At first we talked about anything but the real purpose of my visit, and I found that Karma Paul was a charming man of Tibetan stock, fluent in English and at least four other languages. He had formed an almost indispensable part of all Everest expeditions with the exception of the first reconnaissance, and expected to go again as official interpreter and transport manager with the next expedition planned for 1949. He showed me with great pride an autographed copy of Hugh Ruttledge's book on the 1933 expedition and pointed with justifiable pride to the photographs and mentions of himself.

I was disappointed to find that he was not himself a climbing man, but in any case he was too elderly to be of any active use to me. All the same, he could help if he would, so I unburdened myself of my story.

In brief, I had journeyed alone from Africa with the object of climbing Everest. No, I had no permission to enter Tibet. He looked at me in a strange, incredulous way, and said, without any other words leading up to it, " Impossible! " He repeated himself for emphasis, and then went on to ask if I had any experience as a mountaineer, and knew of the dangers and bitterly cold conditions involved.

I knew why he asked these questions when he began to tell me about the Yorkshireman, Maurice Wilson, who had approached him in connection with a similar mission in 1934. Now it was my turn to be incredulous as I listened to the story of a tall man of about 35 or 36 years of age who had the theory that mountaineers ate too much. He had never gained any mountaineering experience but had accustomed himself to a diet of green, uncooked vegetation—grasses and so forth. He had learnt to fly, and had bought an aeroplane, apparently with the object of going the whole way by air, instead of which he had only been able to proceed as far as India by this means. He had arrived in Darjeeling, and eventually succeeded in reaching Everest, only to find that he had underestimated his task. He died on the mountain.

Karma Paul, as though doubting my own determination, stressed the fact that Maurice Wilson had been a very resolute man. Although he did not say as much, I gathered that he had given assistance, and did not wish to become involved in another illegal entry into Tibet and another possible death on Everest.

All this came as a complete surprise to me, but I could not fail to see the implications and to sense the threat to my own hopes. So I hastened to assure Karma Paul that I was, unlike Maurice Wilson, an experienced mountaineer of very sane outlook who could be relied upon to take care of myself and others. I followed by telling briefly of my expedition to the Virunga mountains, emphasising the fact that no harm had befallen a single man. Karma Paul was anxious that his own chances of going with the official expedition in 1949 should not be jeopardised and I had to assure him most earnestly that nothing would be said to involve him in any way. He took a lot of convincing, but after a while he told me to call again at 11 o'clock the next day, when he would introduce me to a capable Sherpa who might be willing to go with me. In the meantime it would be essential to provide myself with an official permit to enter Sikkim and obtain authority to make use of various Government bungalows. For this I went to the office of the D.I.F. (Darjeeling Improvement Fund) where I was called upon to sign a declaration to the effect that I would not go beyond the border of Sikkim into Tibet. I hated the duplicity that was involved, but it was unavoidable, and for Rs. 25½ I was handed the necessary documents.

It was cold and raining when I kept my next appointment with Karma Paul at his office. Two other men were there, and I was introduced firstly to Tenzing Khansana,[1] who had a slight, faltering knowledge of English and was the obvious spokesman for the two. He had a pleasant face, but the solemnity of the occasion overawed him somewhat, as it did me, and he remained unsmiling. His height was about 5 ft. 8 in. in his heavy boots, and he was well proportioned but not broad—wiry and vigorous rather

[1] Or Khansama. This was the name by which he was made known to me in the first instance, and the name under which he sent several letters in later years. At other times and in other places his name has been given as Tenzing Botia (or Bhotia) and Tenzing Norkey (or Norkay). In other writings I have seen Tenzing given as Tensing, but in the spelling of this name I find that he himself never deviates from Tenzing, and I have his personal signature with a definite " z " in it.

than muscular and powerful. He was 32 years of age (a year or so older than myself) and had been a jockey for two years though he looked too heavy for this.

His Everest record was:—1935 to Camp V; 1936 to Camp IV; 1938 to Camp VI. His performance on this latter occasion of portering to one of the highest camps ever established on the mountain had earned him recognition as a Himalayan Tiger, and he wore on the lapel of his jacket a bronze medal testifying to this achievement. In addition he had been to Nanda Devi, Kamet, Nanga Parbat and other Himalayan mountains with Smythe, Shipton and Tilman. He hailed from Sola Khumbu, and apart from his own Nepali tongue he spoke Tibetan, Sikkimese and Hindustani fluently, and had a lesser knowledge of a few other languages.

His companion was a sturdy individual of about the same height, or slightly less, stronger, but less intelligent in appearance. His name was Ang Dowa, and he also came from Sola Khumbu, in Nepal, where he had been born a year before Tenzing, making his age at this time 33. He had been to Everest in 1936 and 1938 but had not reached as high as Camp VI. It was stated for him that he could speak Tibetan fluently and was an experienced cook. I summed him up at a first impression as a tough, rugged fellow, but not the kind to make a leader.

With the aid of Karma Paul as translator, but sometimes addressing my words direct to Tenzing if the message was plain, I made known my object and the fact that no permission had been gained for entry into Tibet. There followed a long conversation between the three men in which I could not join, and I looked anxiously from face to face in an attempt to divine the individual reactions, becoming more and more apprehensive as I did so. After a few minutes of anxiety I could bear the suspense no longer, and interrupted brusquely to ask Karma Paul what the outcome was likely to be. The reply was not encouraging.

Both men required that Rs. 600 (approximately £50) should be lodged with their dependents before leaving, otherwise they would not consider going. They were married men, it was pointed out, and the risks involved were so great that their families must be provided for to this extent if any further agreement was to be reached between us. I did not wish to argue, and could not, because the uncompromising truth was that my available resources had already been reduced to less than £150, and out of this I had to furnish my return fare to Africa.

Also I felt that Karma Paul, understandably enough, was prompting

the men to hold out for the highest possible terms. Therefore I wished
to make whatever arrangements I could privately, and suggested that the
two men should come to see me in my bleak little apartment.

I did not think of it at the time, but this was the best move I could
have made: the men needed would know that any money withheld from
them was not going into any luxuries for myself, and a glance into my
room would convince them beyond a shadow of doubt.

Karma Paul agreed readily enough, for he had already played the only
part he was willing to play by introducing me to the two men. Beyond
that we must plan, if we could, for ourselves. In fact, after the men had
turned to go, he told me politely but firmly that he would wash his hands
of the affair entirely and did not wish ever to be seen talking with me for
fear of being implicated. My proposed undertaking was sheer suicide, he
said, and he barely restrained himself from exposing me to the authorities.
My saner self entirely agreed with him.

When the two Sherpas had arrived with me at the sanctuary of my
room, I unpacked for them my two tents and let them see the other items
of equipment. Afterwards we discussed a few mountaineering topics,
Tenzing interpreting for the benefit of Ang Dowa. Tenzing's alertness and
intelligence made up for his poor command of English, and I contrived to
make it known that my resources were far less than those of the Royal
Geographical Society and Alpine Club, who had financed all previous
Everest expeditions which he had accompanied. It was made plain that
I could offer no more than Rs. 300 as an advance payment. This would
become their property on proceeding beyond Rongbuk, the monastery
within sight of Everest. After this they would be paid Rs. 5 for each day
spent on the mountain and on the return to Darjeeling. If we were turned
back at the Tibetan border, or if the men should refuse to go beyond
Rongbuk, the sum of Rs. 300 would be forfeited and payment made at
the rate of Rs. 5 per day. This was as much as could be offered.

I held back nothing from the men which would have been likely to
influence them. The deficiencies of my equipment were pointed out to
them and I showed that I had no ice-axes or sleeping bags other than my
own. Tenzing assured me that they had an ice-axe and sleeping-bag apiece
which had been given to them after their last expedition. This information
brought tremendous relief to me, but the pressing issue had still to be
decided. Up to this stage I had made no real effort at persuasion, but the

Ice Pool and pinnacles on Everest

Camp 3 on Everest

The long trail back (the Rongbuk River is on the left)

Tenzing (left) and the author near Darjeeling after their return from Everest

situation now demanded a supreme effort on my part. So I brought into play the one card which I had not as yet revealed.

The essence of what I said to Tenzing was as follows:[1] "If you will accept my terms, which are the very best I can offer, you will stand an equal chance with me of reaching the top of Everest. If you go with a large official expedition you will be nothing but a porter, as in past years when you have carried heavy loads and then had to remain in camp while the white sahibs set out to reach the top. You know from past experience that it is unlikely that you will be given a full share, either of success or failure, if you go with others. Our chances are slender, but if I succeed, you will succeed as well, and if I fail the failure will be just as much yours."

I repeated this, and then said, " Now, tell that to Ang Dowa and let me have your answer."

After a pause in which to think Tenzing turned to Ang Dowa and interpreted what I had said. The two men conversed quietly and earnestly for two or three minutes and then Tenzing gave the reply which I had awaited with so much foreboding. He weighed his words carefully, and at first his tone held an extreme melancholy, so that I expected the worst.

He said: " We know that what you say is true. Both Ang Dowa and I are keen to climb Everest, but although I have been to Camp VI, I have never been able to go beyond. There may be a lot of trouble in getting through Tibet without a pass but we think we may be able to manage."

His expression changed to a half-smile as he added, " We will try."

My feeling of relief was so intense that I can recall nothing else. I can remember nothing of any immediate reaction to this splendid news.

The men called again on the following morning, bringing with them their ice-axes and sleeping-bags, which were of pure eider: instead of only two of these, we should have had at least six, for it is usual to use one inside another on Everest. I had obtained a map of Sikkim, and with the aid of this we roughed out a plan, aiming to leave Darjeeling as inconspicuously as possible on the very next morning, ostensibly on a tour of Sikkim. Both men had shown good sense in keeping their ice-axes out of sight, wrapped in their sleeping-bags, and we agreed to do the same with all mountaineering equipment while there was any need to do so. It must be admitted

[1] This should be considered in relation to the date at which the conversation took place. It was not until some years later that Tenzing, due to his outstanding qualities, came to be given a real chance on Everest. I was, as a matter of fact, the first to grant a measure of equality to any Sherpa.

that our plan of campaign, if it existed at all, was meagre in the extreme. We discussed the use of horses, but the cost was entirely prohibitive and I was forced to rely upon Tenzing's assurance that he would contrive as cheaply as possible with less expensive pack animals. Extra men would be needed at times, but we could pick them up and drop them at successive stages of our journey, or so I gathered, for all our plans were haphazard.

Several purchases had to be made, including boots, blankets, ropes, tinned foods and matches. For the latter we had to scour the town, and until late it seemed that we would be unsuccessful. There was, of all things, a strike at the match factory, and because of it there was a black market in operation. No other Everest expedition could be held up for want of such a trifling commodity, but ours could. On such slender threads did we depend.

I had already opened a banking account in Darjeeling, but all that was left after making the purchases was £120. Of this I drew £100 (1,319 Rs. 9 as.), made up as follows:—100 Rs. notes—6; 10 Rs. notes—15; 5 Rs. notes—40; 1 R. notes—250. The balance of 119 Rs. 9 as. was made up of small coins—8, 4, 2, and 1 anna pieces.

In the afternoon the men came again to my room, this time bringing their wives with them as arranged. I found Tenzing's wife, Ang Nima, to be a quiet, charming person of erect carriage. She did not have much to say, but her calm composure and reassuring smile made me feel that she had confidence in me and would trust her husband to my care. I had strong reason to believe that she would not influence Tenzing against going with me. Ang Dowa's wife remained quietly in the background, but I gained the same impression from her.

When the time was fitting I produced two envelopes with Rs. 300 enclosed in each, and two letters, the contents of which I read and re-read so as to make their meaning perfectly understood. Then Tenzing signed one of the letters and to the other Ang Dowa appended his thumb mark. The letters, dated 21/3/47, read as follows:

" The enclosed Rs. 300 becomes the property of Tenzing/Ang Dowa upon his proceeding beyond Rongbuk in an attempt to climb Everest. Up to this stage his pay is to be Rs. 5 per day.

Beyond Rongbuk, in addition to the aforementioned Rs. 300 he is to receive Rs. 5 per day for all time spent on the mountain and on the return to Darjeeling.

If successful in reaching the summit of Everest, he is to receive a further Rs. 300 made payable to him from my account with Barclays Bank, Salisbury, Southern Rhodesia, upon my return there.[1] At Rongbuk monastery, a letter is to be lodged making over all my personal effects carried on the expedition to the two men, Tenzing and Ang Dowa, in the event of my death on the mountain. Also the money that is left will become theirs in the event of my death.

In addition, in the event of success in reaching the summit of Everest, each man will, on the publication of any book dealing with our Everest expedition, receive a further Rs. 300, thus making a total of Rs. 900 in all.

Rs. 100 of enclosed amount can be used for dependents of Tenzing/Ang Dowa during our absence."

Two other letters were made out and signed by myself, and later deposited in the Bank at Darjeeling for safe keeping. The contents, as follows, were intended as a safeguard for the two men in the event of my death or imprisonment in Tibet:

" This is to state that Tenzing/Ang Dowa was employed by me to act as guide and porter through parts of India, Sikkim and Tibet with the object of an attempt to climb Everest. Tenzing/Ang Dowa agreed to accompany me only if I obtained permission to enter Tibet and he went with me under the impression that I had done so. I therefore take full responsibility for any violation of territorial rights whilst this man was employed by me on this expedition."

This was not strictly correct, but it was not far wrong, for after our original meeting in Karma Paul's office, when conversation had been complicated by the need for interpretation, we never made mention of my lack of official permission to enter Tibet. The second of these documents may have had no validity in law, but the fact of its existence does at least prove the strength of my desire to take full responsibility, and it also gives an indication of my main concern, which was for the safety of Tenzing and Ang Dowa. Quite frankly, and unheroically, I did not care what happened to myself, but I worried at the thought that any punishment should be meted out to others. Imprisonment and torture in Tibet, if travellers' accounts are correct, can be pretty unpleasant.

[1] I had taken care to leave sufficient in my account for this purpose.

XVII.   *Himalayan Approach*

O
N SATURDAY, March 22, the day for our departure, I awoke sneezing
and with a horribly sore throat. My left eye had a painful swelling
at the outer corner and my condition generally was so bad that, if
ensconced in a comfortable hotel, I would most certainly have remained
in bed. But my room was cold and my bed uncomfortable, so I dressed
early and set about the final preparations. A little packing remained to be
done, and there was fresh bread, ordered on the previous day, to be collected.
Also, being a non-smoker, I had so far overlooked the purchase of cigarettes
and tobacco, which I ordinarily keep on hand for others.

A ramshackle taxi had been ordered to take us as far as Tista Bridge,
beyond which we would travel to Gangtok, the capital of Sikkim, by the
ordinary bus service. It arrived, and for the first of many times, I found
myself in suspense. For the tremendous undertaking of Everest there was
pitiably little equipment—all of it contained in only five kit-bags—but we
were supposedly bound for Sikkim, and in that case it might well have
been asked why we were carrying so much baggage.

Tenzing and Ang Dowa had elected to join me later as we did not wish
to cause any comment by being seen together. So, after paying Rs. 32
for my room, I departed on my own, leaving behind a few items of clothing,
my chest expanders, shaving gear, hair brush and cheque-book. For these
I would have no use during the days to come.

Tenzing and Ang Dowa joined me at a prearranged spot and we carried
on over the 22 miles of tricky mountain road which descends in parts as
steeply as 1 in 3½ to the level of the Tista River. The fare cost Rs. 32,
and for a further Rs. 2¼ I relieved the driver of a gallon of petrol together
with an ordinary 3-gallon petrol tin. This was needed for the Coleman
stove, and it had been ridiculous of me to leave this essential purchase until
practically the furthermost point at which it could be obtained.

After a short wait, we crowded into a top-heavy bus and started on the remaining 39 miles to Gangtok. We crossed the river frontier into Sikkim without any difficulty, but we were called upon to present our passes and I was handed a book to sign: consequently I wondered how we would fare at the Tibetan border if there were formalities of this nature to go through.

We arrived in Gangtok at about 17.30 hours (I had no watch and could only make guesses at the right time) and were driven immediately through the crowded market street to the Dak bungalow, or rest house. I was surprised to find an elaborate brick building with electric light, furnished with easy chairs and two beds. From the dining-room window there was a grand view, just before the sun went down, of Narsing (19,130 ft.), Pandim (22,010 ft.), Kangchenjunga (28,146 ft.) and, farther to the right, Siniolchu (22,620 ft.).

Another surprise was to find that the streets were lit at night by electric light, but there was no chance of gaining any additional impressions of the Sikkimese capital because of our late arrival. I could not, as most Everest expeditions of the past had done, receive an invitation to the Residency, for my movements had to be kept as secret as possible, and already I was beginning to grow a beard and adopt the impenetrable guise of a fugitive of long standing. Also there was work to be done in the form of arrangements for the first stage of our journey on foot. With this in mind, Tenzing busied himself at once, and after an initial disappointment, succeeded in enlisting the services of three Sikkimese who were due to go north on the following day with five practically unburdened donkeys. They were bound for Lachen and therefore could take us over four stages of our journey.

This was immense good fortune, the more so because, as pointed out by Tenzing who was already showing consideration for my precarious financial straits, no return journey would have to be paid for because the men were destined to remain at Lachen, where they had come from originally with merchandise for the Gangtok market. This suited our needs admirably and at the same time it benefited the Sikkimese traders by providing them with a paying load for their return journey. I had every reason to feel elated, but my elation at any time was always tempered by the uncertainty of all that lay ahead, so that I could never relax and be carefree.

It would be wrong to give the impression that I gained any knowledge whatever of Sikkim from personal observations after such a short time in the country, but a few general notes will not be out of place at this stage, especially as they are intended to help towards a better understanding of some of the immediate problems confronting us.

The " rice country " as it is known to Tibetans, forms a fairly regular rectangle with its length running from north to south. Its total area of slightly less than 3,000 sq. miles is wedged between Bhutan and Nepal, to east and west respectively: Tibet lies directly north, and in the south there is the Bengal Province of India. Its population at the time of my journey was stated to be nearly 125,000. The original inhabitants were Lepchas, people of Mongolian extraction who called themselves the Rong-pa, or Ravine-folk. The early history of the country is mainly based on the tradition of these Rong-pa, whose characteristics tend to establish them as a tribe which came down from southern Tibet. At the time of which I speak, the Lepchas were only a minority of the population, being outnumbered by immigrants from Nepal and Bhutan.

The Sikkimese (Lepchas, Nepalese and Bhutias) were introduced to Lamaism, the religion of Tibet, during the 17th century, before which they were animists. Until recently they have been guided to a considerable extent by the authorities in Lhasa, and have referred to the Dalai Lama on most secular matters of importance. They are not, however, so preoccupied in their religious devotions as the Tibetans.

It is a land of extremes so far as its topography and climate are concerned. Its numerous unclimbed mountains include Kangchenjunga, third highest in the world, and its largest river, the Tista, is a magnificent stream originating in the far north, with one of its main sources in the snows of Kangchenjau, which rises to 22,700 ft. Much of the country is thickly wooded as well as mountainous, and there is consequently little space that is either open enough or level enough for pasturage or for agriculture on a large scale. Bird life abounds in a great variety of attractive forms, but wild animal life is limited to a very few forest-dwelling species. There are no motor roads beyond the graded dirt track which terminates a few miles north of Gangtok. Travel over the greater part is on foot or on horseback over bridle paths, most of which lead to high mountain passes in the north, east and west. Bridges to the north of Gangtok are mostly crude, while some are extremely primitive and can only be crossed on foot. Dak bungalows are conveniently spaced about the territory, and are available for use by travellers who are in possession of the required passes. These are furnished buildings of brick or wood with a chowkidar, or caretaker, in attendance. In most cases the traveller has only to provide his own bedding.

Until the British withdrawal from India in August 1947 (i.e. shortly after my journey was made) Sikkim was an Indian State under British paramountcy. A year later, India took over the State—which for a short time had gained independence—" in the interests of law and order," after a letter from the local Maharaja to India's political officer in Gangtok stated that the administration could not be carried on satisfactorily without India's assistance. This act of political expediency was prompted by the growing threat of an invasion of Tibet by Chinese Communist forces.

This will be sufficient information about Sikkim to serve as a connecting link with my own story.

We assembled early for our departure, but we had trouble with the original loading of the donkeys, and several halts had to be called within the first mile. The animals were the five most miserable specimens of their kind that could possibly be imagined. Not only were they dwarfish, but they were so bony that no load could be kept in place for long. A single kit-bag was enough to make any one of the beasts sag at the knees, and their sense of direction was appalling. It was all most exasperating, and to make matters worse, there was only one of the three Sikkimese who showed any ability to cope with the situation, so that most of the work devolved upon Tenzing and Ang Dowa. Nevertheless, although the donkeys came in for a remarkable amount of invective, it was grand to be off at last, away from macadamised roads and from the associations which they bring to mind; away to the high mountains which are a symbol of strength without movement or sound. They have not the temper of the wind nor the fury of a storm-lashed sea: these are irresistible forces, but they have no greater strength than—perhaps not as much as—the mountains which hold their silence save when the elements disturb them.

We passed to the right of barley fields and meadowlands, around a hillside from which water trickled, forming into little streams which intersected our path at intervals. There was a strong sun, but the heat was not oppressive, and I found it possible to go barefooted as I had done in the Congo and Uganda. Brilliantly coloured butterflies were there in force, some of them unusually large and capable of swift, strong flight. Squirrels were numerous in the trees, scampering to the topmost branches at our approach.

We had not been on our way long when we passed a large, vertical rock on which Buddhist figures had been sculptured in slight relief and painted in bright colours. There were two large figures of about the same size, and two smaller ones, while there had been a fifth, of which all but the white base had become obliterated. All sat cross-legged, one with outstretched arms and wearing a pointed cowl. The uppermost figure had to one side an earthenware flagon and to the other an indistinguishable white object. This was my first sight of Buddhist art, and fittingly it was in the open, in a setting that was worthy of the high order of the craftsmanship.

Shortly afterwards, we came to a massive prayer wheel set in the same hillside. It consisted of a copper or alloy cylinder about 4 ft. 6 in. long and nearly 2 ft. 3 in. in diameter, set in a wooden frame to which was attached a fine wire netting. The spindle on which the cylinder revolved was encased in a wooden trough, and the whole was contained in a solid structure of stone and cement decorated at the top with lines of prayer flags. The cylinder was inscribed with Buddhist prayers, and along the lower edge were similar petal-like markings to those which formed a base for the figures on the painted rock face. The motive power was water which fell down the hillside amongst dense vegetation, but it was not possible to see the form of blades or wheel upon which the water impinged or to see what sort of bearings were employed. I was to see many other forms of prayer wheels but never a larger one than this.

My bout of illness was now over and, as we walked along at the dawdling pace set by our pack animals, I gave occasional leaps with my right arm up to touch any branches within likely reach overhead. I did this once too often, when I unsuspectingly chose a tree in which a formidable swarm of hornets was nesting. I could not stop in time to save myself, but as soon as my feet had touched ground again I set off along the road, followed by angry hornets, at a speed which startled the others, and even caused the donkeys to break at last into a gangling trot.

At Penlong La (" La " means " pass " in Tibetan and other local languages) we went through a cutting and then emerged to where the narrow path fell away to the right in a precipitous drop. Here one of the donkeys, wandering stupidly to the right instead of keeping with the others, lost its footing and started to fall. Although following only a few yards behind I could do nothing but shout a warning and start to run in its direction. Fortunately the more alert of the Sikkimese was nearer to hand and managed to dash forward and grab a foreleg just in time to prevent the beast from disappearing with its load. Another of the Sikkimese was next to the rescue and in time we were all on the scene, struggling to get the frightened beast on to its four feet again.

At the small village of Penlong, where we rested the donkeys, a young urchin with a running nose danced and sang and clamoured for " baksheesh." Having some small change handy I rewarded him, whereupon his companion, a tiny girl hardly old enough to toddle, came forward with hands extended. " But what have you done to entertain us? " I asked, and although she could not have known what I said, she understood the meaning of my words and started to sing and dance in a simple, childish manner, to the amusement of all who had gathered round.

And so we progressed on our first day, with annoyances, alarms and amusing incidents to shorten the miles.

The Dak bungalow at Dikchu, where we stayed for the night, overlooked terraced paddy-fields, and from it the Tista could be heard below, rushing swiftly and noisily through its deep, boulder-strewn ravine. There was a lawn in front of the wooden bungalow, and in a border a few red and yellow roses were in bloom. Down by the river where I went to fetch water, violets were growing wild, and I stayed sunbathing until the weather changed and a persistent, heavy rain set in. Then, when it was dark, I wrote up my diary by the light of candles and chatted as best I could with Tenzing, who informed me that several expeditions were going out later in the year to Kangchenjunga, Nanda Devi and Kamet.

I gathered, though he did not say as much, that he had sacrificed the chance of going with one of them in order to accompany me, poorly equipped as I was. Not many Sherpas would have done this, and I began to see that he was quietly ambitious and at the same time I began to feel worried because it was not possible for me to offer more for his services. Conversation between us was not easy, but I managed to convey to him the fact that I had always travelled and climbed simply, and with none but natives as my companions. We did not talk for long, but long enough for me to sense that, basically, we were alike in our approach to mountains.

We left Dikchu in a slight drizzle which, however, had cleared by the time we reached the river which gives its name to the locality. This is the Dik Chu (" Chu " is Tibetan for river) and there is an unexpectedly fine suspension bridge just above its confluence with the Tista. The single span consists of a wooden platform supported on heavy iron girders, the width being sufficient to take a large pack animal with bulging loads. The girders, about 60 in all, are suspended from two thick steel wires by vertical wires of lesser cross-section. Large clamps are used for fixing the vertical wires at their point of suspension, and the main wires run on pulleys held by two upright stanchions on either bank. It is a simple enough arrangement, but the effect in this rugged, primitive setting, with tall tree-ferns growing from the river banks, is magnificent.

Only a short distance beyond, as though intended as a distinct contrast of the old with the new, a suspension bridge of the utmost crudity has been thrown across the Tista at a terrifying height. It consists of a crazy structure of bamboo poles lashed together and held in place by rough, fibre ropes which also act as hand rails. A multitude of thin ropes or strings run between the main ropes and the bamboo poles. The distance between banks is considerably more than the height above the river, which at this point is a rushing, roaring torrent. Tenzing, although not lacking in courage, could not be persuaded to venture more than a few yards along the bamboo poles for a photograph, and Ang Dowa would not trust himself to the bridge at all.

Three miles beyond Dikchu we came to Mangan, where there is a squalid little village with a few tin-roofed shops—the last to be met going north. I followed Tenzing into one of the shops and found it to be cluttered with cheap Indian goods, mainly cigarettes, tobacco, sweets, various corns, nutmegs and so forth. There was nothing in the shop to interest me, but Tenzing bought himself a small note-book, which I took to be an encouraging sign of his growing enthusiasm for our venture. There was a level clearing in front of the shops, but one large tree had been allowed to stand, and a circular wall of stones had been built around it. A few tall prayer flags were to be seen but they were as poor and dingy as the village and its inhabitants.

Beyond Mangan, it rained lightly as we passed along the verge of a wood. The conditions were ideal for leeches, which we had not encountered so far, and there were many of them in evidence. I had read a great deal about the loathsome habits of these creatures, and all the worst that I had read proved true. They are small worms of the family *Hirudinea*, of which there are many genera. They have two suckers, one at each end, and they move by looping like a caterpillar. Their sense of smell is extremely keen, and they will anchor to leaves and twigs and weave with a slow, sinister motion, questing for a victim. Their jaws can be moved independently, each on a separate arc, so the bite leaves a triradiated scar, and once they have gained a hold they are difficult to remove, until they fall away of their own accord when sated with blood: hence the expression " cling like a leech," which has not found its way into common usage by accident. It is said that the most effective ways of removing them are by applying a lighted cigarette, or salt, for which they have a natural aversion. They will find their way in a remarkable manner through the thickest of closely knitted stockings, even if two pairs are worn, and they can so attenuate their bodies that they can pass with ease through the lacings of boots or between the overlaps of puttees if these are not tightly bound.

Although I carried small bags of salt, with strings to attach them to the wrists, I found it better on this occasion to keep a sharp eye out for them and remove them before they had gained a hold on the flesh. I had put on boots as a protection against them, but I noticed that many Sikkimese of the coolie class walked barefooted and paid little heed to the bites, though blood flowed freely from their heels and ankles. The strategy of the repulsive little creatures is to attack from the rear, sensing this to be the blind side, and occasionally we would warn the man ahead of a new encroachment, and he would brush the leech away before it could do any harm.

For some reason unknown to me, three of our donkeys had been left behind at Mangan, but the two remaining animals seemed to move more quickly and surely with their double loads, though progress was painfully slow at all times and I was given to wonder how large expeditions with their unwieldy trains of pack animals contrived to make any headway at all. With our two animals it was bad enough. How much worse must it be with hundreds to coax along.

Our progress, despite its irritating slowness, was faster than it might have been because of the sheer insistence of one of the animals for keeping in the lead, as though it was a matter of prestige to do so. It did not want to hurry, or to be hurried, but it simply refused to relinquish the lead. Both were adorned with yak-hair tassels, and their collars were fitted with small silver bells. The constant tinkle of the bells was never out of hearing, like the roar of the Tista River, from which we wandered occasionally only to return. The slower of our two animals was so diminutive that it could scarcely be seen beneath its load, and when walking behind I smiled at the thought of three men and two animals heading for the highest mountain in the world.

The three Sikkimese who were supposed to be in charge of the animals were carefree, good-humoured fellows, and I was pleased to find that they did not spit like Indians do. One of the men, who obviously had the

greater authority, was strikingly handsome, with a light brown face and
a surprisingly fair body, no more coloured than my own after ordinary
periods of sunbathing. He wore a large homespun robe gathered in at the
waist by means of a thong. Very often he would use only one sleeve of
this garment, leaving the other to hang loose, or he would wear it in the
form of a skirt, with the upper part of his body wholly exposed. All had
jet black hair, parted in the middle and plaited at the ends.

The scenery throughout is on a gigantic scale, and most impressive,
but it is not really beautiful in the sense that the Kivu region of the Belgian
Congo is beautiful. There are not the same restful greens and browns, or
the same quiet, lazily-running streams. The mountains are not friendly,
perhaps because they are too cold, and the entire landscape lacks the intimate
warmth of Central Africa. There are no wide open savannahs to give
relief, and the forests themselves are inhospitable places, whereas in Africa
they form sanctuaries for those who go to them. Perhaps that is the real
difference: the forests of Sikkim are dead in the sense that they lack
Africa's wide variety of forest fauna.

The sun never really showed itself during the day, and by the time we
reached Singhik, our next stopping place, the rain had set in once more.
As usual upon arrival at any Dak bungalow I looked over my temporary
abode, though each was basically the same. The most noticeable difference
was a deterioration of standard the farther we went from Gangtok, but this
was understandable enough and caused me no concern. At each stop there
would be the same procedure, which began with the lighting of a fire and
went on to the preparation of a meal and innumerable cups of hot tea.
Ang Dowa was already performing well as a cook, and he surprised me by
using a few English cooking terms.

As when travelling to the Congo for my Virunga undertaking, I had
only one very inadequate map, and as in the Congo, I referred to it as little
as possible because of the agony of finding out what a short way we had
gone compared with what lay ahead. This was of course an irrational
policy, and at Singhik I felt compelled to discuss matters with Tenzing. It
seemed to me that our rate of progress might be stepped up, but Tenzing
pointed out the impossibility of doing so while still in Sikkim. Beyond
the border, he said, we might be able to improve upon the time taken by
the 1936 Everest expedition by covering the distance to Rongbuk in 11 or
12 days instead of 18 or 20. This was as far as we could go with any plans
for the future, and I was pleased to fold the map and put it away. There

is nothing I like better than to browse over maps under more normal circumstances, but at the time a map seemed nothing more than a record of failure to move far enough or fast enough.

Snow-capped mountain peaks ranging up to 18,000 ft. were visible from two sides of the bungalow as we arrived, but within a short time they disappeared. The rain increased and started to come through the roof so copiously that no matter where my bed was arranged it stood beneath drips of water. In the evening and through most of the night a storm raged with an intensity that I have never known to be equalled. Vivid flashes of lightning were followed by prolonged thunder which roared and reverberated between high mountain peaks and swept down in a crescendo of sound to the ravines. It was a powerful display of natural forces, and more than slightly terrifying.

The storm had spent itself before morning, and by the time we had reached a huge sloping rock which ran to a great height at a steep and unvarying angle, smooth and entirely bare, conditions were ideal for photography. Foolishly I decided to conserve my rather meagre stock of films, and I took the same line when we crossed two bridges made entirely of untrimmed logs and twine and situated at widely distant points where deep channels had been cut in the same rock feature.

At what height did the rock terminate, and was there thick forest beyond it? What had caused the enormous disturbance which had led to its exposure? How long had it been lashed by the fury of storms, to be worn so smooth and cut so deep? I pondered all the questions, to which there could be no solution, without pause for investigation, though part of my inquiry was answered when I looked down to the river-bed and found it strewn with fine sand, like powder, which told of centuries of slow wear from the elements.

Waterfalls, one having a sheer drop of more than 250 ft., could be seen on the opposite bank of the Tista, and snow peaks stood out in the far distance to the north-west. At daybreak I had seen them turned to a fiery red and yellow by the first rays of sunlight, but as the morning advanced the colours softened and the snows seemed to recede. Every detail of the landscape was rugged and grandiose—awe inspiring, but not really beautiful, for in Sikkim all beauty is marred by excess.

Shortly beyond Soong, which we passed without a halt, we crossed to the west bank of the Tista by a tumbledown wooden bridge suspended from two steel wires. The course of the river, which wound considerably, was lined by tropical forest and large rounded boulders, and here also the swiftly running waters had made a bed of fine sand. We continued along a narrow ledge where landslides had taken place and others were imminent, and as we did so it began to rain heavily. It burst upon us so suddenly that we were wet through before we could think of protecting ourselves in any way, and so we charged forward blindly with no thought but that of reaching the next Dak bungalow at Chungtang as quickly as possible. We had not been troubled by leeches earlier in the day, so all I wore was a pair of shorts, a khaki shirt, stockings and rope-soled shoes.

For at least two hours we plodded on at the pace of our pack animals, drenched and miserable. My own discomfort was so great that I paid no more than passing heed to a few sharp stabs of pain around my ankles. The path became excessively slippery, and it was with relief that we came into sight of a white bungalow on the far bank and crossed to it over another, but finer, suspension bridge. Even so, we spent fully twenty minutes between sighting the bungalow and reaching it, and then we had to stand and shout for the chowkidar. There was no wood ready for us, as there usually was, and we could get none until I had paid over Rs. $1\frac{1}{2}$ (2s. 3d.) for an amount that would only last two hours at most. I was assured that it was the ordinary charge, but it seemed exorbitant as forest lay around on all sides.

Nothing would go smoothly or well this day and my discomfort was increased when at last I sat down and removed my wet shoes and stockings. As I peeled them off a revolting sight met my eyes. From my left foot three horribly bloated leeches fell away and I hastened to remove the second stocking, which revealed two more. One in particular had so gorged itself that it had become distended to several times its normal size. In fact its skin was so taut under the expanding pressure of blood that the slightest tap with a shoe caused it to burst and disgorge its contents in an astonishingly large pool on the floor.

I have said that I felt sharp stabs of pain in the region of my ankles while on the way to Chungtang. This was certainly the bite of leeches, but some have claimed that the bites cannot be felt. I was soaked with rain at the time, and this may have provided a cause for added pain when bitten. Otherwise I can offer no solution—but I certainly felt the leeches on this occasion. The bites turn purple and itch, and take a long time to heal because of the anti-coagulant which is introduced from saliva glands and walls of the gut of the leeches.

XVIII. *The Ways of the Needy*

I WAS not sorry to be away from Chungtang at early morning. The sun rose behind a mountain which reminded me strongly of Kilimanjaro and at the time of our moving away there was a biting westerly wind. For once we were able to follow along the river bed where it was wide and stony, and after crossing the river at one point we came to a drowned valley which could not have been more than a mile from Chungtang. There was a good deal of water and it was obviously deep in parts, as shown by trees which had been surrounded but still remained erect, though they had lost all but the stumps of their branches. They looked grotesque in their unnatural setting—quite unlike the twelve terns which idled on the placid water, who were thoroughly at home and did not take to flight at our approach. There was unmistakable evidence of a fairly recent landslide in the vicinity, and Tenzing assured me that the valley had been inundated within the past three years. There were snow-capped peaks ahead, feeding the lake, and the whole scene might have been in the Canadian Rockies. This impression was increased by the pine trees clustered on the mountain sides. I felt the water and toyed with the idea of a swim, but we were pressed for time and so I only made a mental note to refresh myself with a plunge before reaching Chungtang on our return.

We skirted the expanse of water to the left by taking to a narrow, muddy trail cut in an almost perpendicular cliff. This took us to another low bridge, and afterwards we left the river for a while to enter a wide glade. Here, I was told, Sikkimese and Tibetan armies had met in open battle some 60 years earlier. It was the first time we had been out of sound of the river, and the silence was most impressive. There was now no sound except the rustling of leaves in the slight breeze. The glade was not at its best at this time of year, but a few magnolia trees bore magnificent cream-coloured flowers, and the short grass was sprinkled here and there with primula and orchids. Rhododendrons could be distinguished by their leaves, but they were not in flower. We rested the donkeys, allowing them to graze for half an hour without their loads.

The glade might have been a paradise, but it was infested with leeches. Whenever I sat down they would advance in hordes, wriggling and weaving in their sinister fashion, and most of my time was spent in retreating from them, taking up a fresh position and then retreating again. This was Mishtong, and for all its delights, I was pleased when the half-hour was up and we were on our way again, this time heading for Lachen, which was as far as the Sikkimese and their two remaining pack animals were intending to go.

Just before we reached the far end of the glade I saw my first yaks. There were eight of them, but as they were being driven in the opposite direction I did not see much of them and will leave my description of their appearance and habits until the time when they become directly involved in the story, as pack animals during a later part of our journey.

A steep ascent, often with steps cut into plain earth or into rock, led us by a series of " S " bends to an entirely new scene at a greater altitude than we had been hitherto. We had gained a lot of height in a very short time and had left the tropical forest and its intervening glade behind as though they were worlds apart. To our left was a wide expanse of burnt grassland, rising slightly, while the mountain side sloped gently to our right before falling away in a well rounded curve. A quarter of a mile farther on we walked through masses of mauve primula (a small flower of the primrose *genus*) which were in such profusion that we could not help treading them underfoot where the trail was ill-defined and narrow. A small belt of coniferous forest came next, and when we emerged from it we were in sight of Lachen.

Two features in the landscape attracted my attention at first glance. Dominating the whole scene was a large monastery set far up on a steep slope which showed progressive signs of barrenness with increasing altitude. Overlooked by the monastery was a village of about 100 houses, which were mostly of wood, and excessively drab because they were unpainted and so alike in size and structure. What attracted my attention here was not the houses so much as the rows of apple trees amongst which the houses were arranged in regimental lines. These Lachen apples are renowned in a small way for their excellent flavour, but unfortunately the trees were bare, although the season here appeared to be somewhat different from that of the forested parts below, as judged by the display of primula.

Another time, I hoped, my arrival would coincide with the fruit-picking season, which is in the months of September and October.

The Dak bungalow, with red roof and white walls, was remote from the village by about the same distance as that which separated the village from the monastery. As usual, the chowkidar had to be called up: these people were never at hand when wanted and never had a fire, or even firewood, waiting. After one had been summoned there was the important matter of pack animals for use between Lachen and our next stopping place, Thang-gu, to be considered. Also there was payment to be made for the donkeys which had been with us for four stages of our outward journey. These were paid for at the rate of Rs. 12 per day, settled before our departure from Gangtok. There were no animals in sight anywhere, and for all I knew Lachen might have been entirely deserted by man and beast. So how were we to get from Lachen onwards?

Tenzing solved the problem by arranging to keep the donkeys and one of the Sikkimese with us for the next two stages of our journey, which would take us within striking distance of the Tibetan border. The charge would be Rs. 36, and Tenzing urged me to accept the offer, otherwise we might be stranded where we were for several days. I complimented Tenzing on his efforts and gave my consent readily, albeit with mixed feelings. The charge was reasonable enough as compared with what we had paid so far, but the donkeys were beginning to get on my nerves. They had been less bothersome of late because they had become accustomed to their loads, but they were still dreadfully slow.

At the same time, I bought a couple of extra blankets from the Sikkimese, and a chicken. I thought it essential to have a little fresh meat whenever possible, but the bird was even tougher than the one I had received as a gift from Chief Tomasi Sebukweto. At Rs. 3 it was a dead loss. I handed it back practically untouched to Ang Dowa, but it was impossible to gather from his inscrutable face if he was pleased to have it for his own consumption or if he accepted it as a slight to his own ability as a cook. However, I made it clear that I would buy no more chickens.

We remained very much to ourselves while at Lachen, and were off early in the morning. There was no need as yet for real secrecy, but our movements might have become suspect if it became widely known that we were intending to go beyond Thang-gu, where there is the most northerly of the Dak bungalows, and beyond which travellers do not as a rule proceed unless openly heading for Tibet.

I had already gained great confidence in Tenzing, both as a guide and as an expert in his handling of animals, at which his two years as a jockey stood him in good stead. He was a handsome fellow with a ready smile and flashing white teeth. His eyes could not be described as oblique, but they were slightly hooded and the lids came to a point at the outer corners. Otherwise, his features could not be said to be typically Mongolian. His jet black hair was swept directly back at all points, forming an oval from ear to ear. His nose was finely, almost perfectly, moulded. I was surprised and rather pleased to learn that he did not smoke at all. My pleasure in this respect sprang from my belief that the margin between success and failure on Everest would remain so small that the slightest detail must be taken into account.

Ang Dowa was not by any means handsome, and did not smile so freely. His hair also was extremely black and was swept back, but it came down in a slight " V " at the centre of his forehead and otherwise formed a square and not an oval. His cheek bones were high and his eyes rather pouchy, but his nose was flattened. No, he was not handsome by any stretch of imagination, but he had a completely frank and honest look about him. Also he had a remarkable popularity, perhaps because he had conversational powers of which I knew little if anything. He had nothing like the intelligence of Tenzing, but he talked much more.

I had a growing admiration for both men, but for Ang Dowa I always had a feeling which is difficult to explain. It may have been a touch of pity, because when things went wrong I would often think, " Poor Ang Dowa." Why I should have felt this way about him I do not know, unless it was that I had a presentiment of his early death. This may sound far-fetched, but the truth is that I held both men in very high esteem, yet for Ang Dowa there was always that underlying tinge of sadness and pity.

Shortly after leaving Lachen, we crossed the Zemu Chu on a decrepit wooden bridge which threatened to give way at any moment. The river originates in the vast Zemu glacier on Kangchenjunga, and a few dozen yards beyond it is a narrow trail leading to the mountain which will surely defy men for many years to come. The self-appointed leader of our two donkeys kept up his habit of striding into a good lead, whereupon he would feel that, honour having been vindicated, he could stand and survey the ground. Then, staunchly refusing to give up the lead, he would plod along and wait again until the other animal had drawn near. If only we could have kept the beast going we would have made better time, but it had a will of its own and could not be persuaded or coerced in any way. At length my patience broke down, and, after a word with Tenzing, I took Ang Dowa with me and we strode out on our own.

We gained about 4,000 ft. during the day, and approaching Thang-gu we went through snow drifts for the first time. The weather remained sunny and warm, so that there was no need to wear a shirt, and upon arrival at the Dak Bungalow, I lay and sunbathed while my boots and stockings were being dried. The chowkidar was slow to put in an appearance, but I did not mind under the circumstances and remained out of doors after the others had arrived, busying myself by mending a rucksack and a pullover while Tenzing and Ang Dowa carried out similar repairs. We were entirely surrounded by snow, and there were high peaks on all sides, but until late in the afternoon we did not need to take shelter inside the bungalow. When we did so I noticed that the living-room walls were decorated with numerous worm-eaten pictures of fashionable beauties which had been cut from numbers of the *Sketch* dating back to the very early 1900's. They were not pin-ups after the modern style, for all the ladies were very refined and dressed with the lavishness of their period, but until I saw them I had not realised the pin-up habit had such a venerable history.

This was the last civilised abode we were to share for a long time, and the last that would not have to be searched for and bargained for. Here, too, we were at the end of the bridle path. Beyond, there was only a narrow track, ill defined if it was defined at all. At Thang-gu we were 12,800 ft. up, but we had to go much higher before reaching Rongbuk. I could now put away my map and never refer to it again, for the country ahead was not marked on it, and had never been surveyed in full beyond the border which we were approaching.

Now was the time to take stock for the last time before committing myself fully and irrevocably. So, like a miser counting every coin, I checked what was left of my money and then consulted Tenzing. There was less than I had thought, and at the present rate and cost of travel we could not possibly reach our objective, let alone return. It would have been galling in the extreme to have had to turn back after progressing so far, but there could have been no other course open to me without Tenzing's entire co-operation. The position was explained to him fully and frankly and the question put: " Do we go on, or do we turn back? " ' It is better we go on," he said.

Setting off from Thang-gu to a very early start, we had more snow to wade through, and the morning remained bitingly cold until the sun appeared from behind the mountains which had robbed us of its warmth by forming an unnaturally high horizon. Waterfalls and swift torrents could be heard but not seen, and we carried on through verdant country, until we swung left into a transition zone in which vegetation dwindled gradually to a mere stunted growth. We kept on for longer than ever before, never stopping once during the whole of the day, and to pass the time, I amused myself as best I could by practising the conservation of energy to its utmost. I often do this on long treks, especially when there are steep gradients to be dealt with. The object is to expend as little energy as possible by taking evenly spaced rhythmical strides and selecting each footfall with precision. I had eyes and thought for little else on this day because of the general uncertainty. On such occasions it is possible to go inattentively through the most delightful scenery and pass significant landmarks without noticing them.

We came to the partly frozen Lachen Chu, crossed it on stepping stones and then kept to its left bank until we emerged into a wide, desolate valley in which was a small cluster of stone hovels. This was Donkung, according to Tenzing's information.[1] It was situated at the base of a mountain slope which seemed entirely barren, though yaks were grazing on it, scattered over a wide area and apparently finding vegetation of some sort that was invisible to all but themselves. Tenzing went from one hovel to another while I waited, miserably cold and anxious. We had our tents, but we preferred not to use them if at all possible because of the time that would be taken in making and breaking camp. The sun had disappeared behind the mountain slope and a cold wind had sprung up from which there was no protection. Tenzing seemed to be engrossed in tediously protracted arrangements but eventually he beckoned me to the last of a line of four ramshackle hovels, where he stood talking to a Tibetan woman. The room was unoccupied and we could have the use of it for a small charge.

"It is the only hotel available," said Tenzing without a trace of a smile.

I looked inside, but it was so dark that at first I could see nothing. The only light came through the low opening, in which there was no door,

---

[1] I have seen the name given elsewhere as Gyagong and Gayokang, but I am keeping to Tenzing's version, right or wrong. He repeated the word for me many times, and I could make nothing of it but Donkung, which is far from either Gyagong or Gayokang in pronunciation.

and in between the stones. As my eyes became accustomed to the gloom, I discerned the carcase of an animal hanging in the corner to my left. I went inside, bumping my head as I did so and bringing down a shower of dirt. The room was about 10 ft. square and so low that I could not stand upright without bringing my head into contact with the ceiling and unsettling more dirt. The floor was of bare earth. A woman entered and began to sweep, using a bunch of faggots and disturbing the dust in clouds. She kept it in partial check by spitting to left and right. I hurried outside, catching my head again and releasing more dust.

When the woman had finished sweeping, a fire was kindled in the centre of the floor by bringing in glowing embers from another fire. Fresh fuel was brought in by the woman, who appeared to be caretaker, or had appointed herself for this occasion. It consisted of dried cakes of yak dung which she carried in a fold of her apron. My bedding was arranged along the east wall, but I could not take refuge from the biting wind because each time I tried to enter the smoke would drive me outside, gasping and choking and blinded with tears. Tenzing and Ang Dowa did not fare any better, and it was long before we could start to prepare a meal, for which we were well ready, having gone the entire day without anything to eat and with nothing but river water to drink. The night was torture and I hardly slept at all.

In the morning, we bade farewell to the Sikkimese and his donkeys. He had spent the night in another hovel, and judging from the hour of his departure he intended making the entire return journey to Lachen in a single day. The feeling of solitariness when he had gone was depressing, for it meant that we were being left in this desolate valley without any means of transport. Tenzing, who had been out on an early foray, came back to say that we must be prepared to leave in company with a party of Tibetan traders who were bound for the first village beyond the border. The thought of getting away so quickly was heartening, because I was convinced that no place in the world held greater discomfort than Dunkung. Little did I know!

I became very depressed again when Tenzing announced later that negotiations with the Tibetan traders had broken down and we would be forced to remain until some other arrangement could be made. I saw the traders preparing to leave with about a dozen yaks, and it was not clear to me why they refused to allow us the privilege of going on with them. But refuse they did, to the accompaniment of a few obviously rude words.

Tenzing, having used all the persuasiveness at his command, had become silent, and his face showed displeasure. Ang Dowa scowled, and at one particularly ugly moment I thought there might be violence. It was evident that our baggage, which sprawled on the ground, was not too much of an extra burden for the yaks, but the Tibetans remained adamant, even when my own mute pleadings were added in a last vain attempt to save the situation. The only possible deduction was that their suspicions had been aroused: either this, or they were wanting to demonstrate their power by refusing to help, and by doing so had involved themselves in this show of truculence.

When they had gone, the place seemed very empty; there were no yaks left that I could see, and from this I gathered that we were doomed to remain unless other traders came in and proved more co-operative. At the worst we would have to pack our own belongings back to Thang-gu. It was a frightful predicament to be in.

XIX. *Into the Forbidden Land*

I HAD little enthusiasm for anything, but another night could not be spent like the first, so I set about making my sleeping quarters as comfortable as possible in preparation for a long, enforced stay. We were still in Sikkim, but the small population was almost entirely Tibetan. There were probably 30 stone hovels in all, and though ours was one of the worst it would be misleading to call the best of them houses. The village looked on to the great mountain slope, for all the doorways faced in that direction, away from the prevailing wind which blew from the east, where there was a wide, stony wasteland, barren of trees and shrubs and cut by numerous small waterways. Most of these were covered with ice, and elsewhere there was a good deal of swamp. A lofty mountain, with only a little bare rock visible, stood in the south-east. I thought it may be Kangchenjau, but Tenzing gave me some other name for it which I could not distinguish sufficiently clearly to be able to write it down.[1] From this direction it would be an easy mountain to approach, but extremely difficult to climb.

There was a strong sun during the late morning, so I sunbathed and exercised, to the great interest of all who gathered round. Afterwards I took a towel and a cake of soap and went down to one of the frozen streams, watched by a group of giggling Tibetans who looked as though they had never washed in their lives. I tried to ignore them, but felt very conscious of their glances and their giggles. At a stream which could be approached without wading through any swamp I stripped. Then, after clearing a small area of its thin coating of ice, I took my last complete wash for a long time. I felt cleaner and fresher, but not for long. Going back into the hovel I struck my head, as always, and brought down a mass of

[1] I was able to confirm later that it was Kangchenjau, but perhaps Tenzing did not know it by this name, and used some other by which it may be known locally.

167

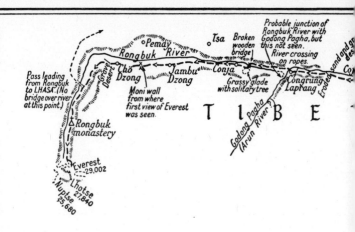

Pass leading from Rongbuk to LHASA. (No bridge over river at this point.)

Rongbuk River

Pemdy

Chö Dzong

Jambu Dzong

Conja

Tsa

Broken wooden bridge]

Probable junction of Rongbuk River with Godong Pagha, but this not seen. River crossing on ropes.

Congrung Laprang

Moni wall from where first view of Everest was seen.

Grassy glade with solitary tree

TIBE

Godong Pagha (Arun River?)

Rongbuk monastery

Everest 29,002

Lhotse 27,840

Nuptse 25,680

N E P A L

Author's route through

SIKKIM AND TIBET
TO EVEREST

APPROXIMATE SCALE

0   5   10   20   40 Miles

Heights in Feet

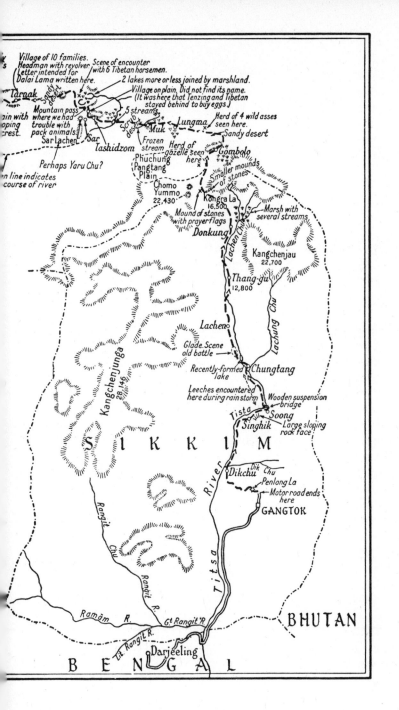

Village of 10 families. Scene of encounter
Headman with revolver with 6 Tibetan horsemen.
Letter intended for
Dalai Lama written here. 2 lakes more or less joined by marshland.

Tarnak Village on plain. Did not find its name.
(It was here that Tenzing and Tibetan
Mountain pass 5 streams stayed behind to buy eggs.)
ain with where we had
oping trouble with Herd of 4 wild asses
crest. pack animals. Muk Lungma seen here.

Sar Lachen Sar Sandy desert
Tashidzom
Frozen Herd of
Perhaps Yaru Chu? stream gazelle seen Gombolo
Phuchung here
n line indicates Pangtang Smaller mounds
course of river Plain of stones

Chomo Kongra La
Yummo 16,500
22,430 Mound of stones Marsh with
with prayer flags several streams

Donkung

Kangchenjau
22,700

Thang-gu
12,800

Lachen

Glade.Scene
old battle

Recently-formed Chungtang
lake

Leeches encountered Wooden suspension
here during rainstorm bridge

Tista Soong
Singhik Large sloping
rock face

S I K K I M

Dik Chu
Dikchu
River Penlong La
Motor road ends
here
GANGTOK

Kangchenjunga
28,146

Rangit
Chu

Rangit R.

BHUTAN

Ramam R.
Gt Rangit R.
lit Rangit R.
Darjeeling

B E N G A L

dirt, which clogged my hair and littered itself on parts of my body which
had only just been washed. A distinct outburst of laughter came from a few
yards away to my right, and out of the corner of my eye I saw a number
of youngsters scampering out of sight. How right they had been to giggle!

A fire had been lit and the room was filled with smoke for which there
was no outlet in the roof. Nor was there any window. It was impossible
to stay inside, but the sun had gone in and the air was chill outside. Tenzing
and Ang Dowa put on their snow goggles and I tried to make do with
a pair of ordinary sun glasses and a handkerchief knotted to form a mask
over my nose. It took the yak dung more than an hour before it would
burn brightly enough to keep down the smoke.

When the smoke had subsided sufficiently for us to be able to remain
by the fire, I learned from Tenzing that he still hoped to get us away from
this awful spot, but that we would be forced to go by an indirect route
over the Kongra La. The nearer route, and the one taken by ordinary
Everest expeditions, was by way of the Sebu La, but Tenzing had been
informed that the pass was snowed up. Also it would be safer, he explained,
to go by the Kongra La and thereafter keep away as much as possible from
the normal route to Rongbuk. It would mean a longer and harder journey
but the risks would be lessened. The towns of Phari Dzong, Kampa
Dzong, Tengyke Dzong and Skekar Dzong, which form the normal
route, would have to be avoided because these places are forts, as the
Tibetan word "Dzong" indicates. We had to sneak in by a back door,
as it were, and keep away from wherever police, militia or officials might
be expected.

The prospects were exciting, but the uncertainty was too great for
enjoyment. I already had a considerable growth of beard which I thought
might help, if only for the reason that a beard covers up a lot of facial
expression and thereby lends a feeling of security. It was arranged between
us that no mention should be made of Rongbuk until we neared the
monastery. All talk of Everest was of course taboo, and whenever necessary
to excuse our presence in the country it was to be given out that I was an
American missionary travelling to some convenient place along the route
which could be changed from time to time in order to suit our advance.
I chose to be an American because I thought that that country would be
more likely to be known by Tibetans than any other.

Our plans were laid, and as though to suit the moment our fortunes
changed when we awoke next morning. A Tibetan had entered Donkung

with a sizeable herd of yaks some time during the night or at daybreak. Where he had come from or what his business was I did not know, but Tenzing lost no time in seeing him and coming to satisfactory terms. It was not fully light when I was woken by Tenzing, and while still drowsy I could not realise that he was telling me to get up, and waste no time.

When I first looked outside there was a solitary Tibetan standing nearby with nine yaks, but, by the time I had packed, he and his animals were fading into the distance and I feared he might be going without us. Everything was happening with such swiftness and silence that I could not make out what our movements were to be, but on seeing Tenzing and Ang Dowa shoulder a load I picked up what was left, and stumbled blindly but willingly over the rough ground until, after rounding a hillside, we came upon the Tibetan and his yaks. Two of the animals were loaded with our equipment and we went on together without noise or fuss. The border lay about eight miles ahead and we had a full journey of about 18 miles to do, but for some reason which Tenzing did not make clear, the yaks would not be allowed within 8 miles of *Gombolo*,[1] the first Tibetan village we would encounter. How we were to proceed beyond the 8-mile limit was a mystery to me, and I did not know how the border would be demarcated or if it would be manned in any way.

We started to climb in earnest along a narrow, stony path, and I thought of a current hit tune, *Don't fence me in*, as giant snow-clad peaks closed in on us, though it was we who were advancing towards them. Far away to our right was a mountain, higher than the others, which I did not know by name, and nestling at the foot of it was a long, narrow tarn, or lake. Some waterfowl, of a species which could not be distinguished from so far away, were drifting lazily in one corner. It was a wonder that the water should be free from ice, but it completely astonished me that birds should be content to remain in the vicinity. We turned to the left, and a feeling akin to claustrophobia gripped me, for not only did we have the mountains hemming us in but we were rising above the snow line, and so had to

---

[1] It is necessary to explain—even if only as a safeguard to my own integrity—that I had no guide as to the real spelling of some of the place names, etc., along the little-known route which we followed through Tibet. It must be borne in mind that I was without a map, and indeed there is no comprehensive map in existence to this day. Nor had I any knowledge of the Tibetan language. At the time I had no check beyond the constant repetition of a word by Tenzing, though I have since been able to align my spelling of certain place-names with that of other authorities. Apart from this, my spelling of place names, rivers and so forth must remain phonetic. In such instances, as with Gombolo, the word appears for the first time in italics, after which it is given in ordinary roman type.

contend with the shortening of breath which comes with increasing altitude.

Lower down, in line with the tarn, there had been short, tufted grasses, tending in parts to be morassy, but as we went on there was nothing but loose stones, completely bare and without the semblance of a defined pathway. Then we came to a mound of large stones, built up to a height of about 3 ft. In the centre, leaning to the west under the effect of the constant wind, were a number of tattered prayer flags attached to slender sticks. Smaller piles of stones lay to left and right. Tenzing confirmed that this was the border as defined at Kongra La, the 16,500 ft. pass leading from Sikkim to Tibet.

We pressed on at the speed of our yaks, never pausing. To our right I noticed a fine group of mountains, one entirely covered with deep snow. There was not a sign of bare rock to be seen from summit to base, even where its sides were vertical. It rose from the bare plain like an unironed sheet billowed out by the wind. Another unclimbed monster had a rounded peak and a sharp spur, both hidden under a thick mantle of glistening white snow. They were chill, forbidding mountains. Although for the most part covered with snow, they were, in essence, naked. Far too naked to be beautiful, much too cold for affection. But they inspired respect, awe, amazement. Ahead lay a desert of small stones.

We were in Tibet.

I did not spare a thought for right or wrong at the time. There are some who will criticise me, as some may have done already, but who are they to judge if they cannot see beyond a mound of stones set in place by men?

I suffer from no misgivings where my deceptions are involved. It is undeniable that I violated a code of honour when I put my name to a slip of paper bearing the words: "I promise on my word of honour that I will not cross the frontier into Tibet, Bhutan, or Nepal." [1] I was, if you like, a trespasser without heed for any political and religious ethics, but I was not entering to conquer a country or to subjugate its people. I was a traveller pledged to be true to an ideal which, rightly or wrongly, I held to be as lofty as the highest political or religious code. Are not the real wrongdoers those who place the tools for crime into the hands of others? I recall the words of Sven Hedin, that great explorer who entered Tibet before my time. His view on the subject was as follows: "I laughed heartily

[1] The actual words of the declaration signed on 19/3/1947 in the Darjeeling Improvement Fund Office.

at those amiable diplomats, who wrote laws for me at their green
tables. . . . I would travel in disguise."

And Marco Polo, could he have undertaken his incredible journeys
to-day? Or would he have found our customs restrictions, passports,
visas, violent nationalism and other restraining factors to be more oppressive
than the brigands, storms and lack of information which were the drawbacks
peculiar to his time?

Let us leave it at this: I do not set myself up as a hero, but neither
do I deserve castigation as a criminal.

The boundary stones were not placed at the highest point of the rising
ground, but slightly lower down. We had to continue for several minutes
before topping the rise, and then we came to slightly more open country
with the beginning of a deep cleft to our right and low hills to our left.
At what was supposedly the 8-mile limit we stopped, and though there
was no village in sight, nor anyone coming in our direction, the Tibetan
went to the top of a stony hillock and peered into the distance. Tenzing
and Ang Dowa followed suit while I remained wonderingly and apprehensively with the yaks, which were big, quiet beasts. Nothing happened,
except that a violent, cold wind sprang up suddenly and I became chilled
to the bone. After a while we continued slowly, and at each hillock, one
of the men would scramble to the top and consultations would take place.
Tenzing said at length that we would go on for four miles. We did so,
and similar hills remained to our left, but the cleft to our right deepened
and broadened until it was a large chasm. Then we stopped finally, and
Ang Dowa, taking an ice-axe, strode off on his own at a very fast walk,
going rapidly out of sight.

When he reappeared he was with a lone Tibetan and as many yaks as
were in the herd with us. Conversations followed, in which I noticed that
Tenzing and Ang Dowa spoke with as much fluency as the Tibetan. The
outcome was an arrangement that our equipment would be taken on to
Gombolo for Rs. 2, which was a reasonable charge. Also noticeable was
the fact that the two herds of yaks were kept apart. This, presumably,
was a safeguard against transference of bovine diseases, but I could not be
so sure of the laborious change-over of loads which followed, though it
may have been a similar safeguard. Our own equipment was easily and
speedily dealt with, but seven of the yaks had been brought from Donkung
with sacks of grain weighing about 200 lb. apiece. These were opened

carefully and the contents emptied into identical sacks which were then sewn up securely. All the sacks appeared to be brand new, so why this time-devouring change-over of contents?

While all this was taking place, I put on two of the most useful garments I had brought with me. The first was a leather jacket with long sleeves, completely fleece-lined, and fastened on the sides by means of tapes. There was an extensive overlap at the side, so that the effect was to give full protection all round without any gaps through which the wind might penetrate. The second item was my " burneeta," [1] which had been with me on each of the Virunga mountains and had been in constant use all through Sikkim. Its original duty was to provide adequate shade from the sun while camel-riding in the Sudan. For this purpose, it had a very long, broad flap at the back and a longish peak, heavily ribbed for strength. The front peak and the back flap crossed at the sides, thus ensuring the fullest possible covering at all points. It was of heavy khaki material, and although not genuinely waterproof, or intended to be, it could withstand rain for a long time without becoming soaked.

When all was ready, we set off again on our journey with the new team of yaks, leaving the others to return to Donkung with their owner. I was pleased to be on the move again, partly because of the wind, which blew an icy blast with almost gale force, and also because I had feared all along that if the animals became unruly they might stampede and plunge over the steep edge of the chasm. We came to more open country, with the hills to our left losing themselves in a wide gravel plain and the chasm widening and running out to a flat which farther on became a morass.

Vegetation was very sparse on the rough ground beyond the hills, but a herd of about a dozen gazelle had gone there to graze and we could see them standing practically motionless as they kept a wary eye on us, appearing to be unafraid but ready to scamper away at the least sign of danger. They were quite near to us, but the effect of glaring sun and strong wind was to make a haze through which accurate observation was impossible. The only notes which I have to offer, therefore, are given with reservation, and only because it is unlikely that any scientific collecting has ever taken place in this locality.

The predominant colour I would define as fawn or rufous-fawn, and this was relieved by a prominent splash of white on the buttocks. Some of the animals had fine horns which, after rising vertically, curved slightly

[1] An Arabic word for headgear of this type.

backwards. Of course I could not be certain as to their identity, and all I can suggest is that they were *Gazelle picticaudata*, the Tibetan gazelle. The species has never been recorded from this part of the country, but that is of no significance whatever in view of the extreme paucity of knowledge concerning the country's wild fauna. I would say that there were no young ones in the herd. All were in obviously good condition, and although vegetation was sparse there was a sufficient living to be gained from the clumps of brown grass which would provide sustenance enough for these hardy animals. Most of their moisture, if not all, would come from the same source.

Our yaks, I notice, were allowed to set their own unchanging, leisurely gait, and it is remarkable that never once during the whole of this day or any other day did I see a hand raised to speed an animal of any sort. Whips were not carried, let alone used. I offer this information as a contrast, for instance, with Africans, who often belabour their livestock in a brutal manner. It says much for the normal equanimity of the Tibetan character, which at all times seems placid, though I have no doubt that tempers, when aroused, can be vicious.

The yak (*Poephagus grunniens*) is most nearly allied to the European bison (*Bison bonasus*), while its next closest relative is the American bison (*Bison bison*). All these are physically peculiar in that they possess 14 pairs of ribs instead of the normal 13 pairs of all other cattle. Taking the American bison as the best known of this subgenus, the yak differs in the following respects: horns slightly larger but of same general shape; hind-quarters more fully developed and higher; withers not so conspicuously humped; the concentrations of long hair extend from chin and throat to the lower part of the flanks and right along the belly, whereas in the American bison the long hair is concentrated on the head and fore-quarters; the tail is long-haired throughout, whereas in the American bison it is tufted with long hairs at the tip only. There are other differences, but these are the main ones.

The yak is massively built, the shoulder height of a large bull being about 5 ft. 6 in. I have seen it stated that they sometimes exceed 6 ft., but this seems an exaggeration, and certainly I never saw one of this size. Although the shoulders are humped, the back is nearly straight. There is no dewlap. The horns are nearly circular in section, curving firstly outward and slightly upward and then forward and sharply upward. There is a tuft of bushy hair between the horns. The pelage, short elsewhere on the head and upper parts, is blackish brown; the colour is uniform throughout.

Wild yaks still exist—at least in the north-western parts of Tibet—but I have come across no worthwhile information regarding them or their habitat in recent times, and I do not know if Tibetans still capture and tame them, or if new stock is reared entirely from the animals which are already in a thoroughly domesticated state.

The specific name (*grunniens*) derives from the grunting sound which the yak makes, though it has been claimed that this sound is restricted to the domesticated breed: arising from this the subspecific name *mutus* was given to the wild race.

The last four miles seemed endless. In no other country which I know can distance be so deceptive. Once when a village came into sight, I estimated it to be 1½ miles ahead. At least an hour later it appeared to be farther away than ever. It was most annoying. There was my first Tibetan village in view and I could not reach it. In my desperation I put my head down, turned the broad flap of my burneeta to the wind, and plodded on. Tenzing informed me that it was Gombolo ahead, and he set off on his own to arrange accommodation and see what could be done about pack animals for the next day. I remained behind, although a brisk walk would have done me good. Being hungry and cold, I had become surly and disinterested in my surroundings. All I hoped was that our first real Tibetan village would offer comfort and warmth. Donkung had been nothing to judge by, for it was no more than a travellers' halt in a sort of no-man's land. Surely I could expect something of an improvement—a degree of cleanliness, rest, succour? So I hoped as we turned from the stony ground to the morass, picking our way over innumerable small water courses.

Eventually it was clear that we really had not far to go, but night was drawing on and all I could see was a huddle of stone buildings on a hillside. None stood more than a single storey high. The prospects of comfort did not look very promising, but even so the gloom hid a lot that would have been additionally forbidding. A few people could be seen singly or in twos, but none heeded us, perhaps because we could not be distinguished for what we were. No dogs came out to bark.

I was pleased to have the cover of darkness, especially as we approached through a narrow alley on the outskirts of the village, where Tenzing awaited us. He led on for a few yards and then turned left by a low stone wall and guided me through a doorway which gave access to a square courtyard where several sheep and goats had been gathered for the night. I bumped my head severely on the lintel as I passed into the courtyard. A dog jumped forward but was restrained, and I was taken to a room directly ahead. Entering, I collided with another lintel, this time bringing a shower of dirt from the ceiling. I heard an old woman in the room give a cackling laugh. It was very dark inside, but I could see that a space had been cleared for me on the far side of the room. In striding over to it I again struck my head, although I was by now making every effort to avoid doing so. The result was the same as before—a cascade of loose dust and dirt and a cackle of fresh laughter. Whatever their manners, I thought sourly, Tibetans have a tremendous sense of humour.

A small wooden shutter on an outer wall was removed, but it made no difference to the gloom and was hastily replaced because of the fiercely cold wind which immediately penetrated. A three-legged fire bowl was brought in by the old lady, together with a basket of yak dung and an armful of brittle scrub. The glow from the fire, which had been brought from another room and was already burning well, showed me a square room entirely without furniture but containing a number of sacks filled with what might have been small grain. A few pieces of old sacking were strewn on the floor.

The old lady seated herself to my left and was watching my every movement with interest and undisguised amusement. She was dressed in a single-piece garment which reached to her ankles, and was indescribably dirty, and so was the room. She seemed friendly, and handed me some cooked corn, the taste and crunchiness of which I rather liked. It was rather like popcorn, and had a slight taste of peanuts. Each member of the household came to peer at me through a doorway leading to another room, laughing and chattering at what must have been the first white man they had set eyes on, though there was but little of my original whiteness to be seen. There was water available for tea, but not for washing, and indeed I no longer gave a thought to cleanliness.

XX. *Early Infiltration*

TENZING WAS worried. The Tibetan who had brought us over the second stage of our journey from Donkung could not, or would not, provide any of his yaks for further travels. Tenzing had tried elsewhere, but without success, and only one slender hope remained. If this proved of no avail, then we were probably doomed. I was assured that it was vital for us to be away before dawn if we were to go any farther into Tibet. Hardly any of the villagers knew of our presence in Gombolo, Tenzing told me, but by morning the news would be widespread and there would be all the more likelihood of suspicion being aroused and our plans being scuppered. We had crossed the border all right because no one had been there to stop us, but there were men of influence here and we must keep away from them. Gombolo was our greatest danger spot. So Tenzing went off on his rather forlorn little mission, leaving Ang Dowa to prepare tea and a meal.

When he came back, I looked anxiously at his face in an effort to read the news, good or bad, but his face told nothing, and for good reason. There was nothing to tell, except that a decision would have to be awaited, and that we could expect it within the next hour or so. We could do nothing but sit by the fire and worry, and Tenzing's face showed as much of the stress and strain as mine. The old woman left us to ourselves, and I prepared a place in which to sleep if sleep were possible.

What happened to bring arrangements to a satisfactory conclusion I do not know. I never knew half of what went on behind the scenes, but it is beyond doubt that if Tenzing could not succeed then no one could. He was indefatigable.

Did the Tibetan who came to our aid with the offer of two donkeys for a double stage of our journey, to start long before daybreak, really allow himself to be hoodwinked into thinking we were *bona fide* travellers? I never knew: but we were busy packing and loading while the stars were still bright in the sky. When we left, Scorpio and the Plough were both visible and Venus was shining very brightly all by itself, dominating one quarter of the heavens entirely. I felt a strange elation, like a schoolboy playing truant.

Our destination was a village with the uninspiring name of *Muk*, and I knew that it would not fail to live up to its name. We skirted the long promontory extending well beyond Gombolo to the east, and then turned due north as the stars were fading from sight and the first glimpses of daylight crept over the horizon. We felt a new tinge of warmth, and I was happy to think that we would be well and truly in Tibet by the time that our destination was reached. Our pack animals were as small as those which had taken us most of the way through Sikkim, but they were much faster—rather splendid little beasts, in fact.

At first there was rubble to go over, as when crossing the border, but the stones became smaller and smaller as we went along until eventually we were in true desert with coarse sand underfoot. It was the most terrible sand I have ever known, with the greatest resistance to forward motion. For most of the morning I toiled, as the others did, slipping back half the length of a stride for each step taken. The sun burned with a fierce heat, so that I discarded most of my clothing and wore my burneeta for the purpose for which it was originally intended.

One of the delights of our world is that there are compensations wherever we turn; often it is only a case of knowing where to find them, and having found them, how to appreciate them. So it is that deserts have a small but fascinating fauna of their own, even in the most desolate, waterless reaches. As an instance of this, we encountered during the late morning a hare (*Lepus* sp.) and a tiny brown lizard, much darker in colour than the sand. Most exciting of all was the sight in the east of a herd of four wild asses (*Equus kiang*).

I was thrilled to see them, especially because in Africa the wild ass is one of the very few species of large wild fauna which I have never set eyes on. The African species, which is now an extreme rarity,[1] seldom consorts in herds of more than seven, and in fact I have only been able to gather one definite record of a greater number being seen together. Therefore, although the habits of the Tibetan wild ass are not known, it is most

[1] They are confined, as far as we know, to Ethiopia, where there is *Equus asinus aethionicus*, and to the Somaliland territories, where there is *E.a.somalicus*.

likely that our herd of four was a normal rather than an unusually small one. Unfortunately they shimmered so much in the heat haze that it was not possible to tell whether there was a dorsal stripe or not. (I have come across conflicting accounts and illustrations. In one illustration there is a definite dorsal band, lighter than the main body colour, but another shows no sign of a dorsal band at all. It is as well to point out here that zoological observations and collections have never been fully or properly made in Tibet. Many specimens, and even some type specimens—i.e. those from which various local species became known originally—have been attributed to Tibet although they have been collected from Ladak(h), which is in Kashmir, beyond the westernmost border of Tibet. It cannot be stressed too greatly that there is, even to-day, no sound knowledge of the range, habitat and numbers of Tibetan fauna. Therefore it is necessary to say that I would not like my own references to the wild life of Tibet to be accepted as other than an attempt to add a little of interest to a fascinating but practically unexplored field of knowledge.)

The predominant body colours seemed to be a greyish-brown above and white below. Like all members of their species they showed themselves to be extremely shy and wary: thus, whereas the gazelle had stood their ground, the wild asses made off after surveying us for only a minute or two. Their lively action as they swished their tails, tossed their heads and galloped away, was worth noting, for it is claimed by the few who have seen them that wild asses in general are noble beasts, utterly unlike their domesticated and dispirited relatives. Their usual habitat is in sand dunes and low-lying hills—never high mountain ranges—and undoubtedly they had a retreat of this nature close at hand, though nothing was visible to us but entirely flat desert.

Our own pack animals, small as they were, made a brave show of this desert crossing, but they must have been as pleased as we were to see the end of it. We had worn goggles most of the time, not only as protection from the intense glare, but in order to keep out the fine, powdery sand which flew up from the donkeys' heels. At about an hour before noon, we had another annoyance to contend with. This time it was a violent wind which blew up suddenly and swirled dust devils into motion. We were caught in the very centre of one of these, which nearly whirled us off our feet and left us half choked, blinded and with nostrils clogged with sand. The wind increased in force, and as it did so we caught an icy blast which made us put on warmer clothing. One minute we were hot and the very next minute shivering with cold. There was sand and then gravel underfoot, and as we came into sight of a village there were snow-capped mountains on the horizon. This was the true Tibet of the south—bleak, barren and windswept—a land of extremes and of sudden changes. Mysterious Tibet; Land of the Lamas; Roof of the World; the Forbidden Land: it is all these, but it is, I found, neither romantic nor glamorous.

We rested our donkeys at the village, and Ang Dowa contrived as though by magic to produce some hot tea. In the meantime, the entire populace came to watch, gesticulating and laughing without restraint. In Africa, the natives of remote places will squat or stand to one side and observe all that a white man does, what he eats and what he drinks, with quiet, polite interest. Unspoilt Africans are gentlemen, simple, but dignified. In this part of Tibet there was no attempt at dignity, and I must admit that I became annoyed when stared at and laughed at so uproariously. Was I really so funny to look at and were my habits really so odd that they all had to laugh helplessly at me and everything I did? I would have been glad to have their attention and interest, but they did nothing but laugh and I did not like it!

I did not note the name of the village in my diary. It was a very small collection of rude dwelling places on the northern outskirts of the desert, and under ordinary circumstances we should have stayed here, for it represented a full day's march from Gombolo. Instead, needing to put as much distance between ourselves and the border as possible, we had to go on for another full stage of the journey. If one travels unlawfully, then one must take the consequences. There is excitement, but not peace, for the wrongdoer.

There was an area of swamp near the village, with occasional clear streams passing through it. One stream was of fair size, but the bridge spanning it was in such a bad state that our donkeys had to be persuaded to take to it and then had to be guided carefully, step by step. The swamp gave way to a desert of a different kind from the one we had crossed in the morning. It was a tussocky gravel plain for the most part, but in places there were great rifts in barren, heavy clay.

Again there was the interminable trudge, without respite, and my thoughts, to be truthful, were few. They were not of home or parents, for I had none. They were not of Everest, because I refused to think about it at this stage. The terrible journey, with its outrageous exposure to hardship, filth, discomfort, and its everlasting uncertainty, was sufficient of itself.

My mind could cope with no more. We had no friends, no allies, none to succour us, none to encourage us by word or gesture. Defeat lay ahead at every turn, at every stopping place, at each meeting with strangers. The journey, if we had but known, was forever gnawing at our mental and physical resources. We were not battling on a mountain, but to reach a mountain. The real conflict had not yet been joined, and yet we were striving all the time, with a numbness of mind and body as our only armour. There was never a moment that was free from fear.

Others had gone to Everest before us, unrestricted, carefree, smiling, joking. Existence for some is a vital, prosperous round, with gaiety, laughter, songs, rejoicing. For others it is a struggle against adversity which never ceases, a relentless war against poverty which never ends. For the one there is joy, for the other, sorrow, and there is not one amongst us who knows why.

And so it is with any journey. It is not the journey itself which is of significance, but the circumstances under which it has to be made. The way may be pleasurable if there is no load to be carried, but if there is the handicap of a burden, the same journey can be made wearisome in the extreme: each mile becomes many miles, and it is more easy to frown than to smile. Or, as with us, it is easier to go on than to turn back, more satisfying to concentrate upon the next step rather than the next but one, or to-morrow's many steps.

And so we plodded relentlessly on, seldom stopping, seldom talking, and seldom if ever thinking about anything apart from the immediate time and place. We were the poor, who yet have pride; fending for ourselves, able to give no charity, and expecting to receive none. We were idealists, too. Tenzing, in his quiet, smiling way, and Ang Dowa none the less, and I, perhaps more than either. People like us are adrift from our age, and at times this gives us pride, but always, in the process of our pride, we are being hurt. We are like forest animals whose natural habitat is being chopped from around them. We are, indeed, like the last leopards in parts of Africa—few and scattered, searching for mates, who are also few and scattered.

The village of Muk could be seen long before we came to it, and again there was the awful illusion of lengthening instead of lessening distance until our destination could be seen with absolute clarity. On this occasion my despair was made worse by the agony of blistered feet, and I bemoaned my fate more than ever when it was found that we had to make for the far side of the village.

Muk, set on a small hill, was typical of the villages with which we were becoming familiar. The houses, severely square and practical, were of whitewashed stone and daub. The roofs in all cases were flat, and there was no house with more than a ground floor. Some houses had a narrow decorative band of dark reddish-brown running all round the top. The corners, and occasionally the centres, of some buildings were adorned with sheaves of juniper boughs, fixed upright. I have yet to find out what religious significance they have, or how they came to act as a symbol of Lamaism. I can only hazard a guess that their scarcity gives them value, and this value has naturally come to be associated with religion in a land wherein religion predominates in everyday life. So far we had not seen a tree or even a bush growing in Tibet, and therefore it was not surprising to find wood used only for doors and small windows, and sparingly as roof supports.

Courtyards, where they existed, were bounded by stone walls, some of which were not held together with daub. A few prayer flags were to be seen here and there, but again there was a shortage of timber for poles, and no doubt an equal shortage of cloth. This was obviously a very poor part of a poor country, and there was no sign of extravagance anywhere.

The Tibetan who had accompanied us this far was willing to remain with us for another day, so there was no arrangement to be made for transport, but Tenzing went ahead again to find lodgings. When the rest of us arrived there was a room awaiting in which a fire had already been lit. This pleased me immensely, but I was so excessively weary after our long double march, beginning before daybreak, that I was in no state to register approval of the welcome which lay in store for me.

No sooner had I entered than the room became a seething mass of humanity. Young and old of both sexes congregated in the doorway, forced their way inside, blocked up the only window and peered through gaps between the ill-fitting stones of the outer wall. Their chatter was incessant and their pressure irresistible. Each time they were suppressed and thrown back they would gather force and surge in again with renewed clamour. They were crowded in the building itself and in the courtyard outside, and they overflowed to the approaches in all directions. Here, I am quite sure, they had never seen a white man before.

Efforts to remove them proved unavailing, even when I asked Tenzing

to appeal to them on the grounds that I was very, very tired and wished to
be alone. Ang Dowa had a meal prepared in quick time, and the sight of
me eating with knife and fork—instead of with fingers as they do themselves—brought forth the wildest acclamations and the greatest wonder of
all. It was interesting for both parties, but it was altogether too much for
me and I had at length to order Tenzing to clear them out, with force if
necessary. Yet still they remained at the threshold—peering in wherever
they could.

When my meal was finished I required, more than ever, a little privacy,
this time for the normal functions of the body. There were no lavatories,
so I had perforce to make my way to the wide open spaces which serve the
purpose. To do so meant shouldering my way through the surging mob,
which thereupon turned and followed hard at heel. The only alternative to exposing myself further to their unremitting stares was to wait
until dark. It was already turning dusk, so I went back and waited.

Once the crowd had dispersed, I noticed for the first time that we had
another sort of company for the night. Sharing our allotted room were
four sheep and two hens. At least I thought they were both hens until,
heralding in April Fool's Day, one made itself known as a cockerel. The
noise woke us all, and set the sheep bleating and the donkeys braying.
Altogether I was not sorry to leave Muk.

As soon as we set off we were in trouble. The ground was frozen and
the donkeys could make little headway. They shied altogether at a frozen
stream and had to be helped across. I was also in difficulties with my
blistered feet, and for a while I tried to do without boots. The ice could be
endured, but when we came to sand and gravel littered with spiky seeds
dropped from clumps of a scrubby growth I was forced to give in and put
on a pair of light shoes.

The ground was so level that we did not notice a sudden drop until
we were within a few yards of it and found ourselves overlooking a ravine,
with sheer sides in parts, the floor of which was cut by five branches of
a very considerable river. Our donkeys were taken down a shelving side
and led across three of the streams on stepping stones. The other two
streams were turbulent and much too deep for stepping stones. The
water was icy and came up to our thighs, and its force was so great that
we had difficulty in keeping to our feet. Both donkeys, to my surprise,
made the crossings fearlessly and well, perhaps being helped by the weight
of their loads. We climbed out of the ravine and carried on across the

continuation of what must at one time have been a lake bed. There was a large bog to our right, and in the same direction a long, sloping promontory came into sight.

Then we came to what appeared to be a closed valley, with rubble-strewn hills to either side and a range of high mountains confronting us. Tenzing told me we were heading for *Sar* (he rolled the " r ") but he changed his mind and we made instead for *Tashidzom* (which I put down from Tenzing's pronunciation as " Dashigong," or " Tashigong.") Presumably his change of plan was made in the interests of safety, but it meant that we were compelled once more to spend the night in an insignificant little stone hovel in an out-of-the-way village. Sar lay within sight, and I looked at it with longing because within its boundary there were houses of more than a single floor. Quite frankly, I did not like Tenzing's choice of stopping places, but I was aware as much as he that greater safety was to be gained by keeping to the smaller villages.

Sar itself nestles at the foot of a 22,000 ft. peak which is called by some the Nyonno Ri, though this name is unknown in the locality. Tenzing gave its name as *Sar Lachen*, which is more likely, and he said that Shipton had made an attempt to climb it one year, but had failed. We reached our own village of Tashidzom after the customary, seemingly endless plod, and this time the presence of snow-capped mountains in the immediate background served to give an even more exaggerated sense of nearness. To me it was exasperating, tantalizing, cruel, but the Tibetan who was with us gave no heed to time or distance and whiled away the journey by pulling out lengths of wool and spinning them on to bobbins. He paid little attention to his donkeys, leaving Tenzing and Ang Dowa to rearrange their loads whenever necessary while he carried on uninterruptedly with his wool spinning.

Our abode for the night was the worst so far, although I had thought it impossible to go any lower down the scale. Here there were three side walls only, leaving one side entirely exposed to the wind, which blew smoke and fine particles of yak dung from the fire into our eyes, and when I came to eat, it settled on my food. We bought a whole side of sheep, but when offered a mere $\frac{1}{4}$ pint of milk for Rs. 1, I refused hotly. Besides, it was thick with yak hairs and, I fear, the same filth that was being blown into our eyes. The tiniest hens eggs I have ever seen were offered at a similarly exorbitant price. In all our purchases, I found the local sense of money values to be fantastic and everyone either thought I was wealthy or that nothing less than a rupee existed. This was all the more surprising in view of the extremely low values attaching to their own two coins, the smaller of which, strangely enough, was worth twice as much as the larger one. They were of copper, stamped on both sides with Tibetan characters. They had the equivalent value of $\frac{1}{4}$ and $\frac{1}{8}$ anna, or roughly one farthing and one-eighth of a penny.

A wedding had taken place, and all through the night there was a monotonous chant in an adjoining building. No musical instruments were used, but there was an accompaniment of hand clapping which never ceased for more than half a minute throughout the hours of darkness, and was kept up whenever the chanting stopped. It was a marathon effort, but not at all conducive to sleep.

XXI. *A Chapter of Misfortunes*

WEDNESDAY, April 2, was an eventful and almost disastrous day. We had paid off our wool-spinning Tibetan for his excellent little donkeys, and Tenzing had been able to arrange for another man to accompany us with two other pack animals. These I could not identify at first sight. They were massive beasts—larger than any thoroughbred yak I had seen. They were lighter in colour, and their tails were tufted and rather short. There was not the usual thick concentration of coarse hair on the under-bellies and foreparts. In many respects they bore a strong resemblance to yaks, and yet there were these differences. They were, in fact, a breed known as dzos, derived from a mixed parentage of yak and ordinary cattle. Our loads were fitted to them by means of wooden supports and straps.

We had trouble with them from the very beginning, as we cut across an area of swamp to by-pass Sar. They were the slowest animals we had made use of so far, and they were dominated by a strong nostalgia. I would see them turn and look back in the direction from which we had come, and it was obvious that they hated leaving home. They looked as ignorant as could be and yet they had the sense to know that a long journey lay ahead. They did not submit tamely, but did all that was in their power to protest. There could be only one way out of the valley in the direction ahead, but it remained out of view until we reached the end of the headland on our right and turned away from Sar. Then we were confronted with another, wider valley, barren of everything but a village situated more than half-way across. Beyond was a range of high hills for which we were making, hesitantly, as befitted the mood of our pack animals.

Moving now at right angles to Tashidzom, and out of sight of home, the obstinate animals quickened their pace very slightly. While still a few hundred yards from the village we were, as commonly happened,

met by a pack of dogs which set out to harry us. By this time we had
become wary, and never approached a village without an ice-axe in one
hand and a number of stones in the other. Our armament was purely for
defence, and we would hold fire until pressed, whereupon we would hurl
stones and then prepare to do battle at close quarters with an ice-axe at
the ready.

Tibetan mastiffs are the most vicious breed of dog existing in a supposedly domestic state. I say this categorically and without fear of con-
tradiction. They are about the size of Alsatians, with thick, rough hair and
bushy tails which usually curl over the back. The general colour is black,
with sometimes a touch of dark brown. Many are provided with woollen
ruffs, worn in place of a collar, which add to their fearsomeness. I have
seen it stated that these are for protection against wild animals, but I doubt
the entire truth of this. Only carnivores of similar size would attack without
provocation, and carnivores are uncommon at high altitudes as well as in
settled areas. There cannot be many wolves or jackals (lynxes) in this part
of Tibet, and I would rather say that the ruffs are for protection from the
bites of other dogs in the fierce fights which often take place. Tenzing and
Ang Dowa were just as much afraid of the brutes as I was, and what
appalled me most was that their masters, who were the only ones capable
of controlling them, always stood by without calling them off. Some even
gained a tremendous delight from our danger and fury.

We suffered no physical damage on this occasion, and, when we reached
the village, Tenzing and the Tibetan stayed behind to make some purchases.
I did not like the idea at all, but could not object because Tenzing had tried
without success to buy me some eggs at Tashidzom, and apart from these
there was nothing but tough sheep and goat's meat to be bought anywhere
along the route we were taking. So I remained quiet and carried on with
the irksome task of helping Ang Dowa to keep our two pack animals on
a reasonably straight course.

We passed several herds of sheep and goats, which we had not previously seen in such numbers, and made for a long trail which climbed
steeply up and then along the high ridge ahead of us. There was little
vegetation, and the trail stood out like a jagged grey scar against the dull
brown of earth and rock. From below as we approached, it could be seen
that a sheer drop appeared in places, while elsewhere a considerable slope
fell away to one side. Our two animals, not as stupid as they looked, could
see this too, and they tried every device to go left or right rather than

proceed in the direction of the hillside trail. To our right was what appeared to be a great cleft between two ranges of hills, but there was no time to pay attention to anything but the animals, which by now were leaving their droppings at more frequent intervals, and each time the droppings became increasingly relaxed until they were like water—a sure sign of fear.

I cursed Tenzing and the Tibetan for remaining behind so long, and I thought of suggesting to Ang Dowa that we should wait until they had caught up with us. But to Ang Dowa no task was too much, and together we managed to get the two animals started up the trail, and then, by dint of much effort, to drive them higher and higher, yard by yard. It was a painfully slow business, for the beasts insisted upon stopping at regular intervals, when the leader would take a look downwards and sometimes backwards. There was no room in which to turn, otherwise he might have done so. I became extremely vexed and worried. Where were the men and what were they doing? " Damn it," I said aloud, " you might have known better than to leave us to a job of this sort."

To make matters worse, the loads on both animals began to slip. We had by this time surmounted the zigzagging upward trail and progressed several hundred yards along the traversing section leading to the hill crest. Beyond this point, the trail followed straight ahead with only a slight upward gradient. There was insufficient room for two animals side by side: to our right was a steep bank and to our left an almost sheer drop to the plain along which Tenzing and the Tibetan could be seen approaching, though still far away. The worst of our troubles seemed to be over. Only the loads must be re-secured, then we could drive straight on. So, beckoning Ang Dowa forward, I indicated the slipping loads and he started to move ahead in an effort to reach the foremost of the two animals. Then everything seemed to happen at once.

From a stationary position facing forward, the foremost beast turned suddenly and charged with reckless abandon over the steep side, plunging and rolling. At one time I saw it with all four legs uppermost, in the middle of a complete turn. Its load scattered immediately, leaping and rolling, striking protruding rocks and bounding high before continuing down. The second animal only hesitated momentarily before following its leader in an equally mad descent, rolling over twice and then regaining its feet, only to roll over a third time. Then both animals and all equipment were out of sight.

I could do nothing but watch all this helplessly. Then confused thoughts rushed through my mind. What would happen to the animals? And the equipment? Not to mention ourselves and the fate of our expedition? The animals could never survive their fall, and compensation would be claimed: but uppermost in my thoughts was the loss of my irreplaceable equipment. We would, of course, have to turn back at once with our journey incomplete and Everest not even sighted. There and then my visions of the mountain faded. It was the end of everything.

My first reaction was one of extreme bitterness, but fortunately there was work to be done—work in which my feelings of the moment could be submerged. So, Ang Dowa and I scrambled down while Tenzing and the Tibetan, who had witnessed it all, came up to the scene of disaster from below.

The remainder of the picture is not clear in my mind. Things were certainly bad, but much better than anticipated. The animals, badly bruised, cut and frightened, were bleeding in places but were alive and sound in limb. One was led back by Ang Dowa and the other by the two men coming from below. Some of the wooden fixings were smashed beyond repair, while others, together with their straps, could not be found. Odd items of equipment had been scattered far and wide, but the kit-bags had been arrested before reaching the bottom, two of them because they were tied together and the others because they had become lodged on protruding rocks. I felt a tremendous relief, though it could only be partial because of what remained to be done. In particular, I did not know what the descent on the far side would involve when once we had reached the top. If it proved anything like the ascent, we would never make it.

After much delay, we were able to proceed, wiser for the lesson we had learnt the hard way—that if cattle must be used at dangerous heights they must be pure-bred yaks and not hybrid animals.

Our progress became more rapid because the beasts were by now thoroughly cowed and submissive, but to the end of the climb they were led at the end of ropes for safety. I went ahead from this point and did not dare to look behind for fear of what might happen again, when almost certainly the consequences would be much worse. At the top, which we eventually reached without further mishap, we found a group of prayer flags lodged in a cairn of stones. This is common in Tibet, where heights and the passes between them are of importance, to which considerable significance is attached. At every cairn a stone would be added by each of the men. This was a procedure which was never overlooked. We had lunch here and rested the dzos, which were still frightened and very woebegone.

The descent proved easy, and the view that opened up to us on the far side was the most beautiful that we had seen throughout our journey. The hillside sloped gently and evenly to an expansive bowl, more or less oval in shape and practically hemmed in by hills. Directly ahead lay a flat region of dry sand and grass from which a few small boulders protruded. A narrow trail could be seen meandering through to the opposite side, where there was a chorten, or religious edifice. To the right the ground was mainly waterlogged, with some stretches of water of sufficient expanse to be termed lakes. The fact that there was more than a single unbroken sheet of water rather detracted from the beauty of the scene, especially as there were tracts of low grassy swamp visible, but nevertheless it was all a welcome and a lovely sight.

There was an added pleasure awaiting me when we reached the floor of the bowl and made our way over the sandy, pebbly trail. Here we encountered wild life in several forms—but it was not truly wild. We walked along with hares scampering among the rocks no more than a few yards away and birds settling almost within reach. Pied crows hopped alongside and Tibetan geese, most striking birds with brilliant plumage, regarded us attentively but without undue fear from the water's edge. It was a delightful experience—one of the most delightful I have ever known. The sun was warm, there was no more than a gentle breeze blowing, the going was easy and like Hiawatha I walked among trusting creatures of the wilds. It made me think with sad reflection of Africa, where there is a much wider variety of wild life, but of a kind which runs away from its friends because it has been persecuted by so many enemies through centuries of utterly remorseless slaughter. When we reached the nearest expanse of water, I found it to be well stocked with fish, but as I knelt and peered into the water there was no violent commotion caused by fish dashing to safety. They swam away, certainly, but they did so in a completely unhurried manner and did not go far.

Why this tameness of animal, bird and fish life in Tibet? The explanation is that Tibetans do not, despite the poverty of their land, eat the flesh of wild beasts, bird or fish. Therefore they do not kill them, and their religion is strongly opposed to slaughter of any kind. As a result, the wild life of Tibet has not been hunted relentlessly and so has become unbelievably trusting in the presence of human beings. Tibetans are not great meat eaters at all, and confine themselves in the main to sheep, goats and fowl, and it is even said that the slaughterers of these are looked upon as outcasts who are denied spiritual salvation.

It is noteworthy that in this area of lakes, where fish and fowl are plentiful, we were pestered by flies for the only time while in Tibet. That these insects should occur in the one place where they can make enticing meals for both forms of wild life which prey upon them seems a remarkable provision of nature.

So much for our pleasurable interlude, and now back to the trials and tribulations of the journey, for our troubles of this day were by no means over.

We passed the chorten without stopping, and I did not ask about its significance. It was a solidly built stone structure of cubic formation and was probably a monument covering the remains of some local deity. It stood at the very edge of the water, and there was a single prayer flag to one side.

We had not proceeded far beyond the chorten when a great commotion heralded the appearance of six hard-riding Tibetans. They broke into view quite suddenly, shattering the tranquillity of our surroundings as they did so. I knew at once that we were in for trouble. The speed and directness of their approach told that, and their faces as they drew near could be seen to be unsmiling and hostile. They reined their horses in sharply, and without as much as a glance in my direction addressed themselves to Tenzing. They were officials of some sort; that much was obvious by their dress, which was the finest I had seen. Their horses were also superior to any I had seen, or was to see, during the whole of my time in Tibet, for they were adorned with a gay assortment of jingling bells and coloured woollen tassels. The men must have seen us descending from the hill, for we were their objective and they had something urgent to say.

Whatever it was, they said it purposefully and with force, speaking rapidly and in a tone which brooked no argument. Occasionally, one or more would wave an arm irritably and expressively. Tenzing was the only one of our party to speak, but when he did so he said little and seemed to be submitting to instructions rather than putting forward a case for himself. He looked crestfallen, dejected, but I fared worst of all because there was nothing I could do but stand by, useless and full of foreboding I could have demanded an explanation from Tenzing, but instead I held my silence. (A faculty for doing this has often kept me out of serious trouble, and I think it helped on this occasion.) Then, as suddenly as they had arrived, the six men galloped their horses in the direction from which they had come. This manœuvre surprised me, for I had expected that we would be forcibly detained.

The tinkling of bells had subsided before I approached Tenzing for an explanation. We had been forbidden, he said, to go beyond the next village, which was the one to which they were returning and the one at which we should have spent the night. So, we had surmounted all obstacles only to meet with this crushing defeat! A deep gloom settled over our party and we went on in silence.

Why had these men wished to turn us back? Why is there so much reluctance on the part of Tibetan officialdom to permit travellers into the country? Does the answer lie in a guileless desire to exclude anti-traditional influences? This is only half the truth. For the other half it is necessary to take into account the fact that wealth, knowledge, and therefore power are in the hands of a privileged religious sect. Those who wield power, both spiritual and temporal, do so by virtue of their own learning and the ignorance of others. How, then, are these powers to be retained if not in seclusion?

I could not shake off my dejection. It shocked me to think that in a single day we had survived one near-disaster only to meet later with a complete disaster. Karma Paul had been right: it was an impossible undertaking which we had entered upon with more enthusiasm than wisdom. It was no consolation at all to know that we had reached so far into Tibet. It only meant that I, as leader, was broken—and what had we achieved?

The wind came on to blow with icy strength, but it could not chill me more than I was already chilled. My mind could register no more discomfort, no more unhappiness, no greater defeat. The miles passed unheeded and all I remember of them is the dull agony of plodding on at the speed of our pack animals. From my diary of the return journey, however, I gather that we left the floor of the bowl and passed through very broken country, shockingly eroded. Often there was thick, loose sand, and at times there were dunes topped with thorn bushes. That, in reverse, is what we met with on our return, but on the way out I bent my head low and saw nothing but the ground at my feet. Nothing, that is, until at one stage we came to a rise which forced upon me a wider view and brought a first glimmer of hope. From the rise it could be seen that we did not have to go on to the next village, but could pass out of sight and by continuing late into the night, reach a village beyond. A double or treble march on the following day would then take us out of danger if there was to be any escape at all. We did not hold any council of war or come to any unanimous agreement on this plan. We just went silently into action, spurred by a renewed determination. A three-quarter moon came up, and still we tramped on, on and on.

We halted for what remained of the night at *Tarnak*, where we met with open hospitality and friendliness for the first time. We were offered the use of what must have been a storage room for grain. One side was completely open and the ceiling was low, but I knew all about keeping my head well down when entering Tibetan homes. Space was made for us by piling sacks of corn to one side. A fire was brought in, already lit in a crude form of brazier, and we proceeded to warm ourselves and to make tea while a crowd of inquisitive Tibetans filled every available corner and congregated at the open side of the room. Something amused them immensely, and I think it was my beard, for it is a strange fact that Tibetans grow little or no facial hair. In a country as bleak as this it would seem advisable to have a thick beard for protection against the cold, but that does not seem to be the way in Tibet.

Tea was made, and I was taking my first sip when the crowd parted and a virile but rather elderly Tibetan entered and was introduced to me as headman of the village. He appeared huge, but this may have been because of his bulky garb, which consisted of a single-piece garment reaching to the knees and making a double-fold across the chest. His height was increased by the typical thick-soled boots with uppers reaching almost to his knees. He sat himself by my side, nearly forcing me against the fire as he did so. Unlike all others he directed his conversation to me, which was unfortunate, for he held his face close to mine and brought forth a spray of spittle with each word he uttered. What is more, he spoke volubly and seldom stopped for translation. There was no retreat from the fellow, and I was forced to remain under a constant barrage of spit. I offered him some tea, but this was a bad move. He obviously disapproved of the taste and it added to his store of saliva. He professed to the age of 53 years and claimed to be the father of 14 children. To one of these he gave instructions and the lad returned with a cylindrical wooden container bound with brass wires. From this, my drinking glass (I drank my tea from a large, thick tumbler) was filled with Tibetan tea. It was my first experience of the drink, though it had been offered to me on previous occasions and had always been refused because of my squeamishness at the dirt which was inseparable from it. Now I could avoid the issue no longer.

The tea was extraordinarily hot, so that I could take only a sip at a time, but whenever I did so, the eager lad came forward to top up my glass. He remained at my side, never once failing in his duty of replenishment as I sipped, reluctantly at first, and tried to avoid the thick scum on top. The brew is made by adding butter (often rancid), salt and soda to preheated brick tea. The mixture is then churned in its cylindrical container by means of a ramrod with a circular disc at its lower end. The taste has to be acquired, and though I did not really like it at first, I soon came to prefer it for the warmth and energy which it provided. Its high fatty content makes it valuable in the cold climate of Tibet, and it was only a matter of time before I treated the scum and its inevitable sprinkling of yak hair and yak dung with scant regard.

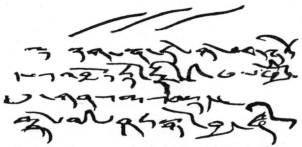

Facsimile of letter written by the headman of Tarnak village. As in Sanskrit, the writing is from left to right. It was begun in pencil, but the pencilled words were crossed out with the three oblique lines.

The headman coveted my fountain-pen, climbing ropes, ice-axe, stove and everything he could set eyes on, but there was nothing of that kind that I could part with. I do not know what reason Tenzing gave for our presence in the country, but the headman's next act was to send one of his children for a pen and some ink. Then, asking me for a piece of paper, and tearing a square from it, he set about writing laboriously in a script somewhat similar to Arabic. He filled in four lines of writing and then handed the small scrap of paper to me. The poor fellow was under the impression that we would be calling at Lhasa and that I would have audience with the Dalai Lama. The letter, which was a plea for promotion to captaincy, was intended for presentation to the highest Lama in the land. I pocketed it with misgivings. The likeable old fellow meant well, and I meant no deceit. Some day, I thought, there may be a chance to atone with a real favour.

Ten families lived at Tarnak, I was told, and the headman possessed a number of horses which it was suggested we should make use of on our return journey. Tenzing had already made arrangements to retain the dzos for our next day's journey, so it was agreed that we should call on our way back, when we would probably be able to come to terms for a quicker means of transport.

I was weary and wanted to sleep, but the headman sent next for a revolver, which he handed to me for inspection. It was of German manufacture, dated 1916, and its chamber contained four bullets. We were given an ominous warning to be wary of bandits. The headman had caught one only that week and had sent him to the lock-up at Kampa Dzong. He wanted to know if I was armed in any way, but I had grown slightly distrustful and avoided a direct answer. He asked through Tenzing how many men I had killed during the war, about which he had heard, and in order to impress him I replied to the effect that in league with others I had accounted for a tremendous number. There was a gasp of wonderment from the audience. It was impossible to make the fellow understand what an aeroplane looked like because he had never seen one and could not imagine anything of its kind. He took a copy of *The Motor Cycle*, which I had bought in Darjeeling, and held it wrong way up. When it was righted for him he turned it back to the reverse position. He had seen a knife before, but not a fork, and he handled mine as though it were a dangerous weapon.

Before leaving, he hung a large curved sword on the wall above my bed. It was a kindly gesture, but I hoped I would not have to use it.

We were up very early, and the headman was abroad to see us off. Knowing him to be capable of writing, I left him all my loose sheets of writing-paper, and we shook hands and parted on good terms. He was the first Tibetan I had shaken hands with. Our trail led around by a steep gorge and then descended to another gravel plain. The going was hard, but our two animals had settled to their task now that they were well away from the beckoning influence of regions nearer home. To our right at one time was a mountain with a long sloping top of such peculiarity that I stopped and made a quick pencil sketch of it. There was an even covering of snow continuing over the gentle slope from summit to base, but the entire side held no snow at all. Its mantle of white, showing up in clear contrast with the brown rock, was as even and smooth as the icing on a cake. Ahead and to the left was a great mountain overlooking several lesser snow peaks. I thought it might be Everest, but Tenzing said it was not.

At one village we were set upon by a particularly savage dog which persisted in following us, snarling and barking, but never coming within striking distance, though it would have sprung upon us in an instant if we had relaxed our watchfulness. As Marco Polo said, " They have also very large mastiffs, as big as donkeys, which are capital at seizing wild beasts." The trouble was that there were insufficient wild beasts for them to seize, so they turned upon us.

On the approach to most villages we came to mani walls, which in these parts were piles of loose stones, usually about 4 ft. high. Some of the stones, especially those set around the base, were smooth-faced and had been chiselled to show Buddhist symbols in relief. Whenever skirting a mani wall, a chorten, a group of prayer flags or any other sacred object it is customary to pursue a clockwise course in accord with the direction in which the wheel of life revolves. Failure to do so will incur the wrath of vengeful gods. At first I did not know this, and invariably selected the shortest route, following my own policy of conserving as much energy as possible. Occasionally we stopped at mani walls for an afternoon rest and something to eat, and I was surprised to find that it was not considered disrespectful or sacrilegious to sit on the stones or to pile them with the paraphernalia of travel.

XXII. *Deep Penetration*

WE KEPT to our intention, travelling all through the day and never stopping until the village of *Cojak* was reached. We had seen no more of the " six horsemen," and I could only surmise that they had been thrown off our trail completely by our double ruse. They may have followed us to Tarnak after finding that we had not arrived at their own village, but they could not have done so until next day and by the time they could have reached there, we were far ahead, travelling slowly but without pause. Whatever happened in our rear, we were by now relatively safe from pursuit.

At Cojak we were kept waiting until an aggressive dog had been chained up. It was more brown than black, and smaller than the usual mastiffs, so that I took it to be a mongrel of some sort with strong mastiff parentage. When its fearsome designs had been thwarted, we were led into an open barn. I objected to this and we were then shown to a small room, much dirtier but at least protected. The ceiling was insecurely plastered with yak dung which descended in showers whenever a gust of wind blew with extra force. The old man who attended to our needs had only one tooth at the front and must have been very poor, but he did his best for us and stayed for a while, watching me with a quieter interest than others had shown. Like the headman at Tarnak, he was attracted by my fork and turned it over and over in his hands.

We were not pestered with a crowd here, for we had made a late arrival and few people seemed to be aware of our presence in the village. But I had my own troubles to face during the night when I felt it necessary to go outside, having previously taken some opening medicine. As soon as I moved to the open entrance, there was the sound of a chain trailing across the ground and a dog leapt forward, narrowly missing me. The night was not dark and I could see that there was sufficient length of chain for the beast to be able to reach me at the farthest part of the opening. There was urgent need to get outside by some means, so I threw a stone and made a dash for freedom while the dog's attention was momentarily diverted. When ready to go back, I had to have recourse to the same tactics. It made me furious to think of big game hunters in Africa who boost their own ego with tales of the danger they undergo when facing elephant and buffalo with a gun. Let them stand unarmed before a Tibetan mastiff and then they would have even less justification for their lurid stories!

This was the worst lodging place of all, so I made it my business to tell Tenzing that under no circumstances must we call at Cojak on our way back. Even so, our fate might have been worse, for we just escaped being stranded there. Our hybrid animals could not be retained any longer, and it so happened that our arrival at Cojak had coincided with the head-man's departure for another village where he was to attend an important function. Nearly every available man and animal had gone with him. The outlook for us seemed hopeless, and I was preparing myself to endure further misery at Cojak, when the old man with whom we had lodged came forward with the offer of his only remaining yaks.

Then there followed some uncertainty as to who could go with us. The village was practically deserted by its grown men, and the old man was reluctant to let his own son go, perhaps thinking him incapable of caring for the animals or of finding his way back. If this was his opinion, then he was mistaken. The lad went with us and we never had a better herdsman. Whereas others had left nearly all the work to Tenzing and Ang Dowa, this youngster kept his father's animals under tight control, never allowing them to wander far from the trail and keeping a constant eye on the loads. He stood no more than 4 ft. 6 in. in his great woollen boots and I estimated his age at 10 or 12 years, though he claimed to be 18. His raven hair—as black as can be imagined—was worn after the style adopted by all the menfolk of Tibet, parted in the middle and gathered at the back into a long pigtail. He was never boisterous, but was alert and energetic, and beneath his dark features there was more than ordinary intelligence. He served us well, and never faltered in his sense of direction.

The yaks were sturdy animals, much more certain of themselves on heights than the hybrids we had previously used, and again we made a double march. After rounding a number of jutting hills, we passed a wide clayey river bed in which the water was divided into several idle streams. Later we started to climb, and for two-thirds of the day we followed the left bank of the *Godong Pagha*, a fast, turbulent river which had cut for itself a deep gorge. There was hardly any vegetation growing on the banks and we saw no sign of animal or bird life during the entire day. There was nothing but rubble all the way, but it was fantastic scenery, in places like a lunar landscape. A strong gale blew up, and during the course of it I was violently sick. I have never once suffered from mountain sickness, and my condition at this stage was due more to an upset stomach than to increasing altitude. It made the long journey an agony, so that at times I felt like dropping from sheer exhaustion. I could keep nothing in my stomach, and the wind blew with such force that nothing would remain on my head. Large, icy spots of rain began to fall. There were precipitous drops to the right of our narrow trail, and I felt relief in the knowledge that we had pure yaks and not dzos as pack animals. At least there was one thing to be thankful for.

Towards the close of day there was a swift stream to cross, but the bridge had collapsed and it was necessary to assist the animals through the water. Then we climbed steeply to our journey's end at *Congrung Laprang*, where there was ice and snow about, and also a few trees, stunted and bare, but trees nevertheless, and the first I had seen in Tibet. There were only a few houses, set in grassy hills and surrounded by towering mountains. In sunny weather it could provide a delightful setting, but we were too late in the day to enjoy the scene at its best. Also, I was in dire straits. It was imperative that I should wash, and clean some of my clothing, and for this purpose I was guided to a frozen stream by a small boy, and here I spent a miserable quarter of an hour in a biting gale with the youngster peering at me from the shelter of a rock.

Fortunately there was some sort of comfort awaiting me. We were unavoidably at a part of the route where official Everest expeditions must call, and therefore Tenzing knew where to find lodgings. The owner of the house was a genial, mannerly fellow of considerably greater wealth than any whom we had met before. He possessed land and several horses, and his house had an upper storey, which alone indicated more than ordinary wealth. He also owned many vicious dogs.

Our room was a mansion compared with previous ones. It was reached from the courtyard and stables by a ladder, and was bare but warm. There was wood for the fire, as well as yak dung. Another incalculable luxury was a lavatory. This was also on the upstairs floor, and consisted of a square

room with a round hole in the centre of the floor. Beneath was a ground
floor covered with straw. It was primitive, certainly, but it gave privacy
and was a vast improvement upon the windswept outdoors to which I had
grown accustomed.

In one corner of the room was a woman grinding mixed corns between
two heavy circular stones. A wooden handle was fixed to the periphery
of the upper stone, and at its centre was a hole into which grain was poured.
The crushed meal came away from the sides in a surprisingly fine powder.
Another woman sat cross-legged on the floor, spinning wool. She had the
raw wool tucked under her left armpit and pulled it out with swift, deft
movements to spin it on a stick bearing a small cross-arm. Both women
had their hair caught up in large wooden frames which extended about
2 ft. 6 in. across their heads. I had seen these supports, or *patruk*, before,
but it appeared that only the women of some wealth and position made
use of them. The two women left the room soon after we entered.

The owner of the house, whose name was *Nombi*, made me a very
acceptable gift of ten eggs. These were all the more welcome because
for two or three days we had been unable to obtain any that were large
enough to bother with. He had provided horses for Everest expeditions in
the past, and he made us the offer of two for Rs. 4 per day. These could
go with us the remainder of the way to Rongbuk. We could afford the
cost at this stage, though only just, and I was overjoyed at the prospect of
making use of a new, quicker form of transport.

I was not so pleased when, descending from the loft at early morning,
I was set upon by one of Nombi's dogs after being assured that all the beasts
were securely chained out of reach. As soon as my feet touched the ground
there was a savage snarl as a black form leapt forward. Luckily I had my
camera in one hand, in its case with strap attached. I swung it round in
a frantic effort to save myself, and instead of burying its teeth into an arm
or leg the beast bit into the leather case. I shouted, and Nombi dashed to
the scene just in time to prevent a second attack. I have never been more
frightened in my life.

We left the house with Nombi and a number of others, departing much
later than usual. There was the river which we had followed on the
previous day to be crossed, and I gathered that there was a strange, complicated technique involved, but I did not know what it was likely to be.
It took nearly eight minutes to reach the river, by which time the sun was
already over the hills. This, I understood, was the reason for our lack of

hurry: the horses would have to swim across on their own, and they would take to the water more readily if the sun were shining. The scene was one of stark desolation. Not a tuft of vegetation could be seen: the banks were nothing but a mass of smooth rocks. The river, torrential and deep, was about 50 ft. wide, and there was no bridge spanning it. The only erections were stakes driven into each bank, supported by mounds of rocks. Three strands of frayed rope were suspended between the stakes. At the centre, there was no more than 3 ft. between the ropes and the water. Tenzing, as though determined to do anything but set me at ease, informed me of a disaster involving the loss of a porter's life at this spot during one of the previous Everest expeditions. Nor was it cheering to hear that the 1936 expedition had taken a whole day over the crossing.

Nombi went down to the river's edge to supervise proceedings, and I clambered to a convenient boulder with my camera. One of Nombi's men took an additional rope, which he made fast to himself. To it was attached a stout piece of wood, something like a coat-hanger. Actually it was part of a pony saddle and consisted of a curved and a straight section bound together with yakhide thongs. The man went to the top of a boulder and, grasping two of the fixed ropes, cocked his right leg over and pulled his way across, hand over hand. He went quickly to the middle, where his free foot almost touched the water, and thereafter he had to haul more strongly to reach the far side. It was a feat of considerable difficulty and daring.

A second man, attached by thongs to the wooden slider, went partly under his own traction, but with assistance from the man on the far side. When he had freed himself after landing, the slider was pulled back. This second man then awaited the horses which were taken down and launched with a firm push from behind. They did not take readily to the icy water, but once they knew themselves to be out of their depth they swam strongly, battling against the current, to land farther downstream.

Next, our kit-bags followed, each being attached singly to the slider and pulled across. I watched apprehensively. " That kit-bag," I thought, " contains our tents. If it falls into the river we shall be able to do nothing about it." Another kit-bag would follow, and it, I knew, contained some other item of equipment which could not be done without. The strain of watching was almost unendurable, for the current was so strong and the fall in the level of the river so great that there could have been little hope of retrieving anything if it had broken loose.

When my turn came to make the crossing, I was roped to the slider and then, grasping both ends, was pulled across. My feet went closer and closer to the water, and I was so preoccupied with my efforts to keep them clear that my neck and hands were scraped along the ropes. My neck was saved by a scarf which I was wearing, but skin was peeled from my knuckles. Otherwise the crossing went well. Not so with Ang Dowa, however. Going next, he had a much more troublesome time. He nearly stopped in the centre and at one stage appeared to be in danger of somersaulting into the water. So great was his danger that I took off two pullovers and stood by, prepared to dive to his rescue. Tenzing made a happier crossing, smiling broadly all the way.

Our entire party, which included a man to take charge of the horses, finished up safely on the far bank; Ang Dowa was the only one to get his feet wet.

Then a Tibetan woman, as though determined to take away our hard-won satisfaction and pride, made the crossing *without assistance from anyone*. She made it look very easy indeed, and I admired her courage so much that I readily pardoned her for detracting from our own performance and gave a spontaneous hand-clap. She smiled broadly at this, and Nombi and all the others seemed pleased too. The woman did not belong to our party, and at once made off on her own.

As an indication of the way in which Tibet has remained unchanged for centuries, it is interesting to recall the words of an Italian Jesuit priest, Hypolito Defideri, who made a journey through the country in 1714. He noted that "In passing from one Mountain to the other, you find no other Bridges over the Torrents, than some narrow, quaking Plank, or Cords, stretched across." His observation was made nearly 250 years ago, and the country has in this respect, and many others, remained entirely unchanged.

Nombi, who had been paid his fee of Rs. 2 for the crossing, waved us a cheery farewell and we took to a trail leading over the right bank and then keeping left. Another trail led to a village over to our right, from which a party of men could be seen making towards us. For a few minutes I was afraid, but for a charge of 8 annas we were allowed to go on our way. This was a customary toll, arising no doubt from the fact that we had entered a different province, or district. Our path continued steeply upwards to the summit of an 18,000 ft. ridge, where we stood well above the snow line and had a comprehensive view. Tenzing gave the name of a prominent peak to our left as *Mogluk*. It was a magnificent mountain.

The most exciting sight of all, though, was a strong river winding through the valley below. The mere sight of it thrilled me, for it had the same name as the monastery which was our immediate goal—Rongbuk. At last we seemed to be making headway. At last we could give our destination openly as the monastery, and Everest lay only a step beyond.

The scenery was not quite so desolate as before. The course of the river was bounded with stones, and the hills around were practically bare, but in parts of the valley floor there were patches of cultivation. A village could be seen a long way ahead and was pointed out to me as *Conja*, our next stopping place. The memory of our near-disaster beyond Sar was still fresh in my mind, so the horses were a great boon on the very steep descent leading to the valley floor. They were sure-footed, but even so, I could not lose my fear, especially as I had only just had the prolonged suspense of our river crossing to endure.

There were a few scattered houses immediately below the ridge, and near one of them, I saw a plough of the most primitive kind imaginable. It consisted of three simple components, and the only metal part was an iron tip, or nose, at the fore-end of the ploughshare.

Nombi's horses, though slow at first, soon settled down to their task, and it must have been only shortly after noon when Tenzing pointed to the spot where a previous expedition had camped. This was not the first instance, nor the last, when we were able to compare our rate of progress with that of full-scale Everest expeditions. On this occasion, Tenzing told me, we would again be covering in a single day a distance equivalent to three days of travel for the previous expeditions which he had accompanied. Of course we were going rather too far and too fast: we were forced to do so by a set of circumstances peculiar to our journey, but others, it was quite obvious, had hampered themselves by a lack of mobility.

Shortly before reaching Conja, we crossed the River Rongbuk on an apology for a bridge. It was made of stones and rough logs, and as the last of us passed over, it fell into partial collapse. Farther on, we came to a small but delightful patch of grass. Primula, the only flowers I came across in Tibet, were in bloom. There was also a solitary fir tree, and this represented another landmark, for it was the only tree of full growth which we had encountered—those at Congrung Laprang could hardly be classed as living trees, and were very stunted. The primula were a dwarf variety,

practically stemless, but they added a touch of brightness to an otherwise
unrelieved drabness. My joy at seeing them received special mention in
my diary. It was one of the outstanding incidents of the whole journey,
simple and unspectacular though it was.

My pleasure will not be gauged by reading this account of it unless
some consideration is given to past events, and to my recent surroundings
and mode of living. Since our illegal entry into the country I had lived at
times as a fugitive in an atmosphere of great suspense, and had travelled
hard through every hour of daylight and often in darkness. I had lived in
the very meanest of Tibetan hovels under most primitive conditions. I
had been long enough in the country to forget what cleanliness meant.
Comfort I no longer expected. My conversations with Tenzing were not
really conversations, but mere phrases with gestures thrown in for extra
effect. There was much to worry me and wear me down, but there was
no light relief and never a word of encouragement. There was no beauty
in the rugged landscape. The winds which blew daily were cold and
oppressive. There were certain things which I did not miss—cinemas,
dance halls, juke boxes, radios, telephones, concrete roads and tenements,
automobiles, chocolates, wines, fine clothes. But there were other things
which I missed very much.

It is at times like this when the simple things of life mean most, and it
was these which I missed—the things which are almost too simple to bring
to mind. A wild flower in Africa or England, or anywhere else, could be
trodden underfoot without a care, but here I tiptoed for fear of damaging
a single primula. It was almost sacrilegious to tread on the grass, because
it was greener, smaller and more lovely than any I had seen in Tibet. Each
blade of grass was precious because it was rare and beautiful. The tree
was the only tree in my world, and nothing would have induced me to
injure it by inscribing my initials on its bark. It is only after submitting
oneself to the sort of chastening experiences I was undergoing that one
learns to appreciate and cherish those small, simple things which are often
the only ones left to us.

Our reception at Conja was distinctly unfriendly, almost to the point
of hostility, but Tenzing managed to find a barn for me to spend the night
in with Ang Dowa and the Tibetan who was in charge of Nombi's horses.
Tenzing had a friend living nearby, and he asked for permission to visit
him and to rejoin us along our route on the following morning. I agreed
readily to this, but asked him to be sparing with the *chang*—the local beer

brewed from barley. At Nombi's, he and Ang Dowa had indulged rather too freely, and one of them—I think the real culprit was Ang Dowa—had moaned and groaned in a shocking manner all through the night.

At the beginning of our next day's journey, we climbed to a narrow valley with steep sides and followed the left bank of the Rongbuk which at this time was an inconsiderable stream. Tenzing joined us at a trail which came in from the left at an opening between the hills. Clumps of low, dry scrub grew in patches, but mostly there was nothing but stones, and we saw no wild life of any sort. In time we came to a huge granite slab forming an obstruction in the hillside, and here Tenzing and I climbed up and continued directly ahead while the others dropped to the valley floor which started to widen at this point. It was Tenzing and I who had chosen wrongly, and we had to turn back in order to reach the others.

We had arrived at a funnel-shaped tract in which the valley opened out to a width which left the far side visible when there was not too much haze in the atmosphere. Thereafter, the two sides ran parallel for as far as the eye could see. Tenzing explained that there were two routes, one to the extreme left and the other to the extreme right. The route on the right was always chosen by ordinary Everest expeditions. It was the shorter and easier way, and led to a number of important towns where there were forts. For obvious reasons, we had no choice but to go the longer, harder way. It was always like this, and I was becoming more than a little tired of being confined to trails which led to small villages and none but the rudest of shelters. On this day, it was particularly annoying to see comparatively fine, big dwelling places over to the right while along our route there were tiring diversions and wide sweeps to be made, and nothing at the end but small clusters of low stone hovels. It will give a useful indication of the state of many villages in this part of Tibet if I explain that on more than one occasion I peered and strained, as on this day, to distinguish between an existing habitation, a tumbledown deserted village, or mounds of earth left standing on a hillside by the effects of erosion.

We had an agonising disappointment in store for us when we reached what should have been the end of our day's journey. Tenzing, who had gone ahead as usual to find lodgings, had failed for the first time. We had already covered two normal marches, and now there was no alternative but to carry on to the next village, *Jambu Dzong*, which took a further two hours to reach.

I was utterly fatigued upon arrival, and in no mood to be met by a

completely savage mastiff. Fortunately it was chained. No rope could
have held it, and I feared that its chain would not withstand the fury of
its efforts. Time and again it hurled itself with terrifying strength to the
fullest extent of its bonds, teeth bared, slobbering and snarling. Nothing
could have restrained it from tearing us to pieces if it had succeeded in
breaking free. One of my greatest regrets is that I never photographed
one of the beasts in this attitude. It would not have been possible on this
occasion because of insufficient light, but there were many other oppor-
tunities which I failed to take.

Another unwelcome attention was from a man asking alms. He was
the first of his kind I had seen in Tibet, where there seems to be little physical
deformity to give excuse to begging. Nor was there any sign of baldness
amongst the men, or of excessive corpulence. Tibetans are hardy and fit
because the ailing could not survive in a climate of such extremes.

Ironically enough, we had our best room so far in this village, but the
sun had set long before our arrival, so that we had no time in which to
appreciate it. All I remember of it, in fact, is that it had a window of
sorts, which was decidedly unusual. This was simply a wooden frame
which could be blocked with a piece of shuttering when necessary. It contained no panes of glass, for this commodity is totally lacking between
here and the Sikkimese border.

XXIII. *Our Journey's End*

WE LEFT Jambu Dzong after quite a haggle about payment, for the owner of the room was extremely reluctant to accept Indian money, which was all we had except for a few odd coins. Hitherto our Indian currency had never been refused, and I assumed that it was preferable to the local coinage. Perhaps reluctance to accept it here was due to the fact that the predominant trade was with Lhasa, whereas up to the Godong Pagha, which is bridgeless and therefore presents a formidable barrier, the main trade is with Sikkim, where Indian currency is in use. I only once saw Tibetan money in actual use while in the country, and never did I see a stamped envelope or any form of organised mail service. There are postage stamps in use elsewhere, however, in a variety of values and colours. Papers of different texture are employed, and there is even an occasional hole. They are not backed with gum, and most are not perforated. Genuine Tibetan stamps are naturally fairly rare, and collectors need to be on guard against forgeries which have been brought out in quantity.

This day—Monday, April 7—was notable because it brought me my first view of Everest. Shortly after noon, we stopped at a long, low mani wall, which was strange in that it was far remote from any habitation. Loads were removed from the horses, and while they rested I propped myself against the wall of loose stones and had a light meal of rusks and cheese. Directly ahead of me as I faced due west was a range of high hills, and above them could be seen a pyramidical peak. Tenzing confirmed that it was Everest.[1]

Only the summit was in sight, and from it a plume of white cloud, like snow, was being driven to the east. It was obvious that a strong wind was

---

[1] It has since occurred to me that the mani wall might have been erected at this spot, miles from any village, for the simple reason that it affords this view of Everest, which is lost to sight within a short distance to either side of the wall.

blowing, but the sky was clear blue, without a threat of storminess. Would
it stay like that for us, I wondered. It was equally obvious that we had not
much farther to go, and that nothing but the grossest of misfortune could
prevent us from reaching the mountain. There was little snow visible.
All was set fair for us. Only the wind—it must have been blowing very
strongly up there. Would it blow too strongly for us? I was not worried
—just perplexed. I was neither excited by the prospect of climbing, nor
frightened by it.

We went on, and at one time we were watched by two wolves which
stood together on the hillside, quite low down. Most certainly I was not
afraid of *them*. They could be as nothing to the greater menace of Tibetan
mastiffs.

A thought which occurred to me later in the day was that our long,
hurried journey had been bad enough with the anticipation of climbing
to spur us on. How terrible it would be, if not impossible, with the bitterness of defeat to dog one's footsteps!

We had left the Rongbuk River, but on our approach to Chö Dzong
(which Tenzing pronounced "Cherzong") we came to a narrowing of
the valley, and the gorge through which the river ran could be seen to our
right. Our day's journey had been the most pleasant so far, but our room
at Chö Dzong was miserably bare, cold and comfortless. The village was
small, but it boasted a monastery, distinguished from afar by its dark walls.
There were three windows with stepped awnings. My evening meal
followed the usual pattern: eggs, if any were available, with rusks in place
of bread. Broken rusks were served up as "pudding" by Ang Dowa, who
revelled in the preparation of a sweet course and the use of one of the few
English words he knew. These puddings were of fine crumbs, heated and
mixed with jam, condensed milk or anything else which happened to be
available.

We had only a single day's journey ahead, and I was pleased to get
started on it. For one thing, I was anxious to reach Rongbuk, and for
another, I had been exposed to a chill wind all through the night. A small,
level plain led to a line of hills on our left, and from the start we were in-
convenienced by one of the horses bolting and scattering its load, which
included the tin of petrol. All the way we had been bothered with this
petrol, which we could not stop diminishing in quantity, due to constant
"breathing" when the sun was hot. Also it had nearly been lost altogether
at the time of our misfortune on the hillside trail near Sar.

Shortly after getting under way again with re-secured loads, we saw dog—which had followed us from the village—give chase to a hare along the gravel plain in the direction of a steep hillside. My sympathies were with the hare, which was a large one, and I watched anxiously as the dog gained all the way along the plain. Would the hare reach the hill in time? I was filled with such loathing for every Tibetan dog that my heart pounded with the thrill of the chase, although, unlike the others who were with me, I was not hoping for any kill at the end. The hare reached the hill with little to spare and then went zigzagging up at great speed, easily out-distancing its pursuer over the steep, rough going. At length the dog, seeing that its quarry was drawing away from it, decided to abandon the chase. I heaved a sigh of relief, and felt a sort of personal triumph, though I had done nothing but stand by and watch. It pleased me immensely to see the hare outmanoeuvre the dog and leave it winded to slink back to Chö Dzong.

We began to climb up after turning left into the narrow Rongbuk gorge. The river was iced over in parts, and the farther we went, the more desolate the scene became. The only vegetation was a small shrub which women had come out from Rongbuk to gather. It came as a considerable surprise when the trail widened into something like a road, bordered in places with continuous rows of large stones. Mani walls and chortens became frequent, and it was obvious that we were approaching an important monastery, the more important because of its remoteness. I became excited at the thought of speaking English to the head lama, who, I understood, had gained a useful knowledge of the language from members of the several expeditions which had called at Rongbuk.

It was not until rounding the final bend that the monastery, and Everest, came into view. The mountain rose almost sheer from the valley in an unclimbable wall of rock, too steep to hold much snow. High ridges blocked the valley in to east and west. It was a massive cul-de-sac from which there was no exit other than by the way we had come. The river, which originates in the Rongbuk glacier on Everest, ran through a 40-ft. gorge to the west. The monastery stood to the east, with a village of small stone houses slightly behind and to the north. Scattered prayer flags were set in the mountainside behind the monastery and the village. A monastery at 16,000 ft. almost in the shadow of the world's highest mountain! Here, I thought, are people who understand mountains, people who revere them.

We stopped within a few yards of the main entrance to the monastery, where there was a chorten. Being very tired, I wondered if it would be improper to sit on the ledge which ran at a convenient height. The temptation was great, but I remained standing until I saw that baggage unloaded from the animals was being dumped where I had so far refrained from sitting. Tenzing set off immediately to find somewhere to stay. He was away for at least ten minutes, and when he returned, my first question was to inquire about the English-speaking head lama. My disappointment was profound on learning that he had died since the last expedition had called at Rongbuk. There was no one at the monastery who could speak a word of English.

Our presence caused no evident surprise and we were left very much to ourselves. Tenzing had experienced some difficulty in obtaining a room in which to stay, but after a while I was taken to a white daub building about 20 yards from the monastery entrance. A flight of seven crazy steps led up to the room—I remember the number clearly, for I was always tumbling over one or other of them until at length I formed the habit of counting every step each time when going up or down. Our room was a rectangular one with a wooden trellis set along one side. This was not of Tibetan origin, but where it had come from I could not say. Its decorative value far exceeded its usefulness, for there was no solid wall to protect us from a biting west wind which swept in with tremendous swirls of dust.

Our intention was to use this monastery building as a base camp, going on from there with all essential equipment and leaving behind everything that would not be of use. For this purpose, it was helpful to find that Tenzing had a sister living at Rongbuk. She was rather handsome, like her brother, and was married to a monk. The news came as a complete surprise to me, and I was pleased to know that Tenzing would be able to renew acquaintances after an interval of several years.

The welfare of Ang Dowa did not concern me so much. He was never at a loss. His popularity was evident wherever he went and he always gave indications of an inexhaustible store of conversation. Nor did I need to bother about him on the matter of cleanliness. It was a commendable thing about him that, in his capacity as cook, he felt bound to keep to a certain standard of hygiene. How he contrived it, I could never tell. My own state was disgusting. My nose, under the effect of sun and wind, had peeled several times, and both Tenzing and I suffered from badly cracked lips. My face was grimed with dirt and adorned with an unkempt beard. The cuts and abrasions on my hands, most of them obtained at the river crossing, would not heal. They remained as reservoirs for the accumulation of dirt.

We had arrived in Rongbuk at about two o'clock, so the remainder of my afternoon was spent looking at the great north face of Everest, taking photographs, exploring down to the river and, generally, in taking stock of my immediate surroundings. There was nothing growing in the vicinity—not a tree or a blade of grass, nor any other kind of vegetation. Not a yak, or a goat, or a sheep was kept anywhere within sight. The simple fact was that there was nothing for them to live on—not even a yak could eke out a living from the mountain sides.

Everything, including fuel for the fires, had to be brought from afar. Because of this, fires were not lit until they were absolutely necessary, and we had difficulty in obtaining sufficient yak dung for our own limited needs. The only thing to do was to put on more clothes if bodily warmth was wanted.

Severe austerity—really severe—was the rule. Religion was the real mainstay. It even made the provision of food from more fertile areas possible. The people were preoccupied with prayer and meditation. Wherever they moved, at any time of the day, they could be seen with their lips moving in silent prayer, or fingering the holy beads strung round their necks, or spinning small prayer wheels in their hands.

These wheels consist of copper cylinders, about 3 inches in length, pivoted and revolving round an axle set in a wooden handle. A cord or chain with weight attached is fixed to the lower edge of each cylinder to provide impetus as the wheel is kept spinning with a circular motion of the hand. The cylinders are packed with scrolls bearing *mantras* in small characters. Of these mantras, or " words of power," that of Chenrazee (or Bodhisatva Avalokita) is the best known. It is *Om mani padme hum*, and it has been credited with the power of bringing about an end to the cycle of birth and death, thus leading to *Nirvana*. In a Tibetan work, *History of the Mani* (of Chenrazee), this mantra is said to be " the essence of all happiness, prosperity, and knowledge, and the great means of liberation." In this phrase the *om*, really having no meaning of its own in the Tibetan language, closes the door of rebirth among the gods; *ma* closes the door among the *asuras* (or titans); *ni* among mankind; *pa* among sub-human creatures; *me* among *pretas* (unhappy ghosts); *hum* among the inhabitants of hell. Each of the six syllables is given a colour corresponding to the light-paths of the six states of existence. These are white, green, yellow, blue, red and black, for the worlds of the gods, titans, humans, brutes, ghosts and denizens of hell, respectively. The mantra of Chenrazee is most popular of all, and predominates on the scrolls of prayer wheels, on prayer flags, mani walls, chortens and other objects of religious significance.

Having become involved in the religion of Tibet, I may as well go on to include a synopsis of the history and principles of Lamaism, which is an offshoot of the Buddhist faith as practised in Tibet. The following account sums up the position briefly:

Buddhist influences reached Tibet from practically all sides—from China, Mongolia, Kashmir, Nepal, India (through Sikkim), and Bhutan. There were already two distinct forms of Buddhism—Southern Buddhism, originating in India and Ceylon, and Northern Buddhism, which was introduced to Tibet from northerly regions—and as a consequence, in the process of assimilation, the original Buddhist teachings underwent considerable changes, being compounded, as it were, and adapted to suit the inherent characteristics of the Tibetan people, with their decided leaning towards animism.

Lamaism, as it became known, holds that the phenomenal world and everything in it has no real or absolute existence. All sensuous things are illusory, chimerical. Every sentient being is bound to the wheel of life. The cycle of birth, death and rebirth is governed by the amount of good or evil done. A person will be reborn into one of many hells as an animal, ghoul, spirit or man, or enter into one of several heavens, only to die there and be reborn again and again. This cycle of existence is broken only by gaining eventual salvation. It is the belief that when an incarnate deity dies, the soul, out of love for humanity, returns to earth instead of retiring to paradise. Reincarnation in human form takes place almost immediately. On the death of a head lama, a search begins for the child into whom his soul has entered. When a child is found who reacts to certain tests, affinity is established. (He may, for instance, demonstrate a preference for colours and objects associated with the previous lama). The search may be painstaking and may go on for months or even years until the omens are held to be incontestable proof of divinity, and the child is then installed as abbot of his monastery, though during his minority all temporal affairs are conducted by a Regent.

In a condensed form, the fundamental teachings of Buddha, in which Lamaism has its origin, may be set down as follows:

There is the *sangsara*, or state of *wandering*, comprising a series of succes-

sive existences. Liberation can only be gained when the devotion, morality
and knowledge of the individual are on a sufficiently high plane to produce
the degree of detachment required. *Nirvana* (translatable as *void*; very
roughly equivalent to the Christian concept of heaven) is reached by gaining
release from the cycle of birth and death, in other words, by gaining freedom
from the state of sangsara. All conditions of sangsaric existence are nothing
but phenomena, and all phenomena are illusory and transitory. These
sangsaric existences are caused by a thirsting after sensation. Liberation
comes as a consequence of renunciation of sensation-seeking in worldly
existence. So long as the cause is not overcome by enlightenment, death
follows birth and rebirth death, unceasingly. Each existence is but a continuation, under changed conditions, and the nature of existence between
death and rebirth is determined by past behaviour. This dream-like state
between death and rebirth is the Buddhist idea of purgatory. It is, in effect,
a world apart, built up of misdeeds, and relieved by the good that has been
done. Enlightenment springs from realisation of the unreality of sensation,
and therefore of sangsaric existence. Emancipation comes from the realisation of Nirvana, which is beyond all earthly or heavenly things. Nirvana
is the ending of all sorrow. It is the only reality, unexplainable but nevertheless there to be sought and found.

Tenzing made arrangements for us to visit the *gompa*, or monastery,
on the following afternoon, when our preparations for departure to the
mountain had been completed. From the outside, it looked very similar,
though larger and more elaborate, than any monastery we had seen in
Sikkim or Tibet. It was built on rising ground, and the outer walls of the
main structure were coloured a deep reddish-brown with a broad band of
black at the upper edges. The only relief was a line of small white squares
running right round as a border between the two wall colours. A similar
checkering existed above the window openings, each of which had an
awning. There were no sheaves of juniper boughs in sight. A large
chorten stood within a few yards of the south-west corner. Its square
base was surmounted by a dome from which a long cone arose, terminating
in a gilded crescent symbol. Whatever artistic effectiveness the chorten
may have had was entirely spoilt by four sprawling steel wires which acted
as supports.

At the entrance, a blind beggar asked for alms, and as we passed through
there were three haggard old women walking towards us spinning prayer

wheels. Tenzing led the way up a rickety staircase towards a balcony on the left. A colourful woollen rug was brought out by two men and I was motioned to sit beside a wooden kiosk. The same two men went inside the monastery and returned almost at once with an amazing array of articles which they placed one after another in front of me. There were several complete torches together with odd bulbs and batteries, an alarm clock, an electric bedside reading lamp, a 4-flag bell indicator box and an assortment of nondescript lamps and other articles of Western manufacture. Prominent amongst the collection was a steel cylinder which had obviously contained oxygen. All these things had been left behind by previous Everest expeditions, Tenzing said, and by signs from the Tibetans it was intimated that a little white man's magic was required and expected.

For a moment I was too surprised at seeing so many useless luxuries to do anything but stare. After a moment I pulled myself together, and concentrated on the gadgets, but there was not much I could do because they were nearly all electrically operated and most of the batteries were entirely dead. I inspected each bulb and changed one battery for another, but all to no effect except that a bell on the indicator box worked feebly. The alarm clock was beyond repair. I wanted desperately to help—to do something spectacular—but I could only make despairing gestures in an effort to apologise.

Tenzing and Ang Dowa took off their boots and stood facing the wooden kiosk. Then both men went down on their knees and bowed three times with foreheads touching the floor. Inside the kiosk was a small boy, sitting cross-legged and motionless. He was the head lama, the reincarnation of the man who had given his blessings to members of previous expeditions before they had set out for Everest. I was, undoubtedly, the first white man to set eyes on him. The child, I learned afterwards, was in his seventh year. He was very pale, almost white, but of a sickly chalky pallor as though he had seldom been into the sunlight. He had a scholarly look, exaggerated by his gold-rimmed spectacles. Spectacles! However had they come to be at Rongbuk unless a member of a pre-war Everest expedition had left them there?

Tenzing and Ang Dowa went forward in turn and deposited a coin at the boy's feet. At this the child put out a hand and touched each man on the forehead. They had received his blessings. Then the Regent, acting for the young lama, conducted us into the monastery. It was very dark inside, and unpleasantly cold—much colder than outside. A window was thrown open and the darkness gave way to a half-light. We were in the main temple, a room containing an altar before which sat a large gilded Buddha with hands on lap, looking serenely into space. On either side were similar figures, but smaller and with hands placed differently. In front of the Buddha and the Bodhisattvas stood an assortment of tiny goblets containing foodstuffs—tsamba cakes, dabs of butter and heaps of corn. Prayer books were pigeon-holed on either side and the head lama's seat occupied one corner. In a partitioned-off portion of the shrine was a litter used for ceremonial occasions.

The child lama's mother joined us, permitting a ghost of a smile as she did so. She was a woman of fine bearing and calm, radiant features. We were led to the right into another room, in the centre of which stood a heavily draped tomb containing the remains of the late head lama. The walls of this shrine were covered with portraits of the Buddha in every conceivable attitude—seated cross-legged, squatting, kneeling, standing, walking, running, riding an elephant, caressing a tiger, playing an instrument—there was no phase of his life omitted. A grotesque black ghoul with fearsome teeth was also depicted. Tenzing informed me that these paintings, done on metal sheeting and highly glazed, were the work of a Sikkimese artist. It was not so much the art which intrigued me as the ingenuity of the craftsman in thinking up so many diverse attitudes for the numerous figures, some of which had three pairs of arms set around like the sails of a windmill. An eerie atmosphere pervaded the place, and I wondered what contributed most to this. Was it the silence (for we walked in stockinged feet), or the strong undercurrent of mysticism, or just the numbing coldness?

After leaving the monastery, I photographed three of the population at the doorway to our room. They were ordinary people of no official standing so far as I could tell. One, whom I photographed afterwards on his own, wore the usual style of robe, voluminous and folded at the middle into a sort of pouch. His head was adorned with a pointed woollen hat with folds tucked up inside which could be let down to cover his ears. His knee-high boots had thick soles, pointed and upturned at the toes. Around his neck was a long string of beads and in his hands he carried a spindle with a ball of wool attached. By all appearances, his garments had been worn a lifetime without being washed, and I doubt if his skin had ever known the touch of soap. He was quite a humorist in his rough and ready way, and in this respect was rather out of keeping with his surroundings.

Back in our room, a raven hopped fearlessly through the open trellis, but there were very few birds about. Tenzing's sister came in, and with her I left a form of " last will and testament " in accordance with the promise which I had made before leaving Darjeeling. She also took the money and other few items which we would not be needing with us. Then we were ready. We were not exceptionally fit, any of us, for we had travelled far too fast; and not so well equipped as some climbers when tackling the Alps and lesser mountains. But we were ready in the sense that nothing else could be done by way of preparation. I slept badly that night.

XXIV. *Defeat on Everest*

WE SET off for Everest on the morning of Thursday, April 10, From then onwards we had to be our own beasts of burden. though I carried only a haversack and the small lightweight tent. Tenzing and Ang Dowa packed a large kit-bag apiece, and suspended them from their foreheads by broad bands of cloth. I had thought they might obtain porters to carry the loads as far as the base of the mountain, but for some reason or other they did not do so. Perhaps no assistance could be gained from the monastery, or Tenzing did not want to arouse suspicion by requesting it, for we were supposedly going only as far as the base to make a survey and take photographs.

There was a distance of between 12 and 15 miles of practically level ground to be covered. The mountain lay directly ahead of us in the rubble-strewn Rongbuk Valley. The great north face, with its massive, pyramidal formation, rose almost vertically in an impregnable wall of rock. A climber could have all the pitons and ropes in the world, but he would never be able to progress anywhere near the top in a vertical assault. If the mountain could be sliced through at the level of Rongbuk monastery and placed at sea-level it would represent a difficult but not impossible task. But rising as it does from the height of Rongbuk to 29,000 ft. it is an impossible climb. The head of the Main Rongbuk Glacier could be seen glistening white, but elsewhere there was surprisingly little snow and ice. An arête and a sloping face to the west held a fair amount of snow, but the north face, too steep to retain snow readily, stood out grey and sombre. A thin, white streamer—the renowned plume of Everest—was being driven away to the east, and extended for a considerable distance from the mountain peak. (The Houston Everest Expedition had reported that, at a most moderate estimate, the plume at the time of their flight over the summit on April 3, 1933, could not have been less than six miles in length.)

The various bands in which the north face terminates stood out boldly. An oblique line running at a slight inclination to the east cut off what is known as the " yellow band " from the great mass of the mountain. What appeared as a distinct black band came next, and, above that, the untrodden " final pyramid." This gave me my idea for establishing proof of reaching the summit, if we should succeed in doing so. My normal habit of collecting small pieces of rock from mountain heights could be put to useful effect. Successive pieces of rock obtained from the various strata comprising the summit block would give reasonable proof of having been that far. I could think of no better proof, and still cannot, for the types of rock from which the different bands are made up must be of very different nature to be shown so clearly from a distance.

We passed nothing of note on the way except occasional hermits' dwelling places, none of which were occupied. It made me smile to think of the imaginative but far from accurate advertisements depicting Everest surrounded by coniferous trees. The scene was in decided contrast with the approaches to many African mountains, where relays of men are needed to go ahead and clear a track through dense forest and undergrowth.

It would be difficult to perceive beauty in Everest. It is no more than a massive upthrust surmounted by snow and ice and blasted by strong winds. N. E. Odell, of past Everest fame, once made the suggestion that expeditions to the mountain should be looked upon primarily as scientific ventures, with an attempt to reach the summit only if conditions proved favourable. No doubt his suggestion was made at a time when there was talk of the Royal Geographical Society withdrawing its support because of an alleged lack of scientific value attaching to the undertaking. Certainly, in my opinion, there is very little of scientific importance to be gathered on Everest. It is essentially a mountaineering project pure and simple. It is wholly a matter of man pitting himself against the highest mountain in the world. Nothing grows there, nothing lives there, and the only thing manufactured in the vicinity is intensely bad weather. Everest is sufficient in itself, and should be accepted as it is—a challenge to man's resourcefulness and inquisitiveness.

As we closed upon the mountain, I could not help wondering why the original reconnaissance party of 1921 had tried to find a way, as I think they did, to the west before attempting to penetrate the eastern approaches. The long arête above the Main Rongbuk Glacier probably tempted them, but to me the difficulties appeared insuperable in that direction.

We followed round the base of the mountain, proceeding beyond an open patch where camp is established by large expeditions which need to keep a base camp in operation—a thing we could not do, even had we wished to. It provided something of a thrill—the only pleasurable thrill I was to experience—when erecting the two silvercloth tents against a background of Everest for the first time. The weather could not have been better, and so we did not hurry. The ground was extremely rocky, but at least it was not volcanic rock as in the Virungas, for the Himalayas came into being as the result of a fracturing and uplifting of the earth's surface. There was no volcanism accompanying the action.

The tents stood firmly and were good to look at. I took some photographs and entered a few words in my diary while Tenzing darned a pair of stockings and Ang Dowa dozed at his side. It was so warm that I even sunbathed for a few minutes without a shirt. Our camp might have been a picnic scene far remote from the Himalayas. Everest was in generous, almost inviting mood. It lulled me into a false sense of well-being. What had passed, had passed. I did not look back and count my blessings. I felt no more than a mild satisfaction, if any at all, with recent accomplishments. It had not yet dawned upon me that what we had already done was about as much as we could do. To have penetrated so far into a barren, inhospitable, closed territory, had been no mean feat. But at the time I thought nothing of it. I did not think to give praise for blessings already received, or to take stock of the series of near-miracles which had served to take me so far from Bulawayo in as little as 53 days of hard travelling.

The precious remains of our petrol—what had not seeped out or otherwise gone to waste—had been poured into an aluminium flask, and from this we filled the Coleman stove. Water was near at hand in a small stream and in patches of snow. Our entire supply of tea had already vanished, despite the use of Tibetan tea during part of our journey. This was the result of a bad under-estimate on my part, and it meant that we had to rely solely upon Oxo and Ovaltine. The stove, when set going, fascinated Ang Dowa, who took his cookery seriously, and together we prepared a meal.

Whatever complacency I had felt was banished when a bitterly cold wind swept upon us with breathtaking suddenness. The sun sank low and we crept into our separate tents, Tenzing and Ang Dowa sharing the larger one, in which we had done the cooking. I was alone, cramped in the very low, wall-less tent, which I wanted to try for size and serviceability. As night drew on, the wind increased and the cold penetrated every nook and cranny. Darkness fell and the hours dragged by, but I could not sleep because I could not derive any warmth from my sleeping-bags. Now and then, during the midnight hours, I could hear the others in their tent labouring for breath and moaning softly as they slept between bouts of wakefulness. More than once I thought of going to join them, but I would not disturb their rest. I was too numbed in mind and body to realise the truth, but this first night was really the beginning of the end.

In the morning there was fresh snow on the ground, and some water left in the tent overnight had frozen into a solid block. I lit some candles for the slight warmth they would give, and as soon as it was sufficiently light outside, I joined Tenzing and Ang Dowa in their tent, where we lit the stove and prepared a meal. Then, without any waste of time, we took down the two tents and moved off to our second camp. There was no need to hang around, for we were already well acclimatised after our journey through Tibet, which had been made at considerable altitudes without a return to lower country.

The going was very rough, over and around hills of loose rocks amongst which it would have been easy to rick an ankle. It was unpleasant enough for me, but how Tenzing and Ang Dowa fared with their heavy loads was something to marvel at. Another thing which amazed me was their almost unhesitating certainty of the route, which is not by any means easy to follow without mistake as it twists and turns through the Lhakpa La. Also, neither man had been on the mountain since 1936—an interval of more than ten years.

The mountain was utterly barren, and there was so much rubble about that I could easily imagine a mass of scree at this point in years to come. Give the frosts and melted snow a few more decades in which to split and wear away the tumbling, crumbling rock and there will be a vastly different scene. There is nothing I hate more on mountains than fine scree, but Everest will have its share of this in time. There are immense changes taking place at present. It does not require much knowledge of geology to tell that Everest, like all other Himalayan peaks, is young in geological terms. It is even said that the mountain is still growing, and this is quite likely.

Poets of all ages have done much to create a vision of immutability by extolling the " immortal mountains " and " changeless hills," but this is all imaginary. There is no immortality in nature. As with civilisation, there is constant modification, alteration and even revolution. Change is not always progressive—advancement and building up—it is also regression and decay. Evidence of change surrounds us in our daily lives: only, because of a natural desire for immortality in some shape or form, we like to believe that the mountains are eternal, indestructible masses. They are not, however, and we who set out to climb them would do well to remember this; it is a sobering thought.

The weather, all-important, remained good throughout the day.

At our second camping site, with a minor peak and tall, fluted seracs forming a background, we decided to erect only the larger of the two tents, in which we could all be accommodated without being too cramped for space. I did not mind sleeping with the others if they did not mind sleeping with me. In fact this joining of forces was entirely agreeable to me, being in line with my desire to make our undertaking a joint venture in which there was no distinction apart from that of employer and employee which could not be avoided. It had the effect of breaking down the last surmountable barrier between us.

Tenzing and Ang Dowa were acting as porters, but I never thought of them in this way, for a climber can only go as far on Everest as the porters, by their own efforts, will permit. Thus there was an ideal bond between us. We were all porters and we were all climbers. Beyond that we were just three men who were striving to give some meaning to a life which otherwise remains meaningless. What *were* we striving for if not for immortality? Most people are content to leave their own progeny as emblems of their own striving. To others this is not sufficient. The name of an individual or of any group of people will be as nothing in the end. It is only deeds which satisfy, and men and women are only remembered for their deeds, whether they be good or bad.

The sole evidence of the progress of previous expeditions on the mountain was provided by the many rusty sardine tins scattered along the route. There was never a jam tin, or a tin of fruit or vegetables—only sardines. Why these should have survived seemed just as unaccountable as a preference for what always strikes me as a most disagreeable kind of food to take on any high mountain.

That we did not encounter wild life in any form whatever was not surprising in view of the absolute barrenness of the scene, but there is no reason why a little problem of wild life should not be introduced at this stage by discussing the likelihood or otherwise of discovering some mysterious mammal in the vicinity of Everest. To put the question bluntly, does such a creature as the Himalayan " yeti " or " abominable snowman " exist?

Much of the news concerning this subject is of recent origin. It seems that a wild man of the Himalayas was brought to the notice of the Western world by Col. L. A. Waddell, who wrote *Among the Himalayas*, published in 1898. But this was only a small start and it was not until the beginning of exploration in the Everest region that attention was again drawn to the possible existence of a wild Himalayan creature as yet unknown to science. It is said that Col. Howard Bury, leader of the 1921 reconnaissance, noticed some strange footprints on the Lhakpa La and referred to them in a message as being those of a Wild Man of the Snows. Then—in the following year, I believe, or perhaps in 1924, when the second climbing party went to Everest—the English-speaking lama of Rongbuk mentioned to Gen. Bruce that there were five wild men living on the slopes of the Rongbuk Glacier.

It was left to a Mr. Henry Newman, of Darjeeling, to popularise the animal. He did this by taking the Tibetan name of *Metch kangmi* and translating *Kangmi* as " snowman " and *metch* as " abominable," thus arriving at the astonishingly apt and captivating name of " abominable snowman." The English-speaking world now had a name of tremendous appeal with which to conjure.

The Mount Everest Reconnaissance Expedition of 1951, with its widely publicised photographs of footprints, did most of all to add to the growing legend, though there were some sceptics who derided the idea of an " abominable snowman " and looked for signs of retouching in the reproductions of the alleged footprints of the animal. Then, scepticism was increased by a highly feasible explanation which appeared in the *Glasgow Herald* and was subsequently reported in many other newspapers. The writer believed the " footprints " to be water blobs caused by condensation and precipitation under the effect of freakish warm air currents. He also suggested " that the study of the formation of these marks in the snow is a matter for a meteorologist rather than a zoologist or demonologist."

It will be interesting to learn the outcome of an expedition which is now being organised with the object of establishing the existence or otherwise of " the abominable snowman."

What are my own views on the subject?

Firstly, one needs to be very guarded, and there are not many naturalists who will commit themselves in any way. The inclination is to deride the idea out of hand, but there is always the thought that some new species of larger mammal may still await discovery. Certainly Sir Harry Johnston, one of the leading authorities of his time, would not have scorned the likelihood of a Himalayan species unknown to science. For it was he who, on the strength of conversations with H. M. Stanley, went in search of the mythical unicorn and astonished the world of natural history with his discovery of the okapi (*Okapia johnstoni*) at a time when zoologists no longer expected anything new, even from the primeval forests of the Congo basin. Johnston's discovery was made at the beginning of the present century, and as recently as 1913 there was the equally surprising find of the giant sable antelope (*Hippotragus niger variani*) by Frank Varian who came across the animal in Angola, where it has its only habitat. So, quite clearly, there is no reason to ridicule the possibility of another unique species coming to the notice of science in the latter half of the same century.

There is also the strange fact that only in the foothills of the Himalayas have any fossil remains been found of a species of anthropoid ape as near the sub-human form as the gorilla or chimpanzee of equatorial Africa. A form of chimpanzee appears to have been known to early Egyptians, but there have been no living or fossil remains brought to light between Central Africa and North-West India, where fossil remains were found in lower Pliocene formations. "From the little we know of it," wrote Sir H. Johnston, " the *Palaeopithecous* of North-West India is rather nearer the human ancestor than any of the anthropoid remains of Europe."

There are greater doubts when considering the nature of habitat. It should not be thought that any large mammal could possibly exist on Everest or any of its satellites. The remarkable photographs of Shipton's " abominable snowman " were taken at a height of about 19,000 ft. on one of the glaciers of the Menlung basin, almost 20 miles due west of Everest. Earlier tales of an " abominable snowman " on the Tibetan side of Everest can almost certainly be discounted. The whole question of occurrence or non-occurrence of the larger mammals resolves itself into one of sustenance and remoteness from human interference. The habitat must provide vegetation of the right kind, and also it must afford adequate shelter, especially for mountain-dwelling species. The scientific study of wild life in relation to its surroundings is known as ecology, and in the entire field of ecology there is no possibility of any chance occurrence as unlikely as that of a large mammal living on Everest.

Some months ago it was reported that a scantily-clad Indian ascetic has been found in good health after spending six months of autumn and winter in an icy Himalayan cave. He, however, had kept himself alive on dried fruits which he had collected during the previous summer.

It has often been suggested that similar ascetics, or men banished from remote monasteries for grave crimes, may be living like wild animals and thereby giving rise to the rumours of an " abominable snowman " or Himalayan " yeti."

In order to uncover the real truth it may be necessary to organise a special expedition in which mountaineers with considerable knowledge of natural history would have to take part. I know from my experiences on the Virunga mountains that one cannot go spooring wild animals while climbing in real earnest. I soon found out that it had to be the one thing or the other, and after that I just kept my eye to the various summits and let everything else go by. And so it is with Everest or any other Himalayan peak.

My second night on the mountain was a repetition of the first, only worse. All night long I tried to pummel some warmth into my cold body, but sleep would not come. My body was numb, and my mind could register nothing but misery. Trying to put my thoughts into words would be as futile as trying to assemble the reactions to death of a drowning man. Each hour seemed a day. Would dawn *never* come?

It did in the end, and we set off early, not because we had to or wanted to, but because inactivity is the killing thing on Everest. One does not have to be on the mountain long to realise this.

Tenzing and Ang Dowa performed prodigies of work in carrying their loads to the next camp. I expected them to complain, but there was never a word of complaint from them. At one time we had to pick our way between numerous tall seracs which rose like giant's teeth from a trough with a flooring of ice and rock. From this trough we turned right, and came later to a glacial pool backed by tremendous pinnacles of ice which were reflected in its mirror-like surface. The North Col was visible and Tenzing said he had never seen it with so little snow.

Beyond the pool we camped at a spot several hundred yards away from the normal camping spot in this vicinity. Tenzing and Ang Dowa, who had hardly rested all the way, put down their loads as though they were only slight encumbrances, like a load of children on a zoo elephant.

There is no praise that can be too high for these men and their kind. They are the real workers, without whose efforts no expedition would have any hope of success. I became convinced more than ever that Everest " belongs " most of all to the Sherpas, and I am delighted that one of them (and one for whom I have such a special affection and admiration) should have been given the first chance of getting to the top.

The weather turned bitterly cold again in the evening, so there was no alternative but to turn into bed after a few photographs had been taken. The sky had been clear until now, but there was an ominous darkening, and during the night a savage wind, like the breath from a Tibetan mastiff, sprang up. I went to bed in all the clothes I could muster, and this time Tenzing shared his sleeping bag with me, and I realised properly, for the first time, how miserably poor we were and what little chance we stood.

By this time I had not much taste for food, and it was almost too much trouble to prepare anything to eat. Cheese was my real mainstay because its taste still registered on my jaded palate. Otherwise the only food to retain any appreciable flavour was milk chocolate with nuts and raisins, in large slabs. It provided me with a pastime, too. At night I kept some within reach and nibbled it when sleep was out of the question. It was a rather tiring business though, involving the removal of my gloves each time I took a bite. Every movement let in a cold draught as I stole out a hand, took a bite, put on my gloves again and lay sucking until the chocolate melted from the nuts and raisins. It was the only pastime I could think of, and to me the nuts and raisins were treasures which had to be unearthed. Even so, time dragged horribly, and in a few hours I seemed to live a lifetime. Occasionally I heard sharp cracks, like pistol shots, from the pinnacles of ice outside as they contracted in the cold air. I do not recall sleeping for a single minute during the night at this, our third camp.

The wind did not relent in the morning, and we pushed on in face of it over rough stones to a long rising slope of alternate gravel and ice until finally we entered the East Rongbuk glacier. On one ice slope we came across a broken climbing boot discarded by a previous expedition. The glistening ice of the glacier was made treacherous by a total absence of snow for our nailed boots to bite into. Tenzing used crampons, but Ang Dowa and I carried on without. We all put on goggles.

After the long climb up the glacier, dangerously pitted with crevasses, we swung to the right, where there was a moraine, and ahead, the North Col. Now we faced the wind in all its fury, and near the foot of the Col we battled to erect our single tent. The men were tight-lipped, but otherwise their faces remained expressionless. I wondered how they felt, but they said nothing and gave no indication of their feelings. The fact that we had to wear more than one pair of gloves made our task all the more difficult. The wind, as though it had a mind of its own, seemed determined to tear the tent from our grasp as we tried to drive pegs into the frozen ground. We worked for brief spells and then stopped to turn our backs to the wind and slap our hands against our thighs. Some pegs we could drive in but others we could not. Where we could not use them we piled huge stones on top of the guy ropes and hoped for the best. Where pegs could be driven in, we also placed stones on top, as heavy as we could carry, for additional safety.

At last we had the tent as secure as we could make it. Before entering I took a good look at the North Col. It did not look as frightening as I had expected. Its slope was less severe than I had been led to believe. Three men could tackle it in safety, but not in the face of the wind as it was blowing then. It must die down or we would be doomed, one way or another.

That night I prayed. " God help me. Help me to do the right thing. Do not rob me of the chance to go forward, but give me strength to go back if I must."

For myself I cared little. I had dedicated myself to Everest. My whole life was Everest. I did not want to live if we failed. I was not concerned about death. There are a million deaths and a million births. It is easy to die; much easier than to live. But we cannot die without fear: either we must fear to die or we must be afraid of living.

So far we had succeeded in doing on Everest what we had done all the way through Tibet. We had gone from camp to camp without stopping in any one place for more than a single night. This is the great advantage to be gained from having a small, extremely mobile party. The 1933 Everest expedition had taken 16 to 24 days [1] to do what we had done in four days.

The chronology of their progress from Rongbuk up to this stage is set out below for comparison:

[1] I do not know for certain how their camps corresponded with ours.

April 16   Arrived Rongbuk.
         17   Base camp established.
         21   Camp I established.
         26   Camp II established.
  May   2   Camp III established.
          8   Camp IIIA established.

As can be judged from this progress, there is a considerable lapse of time between the establishment of one camp and another where a large expedition is involved, and a shuttle service has to be run between the base camp and each successive camp. If there are many camps spread out beyond the base of operations one needs a secondary or intermediate base. The result is that, from something easily manageable, an intricate system grows and grows, and the more time that is spent in establishing and servicing a chain of camps, the greater the time lost in other ways.

For instance, it is necessary to be inside a tent by 4 o'clock, and once inside a tent there is nothing to do but get into bed and stay there. This may mean spending 14 or 15 hours recumbent at a single stretch, and even ten hours is a long time for a normally active man to be abed. Time can become the great enemy in more ways than one. There have been occasions, in the past, when small-talk has dwindled and arguments have led to petty grievances, and in turn to frayed tempers and hostility.

On the other hand there is the matter of acclimatisation to be taken into account. Some may claim that the time spent in establishing camps and stocking them, with intervals between, is all to the good because it provides time for gradual acclimatisation. I do not agree with this at all. We never found ourselves in need of time for acclimatising. Perhaps we might have done so at some point higher than we were able to go, but I do not think so. Or, if we had, a single day would have done much to put us right. Deterioration—both physical and mental—is a worse bogy on Everest than acclimatisation.

All through the night the tent had to withstand a howling, piercing blast from the elements. The guy-ropes pulled, tugged, heaved, strained at their fastenings. The sides flapped vigorously and ceaselessly—flap, flap, flap, flap, flap, flap, flap—as quickly as it is possible to repeat the word. Surely no fabric on earth could stand the stress! If it tore, what then? Two pegs were ripped from the ground. If one more went the same way, there would have been no alternative but for me to go outside in an attempt to prevent a total collapse. It was only the construction of the ground sheet and walls all in one piece which saved us from having the whole tent blown away from over our heads.

I rubbed myself, pummelled and kicked, in an effort to relieve myself of the gripping iciness. The only part of my body to retain any of its heat was at the meeting point between my thighs, and I put both hands there in an effort to give them a share of the warmth. Each minute seemed an hour and each hour an eternity. None of us spoke, but we must have known, as the wind slackened but still continued to rage, that we were beaten.

My prayers turned to bitter oaths. And, as this is a faithful record, I confess that I added some words of blasphemy.

With the first glimmer of daylight, I lit the stove and we all had a drink of hot cocoa and a light meal. Neither Tenzing nor Ang Dowa had slept much, and I had not slept at all. We had no programme mapped out, and we discussed nothing, but we were unanimous in going outside and starting to take down the tent. Then we packed as best we could, our hands numbed with cold. Whatever happened we could not stay where we were. We had to go elsewhere, either up or down, to escape from the full force of the wind. We would not give in so easily, so we went on.

The snow on the Col was not at all as I had seen it in photographs. The wind, no doubt, had blown much of it away, baring the Col to an unusual extent. There were no sweeping, rounded mounds, and not much fine snow. At about the centre of the trough leading to it there was an even, gentle slope to a large pyramid of ice which appeared to have a square base. Beyond this, but diverging at right angles (in the direction of the mountain summit) was a slightly steeper slope, which continued to the top. The obstacle which faced us was, in itself, nothing insuperable—in fact it was not the giant that I had expected it to be. But no sooner had we set upon it than the wind, which until then had relaxed somewhat, gathered up its forces and howled at us with renewed fury. The sky, which on previous days had been clear, was an unrelieved dark mass, almost black. We turned from the height of about 23,500 ft. which we had reached and went back as quickly as we could to the site of our fourth camp on the mountain, but it was obvious that we could not set up our tent there. For one thing, our hands were almost useless. They were on the verge of frost-bite. We held our consultation, if it could be called a consultation. We had played our hand.

I had been critical of large expeditions, but now the scales were turned. No expedition, large or small, could have battled on in the face of the prevailing conditions. But a large expedition would have had a chain of camps, or at least a base camp, to retreat to, there to wait and to try again when conditions had improved. We, for our part, had no reserves. Even if we could have retired to a lower camp, we could not have stayed there for any length of time because we had insufficient food to stand siege. We were a spent force.

Another consideration was that of safety. We had no margin whatever between survival and non-survival. A twisted ankle, a broken leg, frostbite or snowblindness—if any of these had happened to any one of us, the entire party would most likely have been doomed. We had known this from the beginning, of course. It was one of the risks we had been willing to take.

My bitterness was like an open wound as we hastened down, almost running. I refused to consider myself vanquished as a mountaineer by a technical difficulty. There were greater forces, or more elemental ones, to take into account, and I felt deprived by them of the opportunity to demonstrate my capabilities to the utmost.

Had I ever been capable of reasoning, I would have known that my material resources were too slender for the tremendous task which I had set myself and my two Sherpa companions. We had attempted more than was humanly possible. There could be no disgrace in such a defeat, but I felt humiliated because I had been spurred on originally by high aspirations.

I suppose it is all a matter of the store we set on things. To some mountaineers, who go as one of a large party, Everest is no more than a glorious adventure. They do not have to pay for anything out of their own pockets, and failure, when it comes, is shared with others, many others: there is nothing personal about it. To me, however (and I am sure, to Tenzing, and probably to Ang Dowa as well), the physical adventure counted for very little in relation to the underlying motives. I thought I saw in the vision of success a wonderful meaning to life—my triumph over the gross materialism into which our civilisation as I knew it has been plunged. Then, when success did not come, I thought I saw in failure the final crumbling away of anything that was not strictly material. I had always, since childhood, held to my own religion, a very personal sort of religion, elastic and meant for myself, not for whole groups of people who try to bridge their differences; a religion which I found good because it embraced nothing but the good from all religions, and discarded from them all that is stupid or merely pageantry or idolatry. In short, it was the religion of the high mountains. With failure, I saw a world which was not the world as I wanted it to be. I could never become entirely atheistic, but I tried hard at this time to deny the gods of all religions. Yet, even in my defeat, I struggled blindly, groping for a sustaining truth as I groped with my ice-axe, searching with the others for a way down the mountain, stumbling, cursing, hurrying away, trying to hate what I really loved. Seeking to convince myself that life meant nothing and would end in nothingness.

XXV. *The Long Trail Back*

A T RONGBUK we stayed only a day, leaving on the 16th with two tiny donkeys which had been brought in from Chö Dzong. The state of my body was deplorable. My skin had a sickly pallor and was flaking off. It may have been a touch of scurvy caused by a lack of vegetables in my diet. It worried me for a while, but it cleared up by itself. Tenzing and Ang Dowa were taking everything in their stride. There was never a rankling word or a sign of discontent from either of them. I came to like them better than ever because they seemed to understand the things which I could not understand, and they remained staunch at a time when I needed their help desperately.

I caught my last glimpse of Everest as we turned a corner in the trail leading to Chö Dzong. It was snowing at the time, and as I looked back with Tenzing and Ang Dowa there was little of the mountain to be seen. The greater part of it was shrouded in dense masses of grey and black clouds. In my thoughts was the certainty that no one could have survived there under such appalling conditions, and I knew by their looks that Tenzing and Ang Dowa were thinking the same. If we had not come away when we did, we should have perished. There could be little doubt about that, and it helped to soften the blow of defeat somewhat. Even so, I cursed, but as I did so I knew that if the chance came I would go again to the mountain. That was why I was going away. It was why I had not persisted in a suicidal attempt to remain on the mountain beyond the utmost limit of endurance. One more night on Everest and there would have been no return, but there would also have been no defeat to live through, no more striving, no more fruitless searching, wondering, waiting, yearning, and no more unhappiness.

The long trail back! It was a journey without an horizon. There was nothing behind but defeat, and nothing ahead but emptiness. To

232

the one side there was a desert of loneliness and to the other a morass of despair. There was nothing to look up to, and so my eyes remained downcast. I did not want to live, and yet I could not die. A flood of hot tears would have relieved the pent-up feeling deep within me, but I could not even cry. There was no relief of any sort, neither death nor tears, and because there was no escape I went blindly on, aware of the wind and cold, but impervious to them.

Often on the way back and in later years I wondered if it would not have been better to die on Everest. Was I so weak that I could not give my life, or so regardless of posterity that I would not? Or is it true that we only meet death when death is ready to meet us? When we have done our best or worst and can do no more?

If there has ever been a worse journey, then who has undertaken it? Who, if he were mortal, *could* undertake it?

I recalled the time when, on the outward journey, I had given thought to a return under conditions of defeat, and had considered it impossible. And so it might have proved if I had not learned to mellow my bitterness and to catch a glimmer of hope. Would not another opportunity come? Was it, for instance, entirely out of the question to hope for inclusion in some future expedition under the joint sponsorship of the Alpine Club and the Royal Geographical Society? Having gained experience of actual Everest climbing, there was now a likelihood, which did not exist before, but it would mean forsaking my principles in the choice of a small party rather than a large one. Well, I could but try, and in doing so I would not be the first to forsake a principle. On the other hand (and this was more to my liking) there was the slender possibility that I might get the opportunity of going to Everest again with my present companions under more favourable circumstances at a later date. This was only a slight hope, but I clung to it. For is not hope the last thing we have to lose before life itself? Is it not true that when hope vanishes we die?

It is not my intention to tell in full of the long journey back. It was just a hard, wearying slog, but a few of the incidents are worth recording.

We did not stay at Chö Dzong. We arrived there shortly after two o'clock and left half an hour later with three horses. By means of these, which we rode occasionally, we reached a village called *Pemay* (short " a "). We arrived long after dark, and I was sore after my first experience of a Tibetan saddle, made of two wooden rungs set about six inches apart. Also, Tibetans make use of exceptionally short stirrup leathers, and I had been forced to ride with my knees nearly touching my chin. I was horribly cramped, and so cold that, after I dismounted, I could not stand erect. I climbed as best I could to an upper story room which Tenzing had managed to obtain for the night. At the top of the stairs, which were made of round logs that revolved in a most awkward manner as soon as a foot was set on them, I stumbled blindly into a room in which there was a fire. An old woman sat there, and I squatted by her side to warm myself. A man of about the same age came in, and presently a taper was lit in a small container of oil. The old couple smiled and offered me some tea, which I accepted. I was not aware of the fact that I had intruded into their own living-room until Tenzing came to tell me of my mistake.

I would have left at once, but the two old people smiled understandingly, bidding me to stay and warm myself. It was the first time such consideration had been shown to me in Tibet, and I felt a deep sense of gratitude. It was a humble home, but there was friendliness as well as dirt about the place. The words of Mahatma Ghandi came to my mind : " They were burning huts," he had said (speaking of some religious disorders which had taken place while I was in India), " which to the dwellers were as precious as palaces to the princes." These words, ordinarily, would not have conveyed much meaning to me, but in my predicament of the moment they took on a tremendous significance. I did not wish for a mansion or a palace, but my whole being cried out for comfort, warmth and friendliness. I had these, in a humble Tibetan home, dirty beyond description. The homes of the wealthy may be more elaborate and costly than the slums of the poor, but can they always offer as much?

We used two more donkeys between Pemay and *Tsa*. Tsa seemed to be deserted by everyone but extraordinarily vicious dogs, but at length we chanced upon the fine house of *Kasang Chola La*, who obviously was the most wealthy Tibetan we came across. He was not unhandsome, except when he smiled and showed his uneven teeth. His features were hardly Mongolian at all, and he was taller and slimmer than most of his countrymen. His two children, whom I photographed with him, were markedly similar in looks and build. They were, I should say, about 8 and 10 years of age. He was a deeply religious man, always fondling his string of holy beads, and every time he entered or left his house, he gave the three prayer wheels, set in the wall near the entrance, a gentle spin. I never saw him fail to do this. He wore a double-piece garment, and from his left ear dangled a large turquoise stone. He took snuff, and occasionally

I saw him mix it with a pinch of ashes from a fire. He owned five horses, and he offered us three of these for our journey as far as Lachen. Tenzing said we would be nearly seven days in reaching there, so the charge of Rs. 105 was reasonable and I accepted the offer.

The next stage of our journey was to Congrung Laprang, where we made the river crossing in a biting gale. We stayed again with Nombi, who was disappointed to find that we had already obtained horses and would not be requiring any of his as we had previously arranged. However, he treated us well, and I left him a 50-ft. climbing rope with which he was immensely pleased.

I had never thought it possible, but from Congrung Laprang we went to Tarnak in a single day, missing Cojak. Thus we covered two of our outward stages in a single day, during which we had to withstand extreme cold and snow. It was incredibly quick going, but completely exhausting. There was aconite, a poisonous plant, along part of the route, and the horses had to be muzzled. We stayed in the same room as before at Tarnak, but the headman (who had hung a knife over my bed and warned us of bandits on the previous occasion) was away at the time, paying a call at another village. Here Ang Dowa had to crack a mastiff on the head to keep it at bay. We saw nothing of the " six horsemen " who had accosted us on the way out, and we made no attempt to be secretive about our movements. No one was likely to prevent us from *leaving* the country. Kasang Chola La's horses went splendidly over the pass leading to Sar, making light of the steep gradient at which the dzos had baulked. At the top of the pass, the Tibetan who accompanied us left a piece of an old *Bulawayo Chronicle* fluttering with the praying flags. I wonder if it is there to-day?

We by-passed Sar, as we had done before, and also Tashidzom. Beyond the ravine with its five separate streams, we kept too far over to the left, floundering and nearly sticking in the bog. I had a particularly bad time here, and was pleased to reach Lungma, which I recognised as a village at which we had only halted briefly for lunch when journeying in the opposite direction. Between Muk and Gombolo we again saw a small herd of wild asses, which may have been the ones we had seen earlier. At Gombolo we had the same room as before, and again we arrived after dark and left before dawn. It was best, at this stage, not to take any avoidable risks.

The morning sun was trying, the afternoon winds cruelly penetrating, and we arrived cold and tired at every destination. There was barely time to keep my diary up to date. I half expected a warrant for my arrest to be awaiting me at Darjeeling, and I was anxious to get the whole business over and face whatever consequences there were to be faced. Tenzing and Ang Dowa, for their part, wished to be back with their families as quickly as possible and perhaps to be in time to go out with other expeditions before the climbing season was over.

We went via the Kongra La to Donkung, where we stayed, for a change, in a room with a chimney leading from the roof. We heard the disturbing rumour that a large party of Englishmen were at Thang-gu. Whether this was true or not, I never knew, for we left Donkung very early, travelling the first few miles over frozen ground by torchlight. We passed Thang-gu and did not stop until reaching Lachen, where there were still no apples on the trees. Here we had to part with the horses and the Tibetan who had come with them all the way from Tsa. This man had never been across the border into Sikkim before. It was a totally new experience for him, and I often wondered what he thought of the dense forests, grasses, flowers and other vegetation. He had a pleasant disposition and never complained about our hurried rate of progress. Often he walked along with one sleeve of his long garment dangling loose, while at other times, when warm enough, he tied both sleeves round his middle. At night, like others of his race, he simply pulled the whole garment over his head and round his feet.

Tenzing arranged with the Sikkimese herdsman who had come with us from Gangtok to Lachen to take us in the reverse direction for Rs. 62, using a mule and a donkey. I was pleased to have him with us again. Like the Tibetan from Tsa, he was pleasant company and a willing worker. He wore his black hair parted in the middle and arranged in a number of small pigtails at the sides. His skin had a coppery colour.

An incident which took place between Lachen and Chungthang stands out in my memory. Other people may think little of it, but to me it typified the monstrous selfishness of our age, and indicated that all is not well with those who profess to be followers of one religion or another.

I was looking forward with eager anticipation to my first meeting with a white man, for I had seen no one with whom I could converse freely since leaving Darjeeling. We were following the west bank of the Tista at a particularly narrow part of the trail when we came face to face with a white man mounted on a large grey mare. There was only room for one horse, so we stood aside to let him and his Sikkimese porter pass. I expected some recognition for our courtesy if for no other reason, but the man brushed past with head held high and a look of complete self-satisfaction on his face. He gave no sign of recognition whatever, and left me wide-mouthed with astonishment. Perhaps he was a missionary, which would make the sin of omission more odious than ever. Tenzing gave a quick glance in my direction, without speaking, but I knew what was in his thoughts.

With our Sikkimese muleteer we reached Gangtok on Sunday, April 27. Here our trails had to part. The muleteer had to return with his animals to Lachen, while we others had to go on to Darjeeling where we arrived during the afternoon of the following day. I went again to my bleak little boarding-house, where there were no questions asked, and where I kept out of sight as much as possible.

We finished in the same bedraggled manner as we had started. There had been no send-off, and there was no welcome back. We were of no consequence except to ourselves. We did not wish it to be otherwise: indeed, we considered ourselves fortunate to be left in freedom. Only a lack of communication between Tibet and the outer world made this possible, as we were to find out later.

At my last meeting with Tenzing and Ang Dowa, I asked for a few details of Tenzing's adventurous career. He informed me on this occasion that he had accompanied four Everest expeditions.

" But I understood you to say only three when I asked you previously," I remonstrated.

" 1935, 1936, 1938—and Everest 1947," he replied.

I was deeply grateful to him.

XXVI. *The End—or the Beginning?*

WHAT REMAINS of my story will not take long to tell. I left Darjee-ling at the first opportunity and made for Calcutta, where I was told that no passage to Africa was possible for several months to come. Whereas on my outward journey I had been lucky at every touch and turn, I now drew nothing but blanks. It was not possible for me to take up employment in the country, so I eeked out a bare living by writing articles for Indian newspapers and magazines, during which time I haunted the shipping companies' offices and kept a close watch on the docks for every incoming and outgoing vessel. Even with my writing I was handicapped, for I did not consider it safe to publicise my Everest expedition because of the likelihood of unpleasant consequences for Tenzing and Ang Dowa. My plight had become desperate by the time I found a passage on the S.S. *Amra*, which left Bombay on Friday, June 20.

There were three notable passengers on board, and because they had come from Sikkim and had a story to tell of suffering which could be alleviated in others of their kind, I will introduce them here.

They were three sloth bears, *Melursus ursinus*. The outstanding charac-teristics of the species are an elongated muzzle, very mobile and useful—together with a strong power of suction—for indulging a fondness for ants and their larvae; short hind legs; greatly curved claws, longer on the fore-feet; long, coarse, unkempt black hair; the weight of large adult about 300 lb. Their food consists mainly of fruit, honey and insects.

The destination of these particular animals, as marked on their cages, was " Zoo, Pretoria, South Africa." It is impossible to say how long they had been in transit, or under what conditions they had been kept in India after their capture. On board ship they were left to the well-meaning but totally unskilled attentions of the crew. No instructions had been given as to food, about which there was total ignorance. They were housed aft, in cages which were so small that they could not stand upright. These cages soon became dens of indescribable filth, and the beasts developed running sores which, to me, were mute protestations against their pitiable, unnecessary sufferings. One animal, more fortunate than the others, died.

It is true, the survivors would be cared for at the end of their journey —cared for, fed, housed, and protected from all enemies. But no one is made to care about the methods of capture or the problems of transportation. The crowds who gather to view the beasts behind bars or in pits are often indifferent to the circumstances which have led to their own selfish pleasure. What does it matter to the zoo visitor if there is suffering, so long as the suffering itself is not paraded or made obvious in a cage or pit? What does it matter if ignorant blacks or brutish whites, entirely lacking in principles, have captured the animals by means of primitive and cruel methods? What does it matter if the captive beasts have been forced to await transit for weeks or months and then be transported, perhaps for thousands of miles, under the most deplorable conditions imaginable?

Surely, if zoos are a necessity, then it should be compulsory for zoo authorities to care for animals from the time of capture to the journey's end. It would not be possible for each zoo to employ a specialist for the capture and transportation of all zoo exhibits, but there could be a pool of skilled certified animal capturers in the collective employ of many zoos. This should be arranged, in spite of the extra expense all who consider zoos necessary for the pleasure and education of themselves and their children.

I have always felt strongly on this point, and never more strongly than when forced to gaze daily, for weeks, at animals who were dying slowly and painfully before my eyes, myself powerless to raise a hand to alleviate their sufferings.

After calling at the Seychelle Islands, Mombasa, Zanzibar and Dar-es-Salaam I landed at Beira and then proceeded by train to Bulawayo, where I arrived on Tuesday, July 8, with exactly £1 in my pocket.

I wanted desperately to forget all about mountains. I never wished to set eyes on another unless it should be Everest, and of that there was little hope. Most of all, I wanted to be released from the last shred of ambition.

It was, of course, a losing battle. One of the letters awaiting me was a reminder of my Virunga expedition. It was from Chief Tomasi Sebukweto, and was evidently written by his clerk, John Mbonigaba. It read:

Dear Mr. Denman,

Many thanks for your letter and the photographs you sent me down.
I got them safely.

Dear Sir, Happy Christmas and a New Year!! May the year 1947
bring you much happiness, Blessings and Well-being. Many greetings
and good wishes from John Mbonigaba.

I remain here,   Yours respectfully,
(Signed) TOMASI SEBUKWETO

Thus, when I tried to forget my mountains I was forcibly reminded of
them and of the fine people inseparable from them. So, rather than swim
against the tide of events, I decided to drift with it. This state of affairs
could not, and did not, continue for long. An ambition as strong as that
which drives a man to Everest cannot be laid aside easily, and certainly not
for ever. And, when once the ambition had reasserted itself, it was no
longer sufficient to drift, for nothing ever happens to an inactive dreamer
to make his dreams come true.

The only action that could be taken during the remainder of 1947 was
to submit an application to the Alpine Club, London, for inclusion in the
next Everest expedition to be organised by them. This I did with some
trepidation and with practically no hope of success!

I was right outside the ranks of mountaineers from which future Everest
expeditions would be made up. I was not even sure I wanted to join a
large expedition. I shall always remain very much averse to the whole
principle of large organisations where Everest or any other mountain is
concerned. I only tried for inclusion because I was determined not to be
at fault for allowing any opportunity to go begging.

Would I have been happy to serve under a leader after being an inde-
pendent mountaineer? I would, of course, have been happy to have all
expenses paid, but I would never have felt at ease stringing along with
a party of men and long trains of pack animals to do a job which I stead-
fastly believed could best be accomplished in a quiet manner and with a
very small party.

My 1947 Everest expedition was not publicised to any great extent,[1]

---

[1] *The Mountain World: Everest* 1952 carries a short account of my expedition. I do not
wish to cast aspersions on an excellent book but it seems unfair to draw from the fact that the
Krenek–Tenzing story does not agree in every detail with my own conclusion that my
version is in any way embroidered." Differences in detail are inevitable: no one remembers the
same things with the same intensity. My own account here presented is as honest an attempt
to recount a true adventure as lies in my power.

but it became known here and there, and, arising from the spreading of the story, I was given the opportunity to go out again and to renew the struggle with adequate equipment and sounder finance. This time I had the benefit of actual Everest experience to draw upon, and preparations, which took nearly five months to complete, were begun in earnest. I had, too, the help and encouragement of Mary, to whom this book is dedicated. I was no longer entirely alone in my efforts.

No sooner had I laid the foundations for my own plans than there came the news of an expedition to be led by Group Captain A. F. Bandit. I had not previously heard of the leader and did not know if his activities in the proposed venture were to be confined to flying or if he was one of the intended climbing party. Also I could not gather if the Group Captain had any connection with the Royal Geographical Society or the Alpine Club. However, in a letter from the Alpine Club, I was informed: " I can assure you that Group Captain Bandit has no connection whatsoever with either the Alpine Club or the R.G.S."

It was reported that a team of picked men was undergoing tests in special chambers which had been designed to reproduce the conditions to be encountered on Everest. Oxygen was to be used, and also lightweight clothing with self-heating apparatus incorporated. Tent pegs were to be of magnesium. Army pattern cans of food with individual heating units attached were to be tried for the first time. One of the most important innovations was the use of transport planes to fly men and equipment to a convenient marshalling point. Thereafter, helicopters were to be employed for transportation to the base camp. The only known route at this time was from the Tibetan side, which meant gaining permission from Lhasa.

Sensational news came through from Tibet which quashed this venture and placed my own attempt to return with Tenzing and Ang Dowa under a new light.

Casting a horoscope for the birthday of the young Dalai Lama, priests found he was to be threatened by strangers. Foreigners were consequently to be banned from the country until 1950. Later it was announced that war between the great powers was possible and Tibetans did not want their country to become involved. For this reason, the presence of foreigners was not desirable and the ban was extended for an indefinite period. The expedition planned by Group Captain Bandit had to be abandoned, and my own plans had to be altered. Whereas I had intended to seek official permission, I was forced either to give up for all time the idea of a lone attempt or try as before to reach the mountain secretly. So much time and effort had gone into preparations that I decided in favour of the latter course. One of my most important innovations was the provision of special high altitude boots with fleece linings and rope soles. This time I had medical supplies, including vitamin tablets, and several manufacturers supplied me with items of equipment, mostly foodstuffs. I had proper windproof clothing, adequate sleeping-bags, and in all respects I was better provided for than before.

I left Africa, this time from Durban, on January 15, 1948. My port of disembarkation was again Bombay. My route across India was the same as before. A rioting mob had attacked a train near Calcutta, but I managed to avoid all troubles of this kind, only to embroil myself in greater trouble upon arrival in Darjeeling. Tenzing, who was under the impression that I had gained permission to enter Tibet, awaited me. He was all smiles. I wasted no time in disclosing the fact that I had been unable to obtain a permit from Lhasa. His smile faded. He hurried to disclose the latest news —of which I was unaware until then—that we were wanted men in Tibet. A close watch was being kept at the frontier, and neither he nor Ang Dowa dare undertake the journey again without full authority to do so. Nor would any other Sherpa risk the consequences of capture and imprisonment in Tibet. It was shattering news, and for the first time I came to realise fully and clearly the immensity of our 1947 undertaking, which had certainly bordered on the impossible.

Poor Tenzing and Ang Dowa! They wanted to help, but could do nothing. And so I left them, sadder but wiser, to return to South Africa. It was the last time I was to see either of them.

All my equipment was left with Tenzing. Even my treasured ice-axe and Arab burneeta were left behind in the unwarranted hope that I might be able to obtain the necessary permit within a year or two. Also I persuaded myself that I did not wish to climb any other mountain if I could not climb Everest.

The shipping situation had eased considerably during the past year, and consequently I was able to return to South Africa without delay.

An official of the Alpine Club, London, announced that the whole idea of a British expedition under their sponsorship had been shelved. In the immediate post-war years there must have been many eligible Alpine climbers, and some with Everest experience, who feared that they would be too old to achieve their ambition before the opportunity came. It was an era of iron curtains for high altitude mountaineers as well as politicians. Then, at a time when Tibet had become more than ever a forbidden land, a change of attitude was shown by the Nepalese Government, which hitherto had remained determinedly isolationist. From 1947 onwards, a number of mountaineering expeditions were permitted to approach various parts of the Nepal Himalaya. One of these was of particular importance because it did much to focus attention upon the possibility of an approach to Everest from Nepal. It was only a small party, but it included Dr. Charles Houston and H. W. Tilman, who explored the little-known upper Khumbu district in the autumn of 1950. Previously it had been the general belief that Everest was totally invulnerable from Nepalese territory. A letter from Tenzing, dated October 11, 1949, sums up the attitude which was predominant at the time. He wrote: " There is only one route to climb the Everest.[1] That is the route from Tibet. But from Nepal creates many troubles. There is some route which is too stiff and narrow. It is impossible to reach the Everest from Nepal."

The gist of this letter represented the popular belief: but, with Tibet finally and irrevocably closed to Westerners after the Communist invasion, there was need to turn elsewhere. The Houston-Tilman expedition undoubtedly played its part in drawing attention to the feasibility of an attempt to reach Everest from the south. The first definite step in this direction was taken in May 1951, when Michael Ward proposed to the Himalayan Committee that an endeavour should be made to send an exploratory expedition through Nepal later in the same year. Permission was granted by the Nepalese Government, rather unexpectedly in view of recent political disturbances, and Eric Shipton was appointed as leader of what became known as the Mount Everest Reconnaissance Expedition, 1951.

This expedition, which was an equivalent of the 1921 reconnaissance through Tibet, left Namche Bazar on September 25. The objects of this reconnaissance expedition were accomplished with resounding success. A practicable route to the summit was observed by way of the Western Cwm, and the ice fall giving access to the Cwm, in spite of adverse conditions, was successfully negotiated. The expedition was finally brought to a halt

[1] No doubt Tenzing had this letter written for him by an Indian, for Indians invariably use the indefinite article and make it " the Everest " instead of simply " Everest."

by a crevasse, 100 ft. wide at its narrowest point, which lay beyond and above the ice fall.

Rumours became rife. Firstly it was said that a team of Mexican climbers were in training, and later it was said that Russia was to launch an attack. Switzerland, Britain and France were " queued up." A new phase was in the offing. Everest, from being a purely British undertaking, was about to become a centre for international competition. Some people were frankly uneasy about the prospect, fearing that mountaineering would lose much of its earlier meaning. First in the field[1] was a Swiss expedition, sent out by the Swiss Foundation for Alpine Research with, it was stated, a fair amount of Government backing. The leader of this first non-British expedition was Dr. Edouard Wyss-Dunant. After setting their base camp near the snout of the Khumbu Glacier, the Swiss established seven further camps, with the highest at 27,550 ft. Sardar Tenzing[2] was the outstanding Sherpa and, indeed, one of the outstanding figures in the whole party. With Raymond Lambert, an experienced Swiss Alpine guide, he went up to 28,215 ft., the highest so far reached. Special oxygen equipment was used.

Undeterred by their failure to reach the summit, the Swiss tried again later in the same year with a slightly different party under the leadership of Dr. Gabriel Chevalley. Oxygen was again used, but on this occasion the attempt had to be abandoned on November 22 because of extreme cold and high winds. The cost in lives was three Sherpas killed and three badly injured. Among the dead was Mingma Dorje, one of the best of the men from Namche Bazar. Tenzing was a member of this second expedition, though he did not play such a prominent part as before. In a report to his sponsors, Dr. Chevalley declared: " It is the storms that have to be conquered and not the mountain." High tribute was paid by Lambert to the qualities of Tenzing as an Everest climber.

The part which I played off and on during these years was a miserably forlorn one, and has little if any significance in the history of Everest. After my return from India in 1948, I wrote again to the Joint Himalayan

[1] Since this was written it has come to notice that a Dane named Larsen made a solo attempt in 1951. According to a report emanating from Professor Krenek of Darjeeling, Larsen went *via* Nepal and thence into Tibet. This, with Wilson's attempt in 1934 and my own in 1947, makes three solo expeditions to Everest.

[2] Tenzing had by this time been promoted to the rank of Sardar, or leader, in recognition of continued good performances with many Himalayan expeditions. He had become sought after by every party going out to the Himalayas, and photographs of him were becoming commonplace in newspapers and magazines throughout the world.

Committee, but to no avail. I went so far as to try to penetrate the so-called iron curtain with letters to the Communist countries, at that time in control of Tibet, thinking that if I could not go *via* Nepal I would try the old route again. There followed a long period of dispiritedness and torpor during which I tried only to forget Everest, and to assure myself that the wild life of Africa was a more deserving object for my energies. I even wished, while the Swiss were so near the summit of Everest during their first attack in 1952, that they would complete the job, oxygen or no oxygen. I knew I could go no further with my lone efforts. I knew when I was defeated (or thought I did) and decided to try to forget the mountain as far as it was in my power to do so. There was a part of my past which I wanted to forget. I wanted *desperately* to forget it. For me it was *finis* so far as Everest and ambition were concerned.

I was not happy during those days, months, years of feigned forgetfulness, but I endured them and could have endured more. I did not write about Everest and I did not talk about it. My photographs remained out of sight, my " pieces of eight " (the stones gathered from each of the eight Virunga summits) and other mountaineering trophies I never handled. There might have been no change from this attitude but for a chance encounter which led to a request for a series of mountaineering articles for a weekly newspaper, and the gift, from the same person, of a book. In glancing through this book (Eric Shipton's account of the 1951 Reconnaissance) I became fired with enthusiasm once more, and convinced for the first time that Nepal offered the best route. It seemed to me that in the West Cwm there was a fair amount of protection from the winds to which the northerly route through Tibet is wholly exposed. It appeared also that the South Col route to the summit was considerably shorter and less involved than the North Col route. Most important of all, the lie of the rock strata gives a decided advantage to climbers approaching from the south.

Another development arising from the same source, without any manoeuvre on my part, was the one which gave rise to this book. My reason for not having tackled the job sooner was that I did not wish .the story to be one of defeat, but of ultimate success. It was pointed out to me, quietly and effectively, that my story already contained the element of success, and I was encouraged to set about the task of writing the book. I did so at once.

So, at a time when I was striving once more to forget my mountains,

I was forcibly reminded of them, as I had been on previous occasions. I became surrounded by maps, drawings, photographs, Press cuttings, articles, books—all on mountaineering. There was no evading them. All these were a part of my past, and so were inescapable. I started to re-live the days gone by and I knew at once that the mountains were indeed a part of me.

I wrote to Tenzing, and his almost immediate reply gave the final encouragement that was needed to awaken me to a full renewal of endeavour. Because of its bearing on the course of events so far as they concerned me, I give Tenzing's letter of January 15, 1953, in full, except for a few opening remarks of no specific importance. His paragraphs had been tabulated, corresponding with my own letter to him.

DEAR DENMAN SAHIB,

Many thanks for your letter of 31-10-52. . . . As per your queries I am replying:—

(1) I don't think that you will be able to get a permission from Tibet. But according to my experiences I think the route of Nepal is more convenient for us. I don't think you will get permission (from Nepalese Government) for 1954, because in 1953 British Expedition is going, in 1954 French is going—this has already been permitted. In 1955 Swiss might go because they are giving permission by turns. Still do try for the permission from Nepal. I am pleased for that and expect to go with you.

(2) The best month for climbing is June if Nepal route is used.

(3) For Tibet route also this very month is best, i.e. before monsoon.

(4) If we go through Nepal, three porters from Darjeeling is sufficient and if needed local porters can be had from Katmandu and climbing porters can be had from Namche Bazar. From Namche Bazar base camp is only three days' walk. *If you get permission, I rather prefer to accompany you than any other party.* I am very much pleased to accompany you. Regarding Ang Dowa, he died a natural death in his house.

Best regards from whole of my family and myself. Please write me back soon.

(Signed) TENZING

I have given in italics the words which I consider of greatest importance. I was stirred deeply by the fact that this fine Sherpa had expressed a preference to go with me again if I should succeed in obtaining permission, even though other expeditions—with vastly superior resources to any I could ever hope to have—held prior claims to his services. I looked upon this as the greatest compliment ever paid to me as a mountaineer.

There is another aspect of Tenzing's letter which deserves more than passing thought. His fourth paragraph showed him to be in full agreement with my original belief that a small party—a *very* small party—was right for Everest. In considering his views on this and other matters it should be borne in mind that (1) Tenzing had already been near to the summit of Everest several times, (2) he was one of the few active mountaineers with experience of both routes, (3) he had a wide range of experience, which included active participation with exceptionally large parties, medium-sized parties, and with one very small party (my own). In other words, he had gained considerable all-round experience of Everest. He was vital to the success of any expedition, if any one man could be called this, and I *knew* within myself that, when the mountain was eventually climbed, Tenzing would be there with his smiling optimism. The mountain " belonged " to him quite as much as to Mallory or anyone else.

The final point to consider from his letter is why he should, with all his experience, prefer to go with me if I should ever be able to lead an expedition again. (I am convinced of his sincerity. The remark in his letter is typical of him and is not likely to be merely ingratiating.) The original deciding factor—that when accompanying a large expedition he would never be permitted to take part in any final assault—no longer obtained. During the past few years, a change had taken place, and Tenzing, notwithstanding his colour and race, had been given every opportunity to demonstrate his fullest capabilities as a high altitude climber. Yet still he was able to state, "... I rather prefer to accompany you than any other party." Why?

The answer, I felt sure, was that Tenzing and I thought alike. He allied himself with Everest, very keenly, and being a simple fellow he would rather have seen the mountain climbed simply, without fuss and noise and wastage—just as we had tried to do it in 1947.

There was nothing wrong with our original idea. All we lacked was the money, and therefore the equipment and the few extra porters, for putting it effectively into action. We were only three men when we should have had the support of, say, six or eight others. Apart from this, we had been sound enough in our methods. There was no occasion when any argument arose between us, if only for the reason that we could not converse well enough for argument to develop. There was never any dissatisfaction, if only for the reason that we shared everything as equally as possible—even our sleeping-bags.

If only we could go again, I used to think. Of course there would be need to replace poor Ang Dowa, and we would require a few additional Sherpas. But our original idea was sound and would call for little modification. Everest could be climbed this way—*our* way—simply, unobtrusively and without oxygen. It could be done. It *could* be done.

I was convinced, too, that it *should* be climbed this way, in what I would call a " clean " manner—quietly, efficiently, without ostentation, humbly. Sir Francis Younghusband echoed a similar sentiment when he wrote (*Everest: the Challenge*):

> " Theoretically it would have been better for some private individual to come forward to initiate and conduct his own expedition as Bruce, Longstaff, and Mumm had attacked Trisul. And the method of running Everest expeditions by Committee has been severely criticised by R. G. Irving in his recent book, *The Romance of Mountaineering*. Mr. Irving is the Winchester master who first inspired the Winchester boy, Mallory, to mountaineer. And he voices the views of many mountaineers when he objects to the system of selecting climbers—selecting them instead of waiting for them to initiate a climb . . . 'By all means let us encourage men to go on their own responsibility to climb the Himalaya and any other mountain, but do not let us set the ring for them as we have begun to do. Our great footballers, our great cricketers have become public entertainers, and we must accept the fact. Mountaineering is altogether unfitted to follow such a trend.'
>
> " Much else Mr. Irving writes in criticism of the initiators of the Everest expeditions. And we may readily admit that there would be more of the romance of mountaineering if some enterprising individual got together some fellow-mountaineers, collected the necessary funds, and set off to conquer Everest[1]."

I had no knowledge of these words when, sitting in camp on Ruwenzori, the idea of a lone attempt to climb Everest first came to me. At that time, in fact, I had not read a single book on Everest. So I cannot attribute the original conception to any stimulus received from others. To the best of

[1] This passage is here reprinted by kind permission of Nelson., the publishers of the book.

my knowledge, the idea just came and grew, and because of the circumstances of my life I was receptive to it.

The story of my failure is not only that of a solitary mountaineer pitting his slender resources against the world's highest mountain. It is also the story of a twentieth century wanderer—or of many such wanderers, each lost in a changing world wherein a grain of corn is now a silver coin. A world which is as false as its immature, unbalanced system of economy.

I did not give in easily. For eight years I persevered with my lone endeavours. I fondly imagined that I *deserved* success in the end, and I also believed that there were many amongst the poorer classes of humanity who would like to know that one man, by his determination alone, could triumph against organisations backed by tremendous wealth and operating on behalf of national enterprises. Others, being detached from the events which have tended to overwhelm me, may be able to see them in a more favourable light than I can. To me, there is nothing but disillusionment and the undermining of all idealism, whether it concerns mountains or not.

At the time of writing to Tenzing, I wrote about possibilities to the British Ambassador, Katmandu, Nepal. His reply was not encouraging.

The British Mount Everest Expedition, 1953, left England in February. It was Coronation year, and for British mountaineers it was a case of now or never in the quest for final honours on Everest. French and Swiss climbers were awaiting their turns to go out in 1954 and 1955, and it was thought that a team of picked Russian mountaineers was setting out at any time to attempt the climb from Tibet, using the old North Col route. Whatever lay in store, it was fairly certain that if British climbers did not succeed in 1953 they would have no further chance, for the constant barrage of weighty attacks was bound to break the mountain's resistance before long. To the countries directly involved—and this could be taken to include Russia—the ascent of Everest had become a matter of vital national prestige. From being a tremendous ideal, the mountain had fallen into the grip of nationalism, one of the greatest curses of our age. The individual no longer mattered. The important factor was the nationality of the individual.

I was not alone in believing that Everest could be climbed without oxygen, but for others to have dispensed with it would have involved them in another uncertainty as well as that of the weather, and perhaps in years of further struggle. Time, however, was pressing. The mountain must be climbed without delay. Therefore, to all Everest planners other than myself, oxygen was an indispensable item of equipment. To my way of thinking, it would have been better to try to reach an agreement to ban its use, thereby making the issue a less urgent one and tending to take it out of the realm of politics. Also, the issue would then have become a plain one of man and his sheer determination against the mountain, instead of automaton against mountain. The chance has slipped by with Everest, but perhaps reason can be made to prevail for the climbing of Kangchen-junga.

From the British point of view, Everest had remained, until 1952, an all-British affair: the first non-British attack had nearly resulted in victory for the Swiss. The Swiss would be going again, after the French, and they would be better equipped than ever, and have the benefit of previous Everest experiences. Therefore, to set the issue beyond doubt for the British, there must be success in 1953.

Quite rightly, under the circumstances—though I disliked the circumstances—the organisers of the British Everest Expedition realised that full-scale army logistics, which had so recently proved successful in a second world war, would be most likely to bring the required success. To this end, leadership was entrusted to Colonel John Hunt, a Regular Army officer and a man of brilliant organising ability, as well as a seasoned mountaineer.

The total party, as it left Katmandu, comprised about 395 men—a veritable army. It was said to have nearly 10,000 lb. of baggage, in which was included a light mortar for use as an avalanche gun, and metal bridges. Oxygen apparatus consisted of both open and closed circuit types. The names of Band, Evans and Bourdillon were prominent among those singled out at an early stage as being likely to be chosen for the first assault.

In trepidation, I awaited the outcome, ready with my own plans if there should be the chance to continue with the idea of another attempt with a small party. The manuscript dealing with my own Everest story was completed and out of my hands. It had, of course, been written with the hope of going again to Everest, either through Nepal or Tibet, and with Tenzing sharing the undertaking with me.

News of the British expedition filtered through. "May 15 Set as D-Day for Everest Assault"; "Everest Assault Starts Today"; "Everest Climbers Plan 'Coronation Gift' Victory"; "Assaults on Summit of Everest now on." The suspense was as much as I could bear.

There is nothing shameful in admitting that, with my selfish interest in the mountain, allied with my fervent desire to have it climbed the simple way, I was anxious for the expedition's failure. Inwardly I rebelled at the thought of Everest being subjected to army methods of assault. I loathe nationalism (though I preferred to think in terms of a British success) and I could not altogether condone even British nationalism where Everest was concerned. There was a horrible conflict in my mind. I knew that the British were right in going all out for Everest. But I deplored the world-wide tendency to drag mountaineering into the political arena.

News continued to come through. On the morning of May 26 a news-paper lay folded on the breakfast table, and I could see that most of the front page was given over to Everest. The mountain had been climbed, then? I unfolded it and read, "First Everest Attempt Fails: Second in Progress." I breathed again. Tenzing had not taken part in this first attempt, and I could imagine the poor fellow's thoughts—as much in a turmoil as my own.

News had become strangely obscure, and I wondered why. Could it be that news was being withheld until Coronation Day? (Many people wondered that, but I understand that there was in fact no question of holding up the announcement.)

"Time Running Out for Everest Party," said another headline. Then, "Fine Weather gives Climbers New Chance on Everest." This was followed with "Everest Assault has Failed, says Katmandu Report." It was even reported that the climbers had finally turned back and that the expedition was "planning a fresh assault in the autumn."

There followed a confused jumble of reports—a groping in the dark by news-hungry editors. Then, while listening to the radio on the morning of June 2—Coronation Day—I heard the announcer commence with the word "Everest," and I knew what was to follow: " . . . has been con-quered." And so it was that the news reached me, in the very words which I had hoped to restrain if I should have been successful, for it would have been, as I saw it a matter of a compromise between man and mountain rather than a conquest.

I was of course pleased that Tenzing had at last succeeded. He so richly deserved success. But with a lot which followed, I was not so pleased,[1] and in particular I thought that more deference should have been shown to the King of Nepal, from whom news of success appears to have been withheld for a while.

[1] I have seen reports of the story allegedly told by Tenzing to Yves Malartic. This seems to me just one more nail in the coffin of true mountaineering.

Later, news came through of an unsuccessful bid, during December 1952, by a Russian expedition in which several climbers, including the expedition leader, lost their lives. This report did more than anything else to justify the absence of " kid glove methods " by the British. In a way, it was a relief that the mountain had at last been climbed.

Still, however, I did not like the new trend of Himalayan mountaineering, and when Nanga Parbat was climbed, with all that was reported to have taken place during and after the climb,[1] I was more than ever apprehensive for the future of mountaineering, and for the outcome in a world which disavowed first one form of idealism and then another. And so it is that I see in some of the world's highest mountains, now, a symbol of decaying faith and a saddening, discouraging triumph for materialism.

Throughout my years of manhood, I have searched for a meaning to life. There has been no one to offer any satisfactory solutions, so I have had to search for myself, and to suffer the injury and unhappiness which any search of this kind involves. I have had to go a long, long way to discover for myself a simple truth. From being an idealist, I have come to know that others—the people who count—are right in setting the acquisition of monetary wealth above everything else, for neither good nor evil can be done without it. And Everest, which once meant so much to me, now means nothing at all.

It should not be thought, because Everest was my goal, that I was leading myself away for all time from the common walks of life. Apart from Everest, I took delight only in simple things—in walking barefoot on warm grass or wet rocks; in probing deep into cool, quiet forests; in days of healthy activity and evenings of restfulness spent beside a warming fire.

I had set Everest as my goal, but the mountain was no more than a symbol of my searching and striving. My defeat in 1947 was really no defeat at all, but my struggle for Everest did not end there, and in the years that have followed there has been no recompense for what, to say the least of it, was a sincere effort.

David, in his day, slew Goliath. Have the times so changed, then? I think they have, and that the modern David cannot slay the modern Goliath. I had hoped that he might be able to, but I was mistaken. I had made the grave error of staying with my childhood heroes—Livingstone, Speke,

---

[1] If reports are true, two climbers disobeyed an order from their leader, and one of these climbers left his companion behind in camp, while he went on alone to reach the summit. Public squabbling and lawsuits arose later.

Burton—who had been able to give so much of themselves to the age in which they lived. To-day it is necessary to be one of a team or one of an army. That is the crying pity of our age. We have lost the value of self-expression.

So this is the ending? Here in a world of despair for each of us? Here, in bewilderment, where no mountain beckons?

It is the end, but it may also be a beginning.

There has been a shattering of idealism, but from the broken remnants some good may yet be resurrected. When the warriors have finished reshaping the boundaries of our world, then there will be freedom to come and go as we wish: when the perverters have finished with sex and have left us with its sweetness, then there will be love: when the conquerors have come down from the mountains, then we shall be able to go to them again, simply and quietly.

GLOSSARY OF MOUNTAINEERING TERMS

Arête: Ridge.

Avalanche: A large mass of snow and ice which loosens and slides down a mountain slope.

Belay: To secure a rope by winding it round a projection of any sort. A firmly planted ice-axe may be used for the purpose if no feature of the landscape is available.

Buttress: A projection, or rib, usually of rock.

Col: Pass.

Couloir: Gully or furrow of ice, snow or rock.

Crampons: Metal frames with spikes, fitted to climbing boots to give extra purchase on ice or hard snow.

Crevasse: A breach or deep fissure in a glacier or snowfield.

Cwm: Large cauldron or basin in heavily glaciated region. (Pronounced "coom.")

Glacier: A consolidation of snow formed into a river of ice.

Glissade: A sliding descent over snow or scree.

Himalayas: I have included this word in the glossary, not for explanation, but for pronunciation. It should be pronounced Him-*arl*-lias and not Him-al-ay-as, as is common.

Ice-axe: A mountaineer's axe principally used for cutting steps in ice.

Massif: Range or group of mountains—a term usually applied to the highest or central point.

Moraine: An accumulation of stones deposited by glacial action.

Oxygen apparatus: Open circuit type: with this the climber breathes a mixture of oxygen and air. Open circuit apparatus has been used on Everest since the first climbing party went out in 1922.

Closed circuit type: pure oxygen is breathed. I think I am correct in saying that closed circuit apparatus was used for the first time on Everest in 1936.

Piton: Metal spike, with ring in head, which can be driven into rock or ice for fixing a rope.

Scree: Slope of small, loose stones.

Serac: Tall pinnacle of ice. Usually associated with moraines and ice-falls.

Spur: Rib, or lateral projection, of rock.

Traverse: To cross a mountain face horizontally.